An Economist in the Real World

An Economist in the Real World

The Art of Policymaking in India

Kaushik Basu

The MIT Press
Cambridge, Massachusetts
London, England

MIT Press books may be purchased at special quantity discounts for business or sales promotional use. For information, please email special_sales@mitpress.mit.edu.

This book was set in Stone by the MIT Press. Printed and bound in the United States of America.

Library of Congress Cataloging-in-Publication Data

Basu, Kaushik.
An economist in the real world : the art of policymaking in India / Kaushik Basu.
    pages   cm
Includes bibliographical references and index.
ISBN 978-0-262-02962-9 (hardcover : alk. paper) 1. Basu, Kaushik. 2. Economists—India. 3. Economic development—India. 4. India--Economic policy—1991–
5. India—Officials and employees. 6. India—Politics and government—1977–
I. Title.
HB126.I43B3727 2015
330.954—dc23
2015011428
ISBN: 978-0-262-02962-9

10 9 8 7 6 5 4 3 2 1

To Alaka

Contents

Preface

From an existence totally immersed in the world of research, and with little forewarning, I was transported or, more aptly, hurled to the post of chief economic adviser (CEA) to the Government of India, at the Ministry of Finance, in December 2009, in response to an invitation from the then Prime Minister Manmohan Singh. Despite the disorientation of the initial months, this turned out to be a remarkably enriching experience, giving me a view that neither the career bureaucrat nor the traditional researcher has. This monograph is an account of the economy of contemporary India, ranging from the large macroeconomic questions to the granular, microtheoretic ones, all viewed from the perch of my office in Lutyens's Delhi. It is a book on the Indian economy and the art of policymaking, blending economic theory with personal experience.

My two and a half years in government convinced me, and this is the theme that recurs throughout the pages of this book, that economic policymaking is like an engineer's work but with a twist. Crafting economic policy is like building an aircraft where the onlookers take an interest. In building an airplane, for example, onlookers typically take no interest. If they did, the task would be vastly more complicated. If the engineer went along with the popular view, making the wing span according to majority preference, giving the nose of the plane the tilt that the lay majority demanded, and so on, chances are the plane would not fly.

In making economic policy, in most areas, from setting tax rates, through changing key interest rates, to designing how a subsidy should be given out, people have views. This makes the task much more complex, for one has to combine technical knowledge with attention to how people think and what they believe in (which unfortunately also determines how they vote). Effective economic policymaking requires awareness of the fact that economics lies at the intersection of politics and society. This is not license to ignore the laws of economics and hard data, but simply means that the task is more challenging than may appear at first sight.

The transition from academe to the world of policymaking was especially hard in my case because, unlike some others, I had not gone into economics with the intention of helping the world. I went in for more selfish reasons, lured by the pleasures of logic and deductive reasoning and the excitement of discovering how much one can learn through pure reason. When I moved to policymaking in government, it was a conscious decision to abandon hedonism and to try to make some direct and palpable contribution to society's economic well-being. It was the sudden move from a life in research to the deep end of actual policymaking and political jockeying that made me more conscious of the importance of the broader setting of economics. Having come to government from outside, I had the one advantage the anthropologist has over the indigenous people—an outsider's perspective. I could see the differences in norms and culture, both the momentous and the trivial, which would elude the more long-term inhabitants of this setting.

Let me begin with the trivial. It took me a while to fully appreciate that in high offices of the Indian government not only that one did not knock to enter someone's office, but also that knocking was considered somewhat impolite. I remember, early in my job, I was about to knock on the door of Pranab Mukherjee, the finance minister at that time (now the president of India), when one of his doormen rushed up to me, alarmed, and said, "What are you doing?" I told him I needed to discuss some important fiscal policy matter with the minister. He looked bewildered and queried why, in that case, was I not simply going in?

I soon realized this was the norm, though initially I found it awkward, especially because in the tropics doors swell up and tend to get jammed. So when they finally yield to one's pressure one tends to catapult some distance into the room. Doing so without the forewarning of a knock seemed inconsiderate. As with most norms, after some time, I got used to it. And later, I even came to wonder if this norm was not actually superior to the Western one of knocking before entering, because it rested on the eminently sensible axiom: Do not disturb a person fifteen seconds before you need to disturb the person.

This is a trivial example but it draws attention to the fact that all economies are embedded in a mesh of intricate norms, collective beliefs, and behavioral habits. These can make or break an economy. While this book is primarily on economic policies, I have tried to weave into it the case for paying much greater attention to the social, behavioral, and institutional foundations of a society.

There is a second running theme that permeates the pages of this book. Over the last two or three decades there has been a backlash against the excesses of economic theory and there has been a chorus of demand for better empirical work, rooted in statistics and hard data. This is a worthwhile call and, fortunately, the profession has responded. There has been a remarkable improvement in our collection and analysis of data. Treasuries, ministries of finance, and central banks, in most countries, now have large research departments that collate and analyze evidence, as do universities and research institutes. This is as it should be; and we still have some distance to go in collecting more and better data, and doing empirical investigation.

However, during my nearly five years in the policy world, initially in the Government of India and now as chief economist at the World Bank, I have come away convinced that the bigger deficiency now lies in theoretical analysis and reasoning. We owe many of our policy mistakes to unreason and poor deductive reasoning. When policymakers talk about the importance of making "evidence-based policy," the tendency too often is to wave at some evidence and quickly jump to policy conclusions, ignoring the fact that the word "based" also has a critical role to play. This is where analysis, theory, and deductive reasoning come in.[1] Once we recognize that economics is embedded in other social sciences, deductive reasoning gets that much harder. But that must not be an excuse to abandon reason. To recognize, as modern behavioral economics does, that human beings often reason poorly must not be taken as license for the *analyst* to reason poorly. Though this book is not an exercise in theory and stays away from using mathematics, it strives to be fastidious analytically and in the use of deduction.

The book might never have happened but for an invitation that came toward the end of my term in New Delhi from Ashutosh Varshney of Brown University, asking me to deliver the first of the O. P. Jindal Distinguished Lectures at his university. These were meant to be three lectures (though I would eventually fit them into two long sessions) on the Indian economy, giving me the freedom to draw on my own experience and also to use the broader social and political canvas I have mentioned. I worked at a furious pace during the summer months of 2012 to prepare for these lectures, which I delivered on November 9 and 16 of that year. I am grateful to Ashutosh and the president of Brown University, Christina Paxson, for giving me the opportunity and to the remarkably engaged audience for its lively participation.

To make sure I do not disappoint readers, the preface is a good place to clarify that though this book is written from an unabashedly personal point of view and there are frequent references to my own experience in government, it is not a diary. I did keep a diary during my stint as CEA in Delhi, when, within weeks of joining, I realized that my experience was too precious to be relegated to the vagaries of memory. Thereafter, during my entire term of over two and a half years in government, I wrote a diary, generally two or three times a week. I had never been a diarist before that but the activity seemed to be sufficiently enjoyable and, in many ways, also therapeutic; so I kept it up. After leaving government and joining the World Bank I have continued with my diary writing, though it has now become rather more occasional, and has taken the form of jotting down mnemonics to draw upon at a later date.

My Delhi diary is too fresh to be published. There are also difficult ethical questions associated with such verbatim reporting so soon after having had the privilege of an insider's view. So while I have dipped into my diary occasionally, for an amusing incident here and an important policy conundrum there, strictly what is expected of a diary—the "revelations" and notes on personalities—the reader will not find here.

The writing of this book was spread over many locales. The bulk of the work, though at that time I did not know it would ever be a book, occurred during my time working in Delhi. I kept notes for myself; I produced several documents in the form of advisory notes for Finance Minister Pranab Mukherjee and Prime Minister Manmohan Singh. I believe I put in much more effort into these than hardened bureaucrats do. I have drawn extensively on those documents.

By far the most productive and concentrated work happened first in Delhi in the summer of 2012 and then in Ithaca, New York, in the two months between the end of my Delhi stint and the start of my job at the World Bank. I returned to Cornell University in August 2012, into a blissful summer. Contrary to what my friends had warned me, that I would find the quiet of academe trying after the high-pressure days in India, I found myself quite at home in the university. Following John Maynard Keynes's sage advice, I did not wake up early. But once up, I quickly got down to reading and writing for this book, doing little else all day, with occasional breaks to chat with students and colleagues and I worked late into the night.

In Washington, D.C., my daily work was so overwhelming that the little writing that remained in order to complete the manuscript occurred sporadically and on the occasional weekend. I feared that though the main work had been done a long time ago, the book would never be completed. So, in August 2014, I took leave from the World Bank, with the explicit aim of putting in the final burst of work to bring the project to closure.

Between the start of my work on this book in 2009 and its completion in 2014, India's political landscape changed dramatically. The Congress-led government was defeated roundly in the election held in May–June 2014. The new Bharatiya Janata Party (BJP) government, with Narendra Modi as prime minister, was sworn into office in June. On July 1 I went to Delhi for a three-day visit. I was conscious of my altered role. I was now coming in as the World Bank's chief economist. The World Bank is engaged in a variety of projects in India. Being Indian and having worked for the Indian government, these are naturally of special interest to me.

I called the prime minister's office just before arriving and asked for an appointment, feeling somewhat uncertain since I hardly knew anybody in the new administration. As I got off the Air India flight from Hong Kong at New Delhi's Indira Gandhi International Airport on a sultry evening, my phone rang. Could I see the prime minister the following day at noon?

When I arrived at the prime minister's residence, 7 Race Course Road, the next morning, it had the same quiet elegance that I remembered. One security guard recognized me and smiled faintly. I sat in the waiting area, under the familiar Laxman Pai painting. The prime minister's meeting room was arranged the same way it used to be. I congratulated him for his election victory and for India's democracy—that such an important electoral shift took place so noiselessly and with the broad structures of office unchanged. It was a quiet transfer of power, so rare in an emerging nation.

Wanting to put all my cards on the table, I began by telling the prime minister that I was close to his predecessor. He smiled and said he was aware of that. I told him I wanted to share some ideas concerning the economy, world affairs, and India's role in a globalizing world. He said he was interested. In the conversation that followed I covered a range of topics, from monetary policy for inflation control to strategies for positioning India on the global stage. We talked about the critical role of infrastructure and the importance of inclusiveness for a nation as diverse as India. He listened with great attention, adding remarks from his own experience, while I persisted with my rather nerdy discourse. When I was leaving, he suggested I write up some briefs with ideas for the economy.

I plan to do so, but at one level the project of India is so complex and so enormous that there is a need for a fuller exercise in which ideas for India are integrated with a primer on development economics. This book may be thought of as such an exercise. I hope it will be useful for policymakers and political leaders to mull over and use, and for any student of economics and the intelligent layperson to read, think about, agree with, or contest. It is not meant to be an abstract research monograph but a user's manual. The book draws on contemporary research, my experience in policymaking, and also, no doubt, my own ideological and moral predilections. If it makes even a small difference to policymaking in India and other developing countries, it will have served its purpose.

During the long haul of writing this book, I have built up an enormous indebtedness. I would be remiss if I did not record at least some of this. The person I worked with mostly closely during my stint in India was the Finance Minister Pranab Mukherjee, who is now the president of India, since as CEA my task was to advise the finance minister. When Prime Minister Manmohan Singh first invited me in August 2009 to join his government as CEA, he had, by way of persuasion, told me that he would have his door open to me at all times, should I agree to take up his offer. I never shied away from this and, as a consequence, I had more regular access to the prime minister than virtually any policymaker outside his front office. I am grateful to him for this.

My predecessors in the office of CEA, Nitin Desai, Bimal Jalan, Ashok Lahiri, Rakesh Mohan, and Arvind Virmani, were sources of counsel and support as were the several members of the Indian Economic Service, which I headed. There were many people who influenced my thinking through discussions or having been part of the annual conference I organized at the Ministry of Finance on some of these topics. For this I would like to thank Karna Basu, Ashwini Deshpande, Jean Drèze, Bhaskar Dutta, Ashima Goyal, Justin Yifu Lin, Kishore Mahbubani, Nandita Mongia, Puran Mongia, Lant Pritchett, Amartya Sen, Mike Spence, Joseph Stiglitz, and Klaus Zimmerman.

In the summer of 2014 I was invited to lecture at the Ecole Polytechnique Fédérale de Lausanne (EPFL) in Switzerland on the Indian economy. This turned out to be a laboratory in which to develop and debate my ideas with a multidisciplinary audience. I would like to record my indebtedness to Florence Graezer Bideau for the invitation, and to Hans-Peter Hertig and Beatrix Boillat for the long, leisurely treks and conversations, and to all my hosts for the warm hospitality. At the final stage, as I worked on successive drafts of the manuscript, I benefited from conversations with and editorial tips from Diksha Basu, Aaditya Dar, Shabnam Faruki, Devajyoti Ghose, Jose Luis Diaz Sanchez, Indermit Gill, Poonam Gupta, Vivian Hon, Zia Qureshi, David Rosenblatt, Emily Taber, Aristomene Varoudakis, and James Walsh.

One chooses colleagues and friends with whom to discuss and share a manuscript; one has little choice in the editor with whom one works. In this I have been exceptionally lucky. Jane Macdonald, my editor at the MIT Press, helped me greatly with her enthusiasm, support, and plain good judgment. Finally, for reading through the entire manuscript and advising me with her unerring literary sensibility, I am grateful to my wife, Alaka Basu.

In closing, let me draw the readers' attention to the fact that there are two ways to read the book. For those with some familiarity with economic policymaking or some prior education in economics, it is easy to read the book from start to finish and that is what I would recommend. However, I would hate to lose readers who may have no experience with policy and no prior training in economics either. For them, one strategy is to read chapters 1, 2, 8, 9, and 10. These chapters constitute a guide to basic, practical economics, and a short history of economic development and policymaking in India. The book as a whole, I like to believe, is more than a treatise on India. Development economics is a discipline that is meant to help people lead better, more fulfilling lives. This places a special responsibility on us to reach out to those who are deprived of minimal living standards. The poor and the marginalized have no race, ethnicity, or nationality; their binding identity is their deprivation. This book is written in the hope that the principles and policies outlined in it can be used for development policy to reach out to them wherever they are, whatever their nationality. In that sense this may be viewed as a book on practical development economics, with India as the illustrative model, but with lessons for all developing economies.

Kaushik Basu
November 30, 2014

1 Arriving in Lutyens's Delhi

From the Slopes of Raisina Hill

Raisina Hill stands in the heart of Delhi, a gentle mound, barely making the grade of a hill. When Sir Edwin Lutyens began to design and construct the main government buildings and some residences of India's British rulers, soon after the capital of colonial India was shifted from Calcutta (now Kolkata) to Delhi in 1911, Raisina Hill was a patchwork of little-known villages. The decision to build the British Viceregal lodge—which is now the Rashtrapati Bhavan and the residence of the president of India, who, as head of state, occupies a special position—atop the hill transformed this nondescript area into one of the most magnificent architectural landscapes in the world.

On the eastern slopes of Raisina Hill, Lutyens and fellow architect Herbert Baker built the most important government offices. There was the office of the prime minister, who as head of government was the person effectively in charge of running the nation. Facing the prime minister's office was the Ministry of Finance, with the offices of the finance minister, the chief economic adviser, and various secretaries and their staff. Next to these, there were the Ministries of External Affairs, Defense, and Home. These ministries were housed in buildings known as the North and South Blocks, depending on their location, on the two sides of the majestic central boulevard of New Delhi, Rajpath, leading up from India Gate to the Rashtrapati Bhavan. The buildings, with their high ceilings, decorative columns, and colossal walls made of cream and dull red sandstone found in abundance in Dholpur, Rajasthan, matched the Parliament House which sat on the plains, just where the hill touched down.

The massive structures were meant to remind people of the power of government—till 1947, the British Crown. After all, as the Scottish philosopher David Hume had pointed out with his uncanny ability to see beyond the facade, a government's power, massive though it may be, was built ultimately on nothing other than people's belief in that power. If everyone thought government was powerful, that in itself conferred power on the government. In violating a government's edict you worried that someone would come and haul you up; and the someone designated to do so—the police, the magistrate, or another official—would in turn do so for the same reason that if they did not punish someone for violating the orders of government, someone else would punish them. It is this hierarchy, built on nothing but beliefs, that gives government its power.[1] Lutyens's massive colonial structures, like the forts and palaces of the earlier Moghul rulers of India, were meant to aid and bolster such beliefs. And they served the British Crown well—so much so that, when India became independent at dawn on August 15, 1947, there was no question of where the government's high offices would be located.

On December 8, 2009, with the early chill of winter hanging languidly over Delhi, I arrived at the Ministry of Finance in the North Block, on the slopes of Raisina Hill, to take up office as chief economic adviser. In joining this office I was marking two important breaks in tradition, one personal and one for the government. I had never before worked in government; in fact, I had never before worked on anything but research and teaching, and I found these so enjoyable that it would be only a small stretch to go further and say I had never worked before. Yes, I had written on economic policy in newspapers, magazines, and, for several years, on the BBC News website, but primarily from my location in universities or research institutes. I had spent one year at the World Bank at the invitation of Joe Stiglitz, who was then the Bank's chief economist and his idea was to have some visiting professors at the Bank. I took that literally and spent the year writing papers, talking to Stiglitz, and sitting in on and giving seminars. Hence, it seems reasonable to say that my record of having had nothing to do with the "real world," as economists call it when on the rare occasions they wish to veer away from their modeled world to the real thing, was without blemish until December 8, 2009.

The other, more important break in tradition was in my working for the government. When I took office as CEA, it was the first time someone occupied that seat with no experience in government. It was, therefore, a bolt from nowhere when on August 9, 2009, at the end of two months of our usual summer break in India, as my wife and I were busy packing up in our Hauz Khas home in New Delhi to return to Cornell University, I got a phone call from a joint secretary in the prime minister's office asking if I would be interested in the job of CEA. I caught my breath and said that, while it was a great honor to be asked, this was too big a question for me to answer off the bat. Since she was calling from the prime minister's office, I requested that she try to set up a meeting for me with the prime minister so that I could ask him what his expectations were. The only catch was, I told her, that I was leaving for the United States the next night. She called me back in ten minutes saying that the prime minister would meet me at his residence the following evening.

So on August 10, after readying our bags for the airport, I went and met Prime Minister Manmohan Singh at 7 Race Course Road—or 7RCR as everybody in government and the media referred to it. I had a thirty-five-minute conversation, about the economy, about what he expected of the office of the chief economic adviser, about the world of ideas and its influence on the world we live in. He reminded me that he had once held the post of CEA and said that he was personally keen to raise the profile of this post, which was the main conduit for modern ideas on policymaking to flow into government. By the end of the conversation I had virtually made up my mind that, should the formal offer come, I would take it. Feeling somewhat lightheaded, I went home, collected our bags and suitcases, and my wife and I left for the United States.

It all happened so quickly that the adjustment was hard. I took up office on December 8, 2009. As I got out of my government car, laptop and briefcase slung over my shoulder, a man came charging and snatched these from me. Since I'd experienced a similar incident when my wallet was taken from me near St. Marks Square in Venice, I had to resist the urge to run after the man and wrestle him to the ground. I did not know then that he was one of my two "men Friday," who would be lodged in my adjacent office for the duration of my term as CEA and loyally run minor errands, thereby contributing to a small improvement in India's unemployment statistic.

The big reminder that I was in a different setting came later in the same week. The driver assigned to ferry me around in my government-given white Ambassador car was a senior member from the Finance Ministry's

.

retinue of chauffeurs. The first time I got into the front seat and reached for my seatbelt, my driver, who knew that I had come from academe to high government office, turned to me and said helpfully, "Sir, now that you are the chief economic adviser, you don't need to wear a seat belt any more."

I stress the difference, fully aware that differences between societies and settings are almost always less than they appear at first blush. Indeed, over time, what caught my attention more frequently were the similarities between the two settings in which I had worked—in India and in the United States, once I learned to look beneath the surface. Nevertheless, during the first month or two, my new government setting appeared totally alien to me. The only way to survive, I told myself, was to play the anthropologist or the scientific observer. If Malinowski could spend three years in the Trobriand Islands, observing and taking notes on the mores and rituals of the Islanders, and Darwin could sail off on the Beagle to uncharted lands and eventually to the Galapagos Islands to study the fauna and flora of those places, surely I could survive two years in the North Block, if nothing else, observing the bureaucrats and politicians.[2]

This self-disciplining ploy, important in the beginning, would soon become redundant as I began to enjoy my work, and I mean not just the work of observing the tribals of North Block but also becoming one. It nevertheless helped put a distance and perspective in what I did and gave me the observer's advantage and the impetus to maintain a regular diary despite the grueling work hours.

Speaking in Subsequences, the Extended Sen Rule

This book draws on my experience—both the joys and frustrations—to describe and analyze the challenges of making economic policy in a setting where political considerations are in the driver's seat. The setting of course is India. But India in this book plays two distinct roles. One is in the object of this book, which may, therefore, be viewed as an introduction to India's economy in our times. But the book also uses India as an instrument, a lens through which one may understand the basic principles of economics. Hence, the book may be viewed as a practitioner's introduction to economics.

When I joined the government, India's food price inflation was close to an all-time high. Food prices were rising on average by 20 percent per annum. The prime minister called a meeting of five or six principal economists in government to discuss what we should do about this. So I went to 7RCR, and as per standard security routine, got out of my car at the main entrance, and got ferried in one of the fleet of cars that wait to do this for all visitors.

I will return to the topic of food and inflation at greater length later in the book. But the gist is that in India, the Food Corporation of India (FCI) is entrusted with acquiring food grain—mainly wheat, rice, and some coarse grains—from farmers, with the intention of releasing some of this grain on a routine basis to poor households and holding the rest in stock for times of food shortages and excessive increases in food prices. Clearly, we were living in a time of food shortages and grain release was called for to dampen food inflation; and indeed FCI was engaged in releasing food grains. The way it did this was to auction bundles of 1,000 metric tons of grain.

It is easy to see however that with such big bundles there would not be too many private agents in a position to make a bid to buy. Hence, what we were doing in effect was creating, through our own actions, a restricted oligopolistic market. There would be just a few traders holding all the grain, which would likely cause prices to be higher than if we managed to release grain in smaller bundles to many more traders, who would then compete among themselves to sell this grain and in the process bring down prices. This "law" of oligopoly was developed in 1838 by Antoine Augustin Cournot in his classic book, *Recherches sur les principes mathématiques de la théorie des richesses*.

Cournot was a remarkable economist. Born in France on August 28, 1801, he was a mathematician by training and worked as a mathematician and a philosopher. He made occasional forays into economics and made this seminal contribution to the understanding of market structures. Ancient books, even if they are classics, are often unreadable because they are written in such arcane style. However, Cournot's *Recherches* is a notable exception. It was far ahead of its times not only in terms of content but also style. It is a highly readable book for anyone with a modicum of familiarity with high-school algebra and calculus. Though Cournot's theory would be challenged in 1883, when Joseph Louis Francois Bertrand published his essay contesting Cournot, the basic terms of the discourse were firmly set by Cournot and would influence the emergence of modern industrial organization theory.

In the meeting presided over by the prime minister, I tried not to let others sense the awkwardness I felt in being the new person as I argued for changing our release strategy. I pointed out the importance of releasing multiple batches of food grain in smaller quantities so as to keep competition more vigorous in the market. A lively and informed discussion followed. The resulting decision to release smaller batches of grain to more numerous traders eventually was implemented. For me this was a fascinating meeting at the cross-section of theory and practice. It was conducted at a level of erudition and openness that must be rare in high offices of government anywhere and certainly in emerging and developing economies. These interactions have made me believe that, immediate turbulence and fluctuations notwithstanding, the future of the Indian economy is encouraging.

Economics is a strange discipline because it has one foot in science and one in intuition and common sense. As a consequence, everyone has a view about how to conduct economic policy. This participation is welcome because it prevents the elite from hijacking all policies for its members' own benefit; and let there be no illusion that, despite such civil society checks, the elite manages to hijack quite a bit in virtually every country. However, this makes crafting of economic policy a blend of science and political persuasion, and this is especially so for democracies. One has to navigate through a thicket of popular opinions, be they right or wrong, to bring a policy to fruition. This, in turn, makes it imperative that ordinary citizens understand the basics of economics. If they are to participate in the design of economic policy, they may as well acquire a modicum of understanding of the discipline. I hope that this slim book will not only inform and entertain but also contribute to such an understanding.

Interaction with a cross-section of ordinary people, however, creates special challenges. Working on the frontline of national policymaking, with the lively Indian media tracking your every word closely, you have to be careful with what you say. It was Amartya Sen, with his wide experience of public debate and media interaction, who first cautioned me on this. Sen advised me that in my new job I should make sure not only that no sentence of mine conveyed some unwarranted message but also that no consecutive set of words within the sentence conveyed a wrongful message since, in reporting my comments, the media, in their eagerness to make news, could drop words at the start and end of my sentences.

I began my job in India by following this "Sen Rule," and it served me well for a while. But eventually I realized that the occasional reckless reporter went further, by dropping words mid-sentence and replacing them with three dots. Hence, I was compelled to develop the "Extended Sen Rule." Luckily, mathematicians have given us a precise term, "subsequence," in order to be able to formally state the Extended Sen Rule: not only must each sentence not convey a wrong meaning, there also should be no subsequence of words in what one says that conveys the wrong meaning.

The one disadvantage of the Extended Sen Rule is that it places such severe restrictions on speech that the temptation is to give in to what many bureaucrats do—say things which sound nice but mean nothing no matter how the sentence is dissected. I like to believe that I never gave in to this and I continued to speak as directly and transparently as possible, at times at considerable cost to myself. Nevertheless, there were self-imposed restraints. In any case, in making frontline policy there is so much firefighting involved that the more thought-through arguments and analyses take a back seat.

I want to make amends for both these failings through this book. To get the best policies in place we need to take the occasional break from firefighting in order to do research to discover new nonflammable materials. That will ensure that there will be fewer fires to fight in the future. This book pushes the reader toward a deeper analysis, the kind of analysis from which new ideas for economic policy could emerge. If that were to happen, the hard work to produce a book like this will have been more than made up for from my point of view.

2   India's Growth Story: Stagnation, Crisis, and Takeoff

Delicious Bengali Dishes

The India story is a tale that has been told often enough, but the same is not true of the Indian *economy* story, the presumption being that that would be drudgery for the writer and the reader, and have no takers. The presumption, at least in the case of this writer, is erroneous. It is a tale of drama, personality conflicts, and, ultimately, decisions that affected human lives profoundly. It is certainly a tale worth telling.

We have a cookbook at home, *Delicious Bengali Dishes*,[1] presented by my mother's friend to my wife, not a Bengali, for her to learn the basics of her in-laws' cuisine. The book is a collector's item for me because of one fish dish, *dahi mach*, in which you are instructed, early, to "grind ginger and onions to a paste." Then you go through other steps like cut the "fish into thin slices and remove fishy smell," mix the "fish with curds, salt, turmeric," cook "over a slow fire," and so on. What is remarkable about the dish is you never again return to the ground ginger and onions. To date I have not been able to decide (nor could I ask my mother's friend for fear of offending her) whether the grinding of ginger and onions was meant to be a mystical exercise to set the mood right, or if the author simply forgot about the paste.

Though this book is about contemporary policy challenges for India and other emerging economies, I prefer to begin with a brief account of the history of thought and economic experience that has brought India to where it is today. This is not essential to the book; but I hope that the reader in a rush to get to our times and the problems of development that India faces today, will nevertheless go through this, if nothing else, in the spirit of the grinding of ginger and onions—a meditative exercise to set the backdrop right. The chapter provides a context for what is happening in India now, and can contribute to an intuitive understanding of the Indian economy, which is so essential for crafting good policy.

The Coffee House at the Delhi School of Economics

Barring an occasional spell in Europe (at the Center for Operations Research and Econometrics, better known as CORE, and the Centre d'Economie Mathématique et d'Econométrie in Belgium, and at Warwick University in UK) and the United States (Institute for Advanced Study at Princeton and Princeton University), I spent the 1980s at the Delhi School of Economics, a disproportionate amount of this time in the Coffee House. Founded in 1949, the Delhi School of Economics was a remarkable institution. Intellectually it had no peers in developing countries, and matched up to leading academic institutions even in industrialized nations. It was a place with little sense of hierarchy and even a certain disdain for those holding high offices in government and industry. There were several professors who served in various capacities in government but they made sure they dropped their high-office swagger for fear of appearing ridiculous when they returned to the premises of the school.

Within the school, the Coffee House had a special place. It was a high-ceilinged ramshackle structure, located between the two buildings housing the departments of economics and sociology. The coffee was good and the food indifferent. There was a lot of excitement when in a rare display of innovation the Coffee House introduced the double-decker sandwich—three slices of bread with two layers of shredded chicken between them. But, over time, for considerations of economy, the authorities began to skimp on the chicken, so much so that the famed sandwich came to be known all over the campus as the "bread sandwich." That was the end of experimentation for the Coffee House. Its hallmark has been its constancy.

Here, through the day, groups of faculty and students gathered around tables with laminated tops and a disdain for aesthetics, and their numbers swelled and ebbed, depending on varying class times; but conversation never stopped. Unlike the famed Coffee House in Kolkata, no overthrowing of regimes, like the British Empire, was plotted here—though there were some aborted attempts to plan the overthrow of the chairpersons of the departments of economics and sociology. While revolution was not the

Coffee House's forte, some of the most important ideas that emerged from the Delhi School of Economics and influenced the landscape of independent India's economic and political policies were conceived here. On any normal day, you could find there, engrossed in conversation and animated debate, a member of the Planning Commission, student leaders with firm conviction in India's need for Maoist-style revolution, Indira Gandhi's economic advisor, the votaries of the Chicago school arguing for government to be kept out of everything, a future Nobel laureate in economics, a future prime minister. I pursued economic theory in my office and at home, mainly in the evenings; but my first lessons on the Indian economy were learned in the Coffee House.

In the Coffee House in the 1980s and even the early 1990s, in all the bustle of conversation, no one ever spoke of India as a fast-growing economy in the conceivable future. We took pride in the nation's vibrant democracy, commitment to secularism, cultural openness, and free media; but no one believed India could be in the lead when it came to growth and economic development. We cherished the openness of our borders as far as books, films, and ideas from all over the world went; but we were quite reconciled to economic closedness. It was very difficult to import goods into India. Sky-high tariffs blocked imports. Scarred by the East India Company, which came to trade with India in the seventeenth century and stayed on to rule the nation for more than two centuries, we blocked foreign direct investment (FDI) from coming in from any multinational corporation to India. And to make sure that these barriers were not violated we strung the economy up in rules, regulations, and permits. India used to be referred to as the "permit raj." As I will argue in more than one place in this book, the culture of "permissionism" still pervades India's economy and remains a stumbling block against better performance.

It is a residue of our history that is not easy to wipe out.

Intellectual Roots of the Economy

Even while our discussions were going on in the Coffee House over tepid cups of South Indian brewed coffee, India was beginning to feel the headwinds of a developing crisis. Through the late 1980s the Indian government was building up a large fiscal deficit—that is, it was spending more than it collected by way of taxes and other sources.[2] Its international debt was also on the rise. All this did not matter as long as the going was good. The First Gulf War of 1990–1991 changed everything. India was plunged into a crisis. For a system resistant to change, nothing is as good as a crisis. Teetering on the verge of a default on its international borrowings, India undertook the most major reforms it had done since gaining independence in 1947.[3]

The crisis was critical, but equally or even more important was the handful of men and women who stood ready to use the crisis to push in a set of new ideas on how to run the economy. The impact was huge; India began growing at around 7 percent per annum from 1994 onward; its foreign exchange reserves, which used to hover around $5 billion for a decade and a half before 1991, rose to around $300 billion over the next decade and a half. By 2005–2008, years in which the country was growing at over 9 percent per annum, it was evident that India's economy game had changed.

Before going into this, it is useful to ask: how did we come to be where we are today and what kept the Indian economy down for so long? While the reforms of 1991–1993 were game changing, is India really out of the woods or will its history come back to haunt the nation?

We must keep in mind that a nation must not be judged by gross domestic product (GDP) alone. The distribution of income matters, as do other nonmonetary markers of development, such as indices of health, and security, and the sense of dignity among ordinary people. These are more difficult to measure and hence it is harder to evaluate a nation in terms of these criteria. India historically has not done well in terms of them, though it is arguable that even on these criteria, the nation's prospects are beginning to look brighter. For a long time, India's masses—despite adult franchise and the many rights of all citizens written into the constitution—were dormant spectators in the arena of policymaking. In presenting the national budget in parliament, with the whole nation watching, the government's aim for a long time was to please the middle and richer classes. The income tax payer was supposed to be happy about what was being announced; the big corporations were to be happy and reassured by the new budgetary provisions; those playing the bourses were to be happy about future prospects on the market. And the poor, who did not fit into any of these categories, were—so seemed to be the presumption—to be happy seeing so much happiness all around. Today the rise in civil society activism has begun to change this. Ordinary Indians, poor Indians, are being demanding in ways that they never were before. In this lies hope but also some risk of political chaos, since an increasing number of voices requires attention. For this reason, the social and political backdrop of economic policies is important; I will turn to this in later chapters. But, for now, let me keep the focus on economic development and, in particular, to the questions raised in the last paragraph.

To answer them, we need to go back to before 1991, to the ideas and actions of India's founding fathers.

John Maynard Keynes, the architect of modern economic policy, in one of the most famous passages in his book *The General Theory of Employment, Interest and Money* wrote: "The ideas of economists and political philosophers, both when they are right and when they are wrong, are more powerful than is commonly understood. Indeed, the world is ruled by little else. Practical men, who believe themselves to be quite exempt from any intellectual influences, are usually slaves of some defunct economist. Madmen in authority, who hear voices in the air, are distilling their frenzy from some academic scribbler of a few years back. *I am sure that the power of vested interests is vastly exaggerated compared with the gradual encroachment of ideas"* (1936, 383; my italics).

As a professor, I liked those lines but I did not really believe in them. To me they seemed too self-serving—a professor, Keynes, saying that what he did was more important than what others did. I treated this as example of the pats on the back we all need to keep our enthusiasm up for whatever it is that we do. In addition, Keynes's literary style was so good that it made for engaging reading.

The most important thing I learned during my nearly three years in government, and this has been reinforced by my subsequent work experience at the World Bank, was the profound truth of Keynes's observation. Ideas, how people think, the beliefs hardwired in them, the mental models people carry in their heads, are more important in shaping our lives than most of us realize, and more so than vested interests.

There were many larger-than-life characters in India in the first half of the twentieth century who shaped the ambition of the nation. Rabindranath Tagore—poet, litterateur, and the first Asian Nobel laureate; Ramanujan—the mathematical genius, who, self-taught and working in isolation as a clerk in Madras (now Chennai), advanced the frontiers of number theory; the scientists, C. V. Raman—Nobel laureate in chemistry, and Satyen Bose—the name behind the particle, boson, in the news in recent times in connection with the God particle; political activists and thinkers, Udham Singh, Bal Gangadhar Tilak, Sardar Vallabbhai Patel, Rajendra Prasad, Subhash Chandra Bose, Mohammad Ali Jinnah, and Sri Aurobindo; and many others would figure prominently in every historian's list.

But in the shaping of the modern Indian economy two characters stood out—Mahatma Gandhi, and the country's first prime minister, Jawaharlal Nehru. It is their thoughts on economic policy, at times in unison but more often in conflict, that shaped the India that was born at dawn on August 15, 1947. Some of the ambiguities of modern India's policies have roots in the differences in the views of Gandhi and Nehru. These differences were never quite looked at in the face; given the iconic status of Gandhi and Nehru, these were differences that Indians found too difficult to confront.

The roots of the inconsistencies between their economic philosophies go back to well before 1947. They can be found in Nehru's education at Harrow and Cambridge, his commitment to Fabian socialism, which advocated a gradual instead of a revolutionary change to socialism and simple living, and in Gandhi's grassroots struggle, experiments in alternate living, and innate convictions. Nehru's early commitment to socialism, which he would later abandon in all but rhetoric, was genuine. As early as 1933 Nehru had confided to his diary: "I cannot understand how [Gandhi] can accept . . . the present social order [and] how he can surround himself with men who are . . . the beneficiaries of this social order." Nehru was more radical in a conventional sense than Gandhi. This was clear from his diary entry: "In many ways I have far more in common with English and other non-Indian socialists than I have with non-socialists in India."[4] Ever the contrarian, Nehru would later laughingly tell John Kenneth Galbraith—Harvard economist, adviser to President John F. Kennedy, and the U.S. ambassador to India—that to understand India he should realize that Nehru was the last Englishman to be ruling over India. It was compassion for India's suffering poor that had drawn Nehru to a kind of Fabian socialism. Seeing the unfolding of Russia's Communism, he, ever the democrat, had balked and kept his own creed very distinct from the fashions of the time.

Gandhi lived life with a minimum of material trappings, but did not believe in socialism—certainly not of any known variety. He viewed Nehru's difference of opinion with tolerance and understanding. Thus in 1937 he would tell some foreign visitors: "[Nehru's] enunciation of scientific socialism does not jar on me. I have been living the life since 1906 that he would have all India live. To say that he favors Russian Communism is a travesty of truth." Gandhi, despite his own beliefs to the contrary, clearly had a way with socialists. Here is Harold Laski, one of the most prominent socialist intellectuals of the twentieth century, in a letter to U.S. Supreme Court Justice Oliver Wendell Holmes (September 27, 1931): "Gandhi is really remarkable; there is no difficulty at all in understanding the veneration he inspires. He is quiet, precise and subtle, and there is an inner dignity about him, which is of supreme quality." In another letter (September 17, 1931), Laski wrote amusingly of Gandhi's appeal to the poor in England. He asked a workman, who craned his neck to see Gandhi in a big London crowd, why he came to see this simple man in his white dhoti. To Laski's dismay, the man replied, "I always come to look at the sights. Floodlighting yesterday, Gandhi today," which prompted Laski's apt observation: "I don't think that even the prospect of losing the empire would disturb the sang-froid of the man in the street."[5]

Gandhi was right in his assessment of Nehru; the economic policies they envisaged for India were very different. In the 1930s and even the early 1940s, Nehru was quite enamored by Marx and Lenin (though not by Russian Communism) and referred to their works repeatedly in his diary entries and in letters to friends. He had shed his Marxism-Leninism and even socialism well before India attained independence, but his faith in megaplanning, heavy industry, modern science, and technology would persist. Along with Prasanta Mahalanobis, the statistician, linguist, and polymath who designed one of the world's earliest national random-sample surveys, Nehru would try to give shape to those ideas in the form of what came to be called the Mahalanobis-Nehru strategy of development.[6]

The actual policy regime that India followed during its early days of independence was a mixture of many competing and, at times, even contradictory visions. Nehru was deeply fond of Gandhi. He admired Gandhi's simplicity, acute intelligence, remarkable political instincts, and, above all, his secularism and universal compassion. At the same time Nehru was clear-headed enough to be aware that they had differences. For one, while Gandhi was a deeply religious person, Nehru was openly an atheist. When he visited temples he made it clear that it was to admire the statuary rather than the Gods. He also treated Gandhi's vision of the kind of economy that India should build, namely, a republic of small, self-sufficient villages practicing democracy, with the people living simple lives amid nature, as a good idea but totally unrealistic. If the whole world could be persuaded to be like that, it would be fine, he believed, but in the world that we inhabit, a nation of this kind is unviable.

Gandhi was the father of the nation. His ideas could not be flouted openly, not at the dawn of the nation, and least of all by Nehru, who was the freedom fighter closest to Gandhi with deep and genuine emotional bonds to him. Nehru was clear in his own head that he would jettison Gandhi's economic ideas overall, but drew on several strands of them such as the effort to protect the small-scale and handicraft sector. Regulation was put in place to prevent large firms and corporations from producing certain basic goods. Nehru sought to carry on some of Gandhi's principles of sharing and trusteeship through government action.

Trying to marry different incompatible ideas meant that often rhetoric got the better of actual action, and there were deep contradictions policymakers tried to accommodate within the same system that would later give rise to fault lines and fissures in the economy and hold up development. A Soviet-style planning system was developed, but without the state having a monopoly of control over the resources. Capitalism was allowed to flourish, but an overpowering bureaucracy was nurtured. Huge investments were made in basic industries but at the same time several special activities were protected as belonging to the small-scale sector. Capitalism was criticized but at the same time it was the system India's economy was based on. Socialism was never practiced but the rhetoric of socialism was the norm, with a burgeoning bureaucratic system acting as the surrogate for socialism.

Ideas played a major role, and in this case the dominant ideas were those of Nehru, trying to accommodate elements of Gandhianism. Nehru was an outstanding intellectual, with a flair for writing that put him in the class of a very limited number of national leaders in world history. He was not obsessive about economic growth the way some other twentieth-century leaders had been, such as Park Chung Hee of Korea and Lee Kwan Yew of Singapore. Nehru and some of his generation of leaders did participate in the economic planning process, but their interests were not so much in the plans as in the prose of the plans. Not surprisingly, while Korea produced some of the most effective plans, India produced some of the best-written plans.

Some advisers and economists sitting in rich countries often recommend that developing countries pursue democracy and then go on to specify in detail what these countries should do, for instance, privatize all sectors, nationalize all sectors, allow capital to flow in and out unrestrained, and so on, oblivious of the fact that to ask for democracy and then to specify what the democracy must choose amounts to a contradiction. Since most developing countries were not democracies they did not face this problem, but India did. Once democracy was adopted, as luckily happened right at the time of the nation's independence in 1947, and people's opinions took shape, there was no way that policies could be dictated to them. Opinions would have to be molded before major policy shifts were possible; or, at least, you had to catch people in moments of doubt or inattention to usher in change and work on persuading them that this was in their interest. For this reason, when economists give advice and try to persuade, there is reason to direct their views at ordinary people and the voters, and not just at the policymakers. Serious change in a democracy can happen much more easily when mass opinion shifts.

That opportunity arose in 1991, when Prime Minister Narasimha Rao, Finance Minister Manmohan Singh, and a small team of advisers seized the moment to make fundamental changes. I will turn to these presently but there were important, though less momentous, changes that occurred between the time of Nehru and 1991.

Nehru died in 1964. After a brief interlude, Indira Gandhi became prime minister in 1966. Though there would be disruptions in her rule, 1966 to 1984 became the age of Indira Gandhi. Her influence on the shape of modern India was profound. It is I think fair to conclude that, when it came to economic policy, Indira, unlike Nehru, had no strong ideological convictions. Her beliefs, such as they were, came from two men in her life. As a result there were two different Indira Gandhis that ruled India. Up to 1977 she was very much Nehru's daughter. Her ideology was a broadly socialist one, though the term "socialism," as always in India, was used loosely to connote a redistributive system with reliance on heavy industry, rather than in the original sense of ownership of the means of production being in the hands of the state. It is during this phase of "Indira Gandhi I" that we find her nationalizing banks and attempting to nationalize grain trade, though she had to subsequently retreat on this after the distribution system began to visibly unravel.

When Indira Gandhi returned to power in 1980, it was "Indira Gandhi II" who was in charge. By then, she was under the influence of her sons, Sanjay Gandhi and Rajiv Gandhi. Indira Gandhi II's ideas were shaped primarily, I believe, by Rajiv Gandhi. Her convictions about what should be done to develop India were very different from what she had brought to the nation's helm when she first came to power. It was during the 1980s that India saw the first moves to liberalize the economy and ease foreign exchange transactions, small moves that would nevertheless set the tone for the bigger reforms of 1991–1993.

The Growth Trajectory

Contrary to what some apologists of empire foretold, independence turned out to be good for India's growth. During the first half of the twentieth century, the Indian economy, measured by gross domestic product, grew annually by 1 to 1.5 percent (Sivasubramonian 1997). This would rise to around 3.5 percent after independence, but the economy would then remain stuck in that groove until the middle of the 1970s. It was so resistant to change that this came to be known as the "Hindu rate of growth." Delhi School of Economics professor and distinguished planner Raj Krishna had popularized the term, jocularly suggesting that it must be written somewhere in the scriptures that the people of this land were destined to never see their economy grow faster than 3.5 percent per annum.

While there is dispute about exactly when it happened, India did grow out of the "Hindu growth trap." Through the 1980s the country's GDP grew at an annual average of over 5 percent, though there were some growth spikes even before this time, as is evident from table 2.1. Table 2.1 is a useful background template for a lot of the discussion in this book. It gives the growth history of the nation from just after it gained independence to now. It also shows the corresponding rate of investment, formally, gross capital formation, as a percentage of GDP, basically the total output produced in the nation. Investment is a major driver of growth and I shall have more than one occasion to refer to this.

In 1975–1976 India's GDP grew by a record 9 percent.[7] Whether this was the start of a new trend or a mere reflection of the dramatic events of 1975 will probably be a never-ending debate. Nevertheless, to understand the trajectory of India's growth it is important to understand 1975.

Indira Gandhi's career had reached a pinnacle in 1971. In the late 1960s she planned and engineered a major agricultural triumph for the country—the Green Revolution, which, by introducing new seed varieties and

Table 2.1
Annual growth rate of real GDP and investment rate, 1950–2014

Year	Growth rate of GDP	Investment rate	Year	Growth rate of GDP	Investment rate
1950–1951		9.3	1982–1983	2.9	19.1
1951–1952	2.3	11.4	1983–1984	7.9	18.2
1952–1953	2.8	8.5	1984–1985	4.0	19.1
1953–1954	6.1	7.9	1985–1986	4.2	20.6
1954–1955	4.2	10.0	1986–1987	4.3	20.1
1955–1956	2.6	12.8	1987–1988	3.5	21.9
1956–1957	5.7	15.2	1988–1989	10.2	22.8
1957–1958	-1.2	14.0	1989–1990	6.1	23.7
1958–1959	7.6	11.7	1990–1991	5.3	26.0
1959–1960	2.2	12.4	1991–1992	1.4	21.8
1960–1961	7.1	14.3	1992–1993	5.4	23.0
1961–1962	3.1	13.4	1993–1994	5.7	22.2
1962–1963	2.1	14.9	1994–1995	6.4	24.7
1963–1964	5.1	14.3	1995–1996	7.3	25.3
1964–1965	7.6	14.5	1996–1997	8.0	23.7
1965–1966	-3.7	16.2	1997–1998	4.3	25.6
1966–1967	1.0	16.7	1998–1999	6.7	24.2
1967–1968	8.1	14.3	1999–2000	8.0	26.6
1968–1969	2.6	13.1	2000–2001	4.1	24.3
1969–1970	6.5	14.6	2001–2002	5.4	24.2
1970–1971	5.0	15.1	2002–2003	3.9	24.8
1971–1972	1.0	16.0	2003–2004	8.0	26.8
1972–1973	-0.3	14.7	2004–2005	7.1	32.8
1973–1974	4.6	17.3	2005–2006	9.5	34.7
1974–1975	1.2	17.5	2006–2007	9.6	35.7
1975–1976	9.0	17.2	2007–2008	9.3	38.1
1976–1977	1.2	17.4	2008–2009	6.7	34.3
1977–1978	7.5	17.8	2009–2010	8.6	36.5
1978–1979	5.5	21.1	2010–2011	8.9	36.5
1979–1980	-5.2	20.4	2011–2012	6.7	35.5
1980–1981	7.2	19.2	2012–2013	4.9	34.8
1981–1982	5.6	18.9	2013–2014	6.6	

Source: Government of India 2014, with updates for GDP data for the last two years. The GDP growth shown is at factor cost, at constant prices, with 2004–2005 as base; and the investment rate refers to gross capital formation as percent of GDP.

techniques of production and fertilizer use, caused agricultural productivity to shoot up, especially in India's large wheat-growing regions. In politics, moral battles are rare but, when in 1971 India got engaged in helping East Pakistan in its struggle for independence from Pakistan, we saw Indira Gandhi at her moral high ground. As East Pakistan was being savaged by the Pakistan army to suppress the independence movement, Indira Gandhi had the Indian army step in on the side of the street fighters of East Pakistan. Tensions mounted when President Richard Nixon, an ally of Pakistan, in an ill-conceived maneuver, ordered the Seventh Fleet to move into the Bay of Bengal to pressure India to step back. What happened next was the very opposite. It steeled Indira Gandhi's resolve and the Indian army, along with Bangladesh's Mukti Bahini, stepped up action. On December 16, 1971, the Pakistani forces in East Pakistan decided to surrender and were taken prisoners of war, the largest number since World War II. Bangladesh, which had unilaterally declared independence on March 25, 1971, was truly independent now.

These successes and Indira Gandhi's socialist rhetoric raised implausible hopes. When the first oil crisis struck in 1973 and India's economy slowed down and inflation picked up, disenchantment set in quickly. During 1972–1974 India's annual inflation breached the 30 percent mark. This kind of inflation had not happened before in independent India, and has not happened since. As the disenchantment grew, there was also an increase in civil-society activism led by Jayaprakash Narayan, and there were court strictures passed against Prime Minister Gandhi. Indira Gandhi also knew, as Katherine Frank so eloquently recounts in her gripping biography of Gandhi, that "she was high up on Richard Nixon's hate list and she was genuinely afraid that she would be overthrown in the same way Chile's CIA-backed Augusto Pinochet had staged a coup against Salvador Allende in 1973" (Frank 2002, 374–375). Nixon was known to have been smarting ever since he was shown to have misjudged the effect the Seventh Fleet action would have on the prime minister of this poor nation.

As she felt beleaguered by all these developments and her innate sense of isolation grew, Indira Gandhi, along with a small coterie of advisers, hit upon an idea. June 25, 1975, was a dramatic day in modern India's history as Indira Gandhi conferred with her advisers, notably, the lawyer Siddhartha Shankar Ray, and her son, Sanjay Gandhi. When Indira Gandhi explained her concerns to Ray, he said he would need time with his law books before he could advise her. He rushed home, consulted multiple sources, including the Indian and U.S. constitutions, and returned to the prime minister's residence at 3:30 p.m. It was soon decided that they would invoke article 352 of the Indian constitution, which allowed the declaration of a "national emergency" in the event of a threat of war or internal armed rebellion. The only remaining catch was to persuade President Fakhruddin Ali Ahmed to sign the order. Since there was no real external threat and Jayaprakash Narayan's powerful movement against the government was not an armed rebellion, there was need for considerable imagination to use this special constitutional provision for the consolidation of power. Fortunately, the president at that time was a pliable person and a decision was taken late in the night of June 25 that early next morning Indira Gandhi would announce the "dangers facing the nation," the need to suspend civil liberties, and the start of what came to be known as the Emergency.

Indira Gandhi went off to sleep well after midnight. Ray stayed a while to discuss with other close advisers the strategies for the following day. One thing they were all aware of was that the Indian press would savage the prime minister for declaring the Emergency without sufficient cause and for arresting opposition leaders, as she would have to order done to quell dissent. Around the same time, Sanjay Gandhi and his cronies in an adjacent room decided that they would arrange to have power supplies to all major newspaper offices in Delhi cut off in order to slow down the transmission of news and dissent. Katherine Frank tells us in her book that an argument ensued, with Ray objecting to this power outage plan as undemocratic, and that eventually Indira Gandhi had to be woken up (Frank 2002). She assured Ray that this would not happen.

The following day the power supply to almost all newspaper offices was cut. The only two papers that came out, *The Statesman* and *Hindustan Times*, did so only because of an oversight by those in charge of engineering the outage. The full details of how this happened are not known but it simply illustrates that totalitarian control is seldom as total and controlled as appears to outsiders. The forces of authoritarian power, once unleashed, acquire lives of their own and, no matter what the original intentions, chart out courses difficult to anticipate.

Thus began two of the most traumatic years in the political life of independent India. Opposition leaders were indiscriminately arrested and several of those leading civil society movements were put behind bars. The opposition movements that survived the initial onslaught soon went underground. Anonymous pamphlets criticizing the Emergency were distributed in the universities. There was a sense that Indira Gandhi's hawkish son Sanjay was getting the upper hand. The prime minister criticized the opposition as a cabal with vested interests, out to foil her from fulfilling her commitments to the poor and the dispossessed. There was conviction in her voice, but conviction, it is known, comes easily and without adequate reason when it is an instrument of survival.

At least to start with, her overall popularity remained high. This was helped by the economy, which seemed to gather strength. In 1975–1976 India's GDP grew by an unprecedented 9 percent. It is difficult to pin down what caused this spike. Trains have a knack for running on time in totalitarian states, at least in the first flush. And there was enough evidence that trains in India suddenly began running on time. Some time ago, the Swedish economist and game theorist Jörgen Weibull and I wrote a paper on why some societies are more punctual than others and we argued that punctuality is, in large measure, an equilibrium phenomenon (Basu and Weibull 2003). If others in your society are punctual, it is worth your effort to be punctual; if others are not, it may not be worthwhile for you to expend the effort to be punctual. In a more elaborate model we may want to append to this the fact that habits get formed, which creates some resistance to change. Hence, change happens, but not instantaneously.

What this formulation suggests—and I still believe this is an important feature of societies' behavior patterns, such as those pertaining to punctuality, and social norms—is that societies exhibiting very different kinds of behavior patterns are, at a fundamental level, much more similar. Societies, a priori, have multiple equilibria and different societies get caught in different equilibria. However, this does not mean that other incentives and exogenous factors do not matter. If you risk being put in jail for running your train late, you are less likely to be late. The Emergency did create these kinds of fears and may have contributed to efficiency.

As it happens, the growth impulse of that year did not last long enough for us to be able to attribute any permanent change to the Emergency. The following year growth plummeted to 1.2 percent. In 1977–1978 and 1978–1979 it picked up somewhat and then in 1979–1980 growth declined sharply, to -5.2 percent. In other words, India's GDP shrank by 5.2 percent. Purely in terms of growth, this stands out as the worst year for India since the nation's independence. Interestingly, 1979–1980 was the last year in which India saw negative growth. In 1991–1992, caused by the economic fallout of the First Gulf War, growth did plummet but it still did not go into negative territory. Growth that year fell to 1.4 percent.[8]

For readers unfamiliar with these kinds of numbers, it may be useful to point out that the fluctuations in growth figures that occurred in India are by no means excessive by emerging country standards. India's government officials always played safe in matters of economic policy. It may have something to do with the country's political institutions that its leaders refused to take major gambles. Hence, India seldom saw spectacular growth but it never suffered large crashes either. China is an interesting study in contrast. The main difference between China and India, especially before 1978, was not in the levels of growth but in terms of the magnitude of fluctuations in growth. In 1958 Mao Zedong started the Great Leap Forward, collectivizing agriculture and taking away the individualistic drive that motivates farmers to grow more. The consequence was not even a gentle leap forward but a massive backlash triggering one of the worst famines humankind has seen.[9] And in 1961 China registered a growth of –27.1 percent, a magnitude of collapse that is hard to contemplate. But soon thereafter, China's economy grew at rates hardly ever seen in any nation, certainly never in India. During 1963, 1964, 1965, and 1966 China grew by, respectively, 10.3, 15.8, 16.4, and 10.7 percent. Over the next two years the economy would again collapse, and shrink by over 5 percent and then 4 percent, respectively. Whatever Mao Zedong's big ideas did for China otherwise, in terms of economic growth they led to volatilities at a level that few nations would tolerate. It is interesting to observe the difference in the range of fluctuations that India and China exhibited. It is possible that this reflected what the political systems of the two nations considered permissible.[10]

To return to the India story, one reason for the fluctuations the Indian economy witnessed between 1977 and 1980 was the instability that occurred in the political theater at that time. Despite the success of the economy, Indira Gandhi's Emergency began running into trouble soon enough. Indians were already too used to democratic rights to tolerate the indiscriminate silencing of voices of dissent and the imprisonment of opposition leaders. The anger started mounting. Then a program of forced family planning, coordinated by Sanjay Gandhi, had a massive negative backlash. The government's popularity was clearly on the wane. In 1977 Indira Gandhi announced something that few leaders at the peak of authoritarian control ever did—a free and open election. Many felt it was her hubris that led her to believe that the opposition to her came from a minority elite and that, put to vote, she would win. As it happened, she lost the election.

Whether she called the election out of overconfidence or a sense of regret for having sullied the democracy her father had so carefully nurtured is a topic that has been debated endlessly. In early 2012, I did a little research into this and learned from a very reliable source that Indira Gandhi told one of her trusted advisers—and there were very few of them—that, based on intelligence reports she had received, she expected to lose the elections, but she could not continue with the Emergency. Evidently, she had begun to doubt if what she had done was right and, minimally, wanted an endorsement from the electorate; and if she did not get that, an outcome for which she was fully prepared, she was ready to relinquish office.

It is interesting to note—and this is a matter not without interest to social psychologists—that Nehru published in 1938, under the pseudonym of Chanakya, an article analyzing Nehru, himself, in the November issue of *Modern Review*, the preeminent journal of the nationalist intelligentsia of India. The article dwells at length on the risks of dictatorship that even committed democrats have to contend with: "Jawaharlal [Nehru] is certainly not a fascist. . . . He is far too much of an aristocrat for the crudity and vulgarity of fascism. . . . He calls himself a democrat and a socialist, and no doubt he does so in all earnestness, but every psychologist knows that the mind is ultimately a slave to the heart. . . . A little twist and Jawaharlal might turn a dictator sweeping aside the paraphernalia of a slow-moving democracy." Was he ruminating on some of his own fears or warning a daughter of how easy it is to despair of India's slow-moving democracy and fall into the abyss of dictatorial control?[11]

The fall of Indira Gandhi and her Congress Party brought to power the Janata Party, with Morarji Desai as prime minister. Morarji was an old-style politician, who led a simple, spartan life. He was a Gandhian and, though they had once been colleagues, by the time he became prime minister, he was staunchly against Indira Gandhi. He worked to reverse many of her policies; in particular, he made an effort to improve relations with the United States, which had soured since 1971. This move would turn out to be useful; it set India and the United States on a trajectory that would yield dividends two decades later. Morarji was also widely noted to be "above corruption" even though there were some journalists who insisted that that claim simply referred to the fact that he lived one floor above his son.

The attempt to reverse domestic policy too aggressively backfired on the economy. It began slowing down and prices began to rise in 1978 and, as already noted, 1979–1980 turned out to the worst growth year for India. Morarji was soon ousted as prime minister by Charan Singh. By then, disillusionment with the squabbling group of people trying to lead India had firmly set in the electorate and, when an election was called in 1980, Indira Gandhi was back in power. As I noted earlier, this time it was Indira Gandhi II who was in power. She was now much more ready to recognize the role of the market, even while retaining her instinctive sympathy for the poor, and her socialist rhetoric was now more muted. She had not changed her mind about any of her fundamental objectives but simply realized that the policy instruments she had earlier chosen were not working. A relatively steady period of growth ensued, even though much of her attention was now beginning to be taken up by the Sikh secessionist movement that was brewing in the Punjab.

Indira Gandhi's eventful era came to an abrupt end on October 31, 1984. I do not know if there is anything called premonition, but on October 30, in an emotional speech in Orissa she said, "I am alive today, I may not be there tomorrow. . . . I shall continue to serve till my last breath and when I die every drop of my blood will strengthen India and keep a united India alive." Returning to Delhi that evening she found herself unusually restless, and interrupted her sleep to chat with her daughter-in-law, Sonia Gandhi, to whom she was very close. The following morning, as she walked across from her residence to her office next door to give an interview to Peter Ustinov for the BBC, she was assassinated by two of her Sikh bodyguards.

Her son, Rajiv Gandhi, who had diligently stayed away from politics, was hurriedly ushered in to be prime minister. A reformer by instinct but with little expertise in economics, Rajiv Gandhi tried to bring in changes as well as he could and the economy responded positively. The 1980s saw India growing at an average rate of above 5 percent per annum. India had clearly broken out of the Hindu growth trap. There was also recognition from American businesses, forever in search of markets, that India was becoming a market-friendly country. They began to bring pressure on the U.S. government to open up more to India. This would eventually bear fruit in the 1990s.[12]

The political history thereafter is not important for my story. Politics is, if nothing else, fickle. Rajiv Gandhi's wild popularity on being inducted, reluctantly, into politics in 1984, led to one of the biggest Congress Party victories in that year. But with some major corruption scandals breaking in 1987, his popularity began to wane; and the Congress Party was defeated in the elections in 1989. Rajiv was out of power but active in politics. There were two years of rule by the Janata Dal and the Samajwadi Janata Party, but these were fractious enough that by 1991 elections had to be called again. On May 21 while on the campaign trail in South India, Rajiv Gandhi was assassinated by a suicide bomber belonging to a Tamil secessionist group based in Sri Lanka.

Crisis as Opportunity

On June 21, 1991, the Congress found itself back in power, with Narasimha Rao as prime minister and Manmohan Singh, a political novice, as finance minister. There could not be a worse time to form a government. The First Gulf War had a disastrous consequence on the Indian economy. In those days the largest source of foreign income for India was money remitted home by Indians working abroad.[13] The big remitters were not the well-off Indians working as engineers, doctors, and professors in the United States and other industrialized nations. They were Indian workers based in the Middle East. The Gulf War led to many of these workers losing their jobs and there was a sharp decline in foreign exchange inflows into India. Coming on the heels of the government's fiscal profligacy of the previous three or four years and consequent large foreign debt, this meant trouble.[14]

One well-known feature of finance is that crises often come in a flash. This is caused by imitative or herd behavior. When several people lend to an agent—be it a person, a company, or a nation, it is considered safe to lend to the agent. If you want to take your money back, you know that the agent will be able to turn to the several lenders it has access to, to draw enough money to pay you back. Conversely, when others stop lending to an agent, you should stop lending to the agent. This looking over the shoulder to see what other lenders are doing can result in sudden, seemingly coordinated halts in lending, precipitating a crisis that need not have occurred. This is what happened to India. India was always considered a safe country to lend to because as a nation it did not take undue risks. Nevertheless, when the remittances began to dry up because of the Gulf War, other lenders also stopped lending money or pulled out their money. When the new government came to power in June 1991, India had enough foreign exchange for thirteen days of normal imports.

There was no option but the politically unpopular one of going to the International Monetary Fund for money. That calmed markets and gave the country some breathing space, which was used remarkably effectively to put together a package of reforms of the kind never seen before. The government also had the wisdom to clear up cobwebs that may not have had much to do with the crisis but needed clearing up anyway.[15]

At that time, India used to have a notorious licensing system. Anyone wanting to start up a new industry or even expand production beyond a certain level had to get a permit or a "license" from the government to do so. This was meant to be an instrument for directing production into socially useful activities and thwart industry from going into areas that the government considered lacking in worth.[16] But, in effect, it led to notorious bureaucratic hurdles and became a breeding ground for corruption. Commentators of all political hues criticized India's cumbersome bureaucracy and, in particular, the licensing system.[17] But, at times, change for the better becomes impossible because of a failure to agree on the best. Everyone agreed that the licensing system ought to be jettisoned but there was no agreement on what the ideal alternative would be. This failure of agreement meant that what was agreed upon, namely the jettisoning, could not happen. This is a bit like America's archaic gun control laws. The ease of acquiring assault weapons in the United States is a primitive custom, justified through an inchoate understanding of what constitutes individual liberty. If this were put to a referendum it is almost certain that the nation would vote for much stricter laws concerning the possession of weapons. Indeed, if the United States had stricter gun control laws, and some distant, poor nation had easy gun control laws like the United States has, popular opinion in the United States would lament the outmoded laws in the faraway region. The failure to agree on what is best often implies that what is better remains unimplemented, and we learn to live with what we have and even justify it.

Luckily for India, the government had the sense to weave the revocation of the licensing system into the package of reform measures announced in 1991.[18] Another part of this reform package addressed foreign exchange transactions and international trade. The highest tariff rates applied to manufacturing goods, called the peak rate, was first brought down to 150 percent in 1991, and lowered steadily thereafter, reaching 15 percent by 2005 (Ila Patnaik 2011).

On foreign exchange India had a naïve attitude. Since India's foreign exchange reserves were so meager the instinct was to have rules to make it difficult, in fact, virtually impossible, to take foreign exchange out of the country in any reasonable volume. What the policymakers did not realize is that if you do not allow people to take foreign exchange out, they will be hesitant to bring foreign exchange into the country. Hence, allowing people to take dollars out more easily could actually result in more dollars being brought into the country.

This inability to do two-stage thinking, as I would later discover to my dismay in the context of corruption control (I shall turn to this in chapter 8), is rather pervasive in policymaking, much to the detriment of nations. Fortunately, in 1991, the Indian government woke up to this folly and eased up foreign exchange flows outward and inward. Several commentators made dire forecasts about how India's meagre foreign currency reserves would soon run out.

What happened was the opposite. Figure 2.1 may well be the most iconic picture of what the economic reforms and liberalization did for India. It shows the dramatic effect of easing up on foreign exchange controls. For at least fifteen years, up to 1991, India was used to surviving with roughly $5 billion worth of reserves. If this rose to $7 billion, we felt comfortable and if it dropped to $3 billion we considered it a balance of payments crisis. But on average the reserves remained stubbornly in the vicinity of $5 billion. The foreign exchange reserve in India was $5.82 billion in 1978. It was $5.83 billion in 1991. After the market liberalization, over the next fifteen years, the foreign exchange reserves rose exponentially, breaching the $300 billion mark in 2008. India was among the five or six largest holders of hard currency reserves in the world. Her balance of payments story had evidently made a gestalt switch. The policy break is visible to the naked eye. In figure 2.1, the best-fit line from the early 1970s to 1991 is a horizontal line, virtually grazing the horizontal axis. The best-fit line beyond 1991, on the other hand, lifts off precipitously.

Changes were not confined to the external sector alone. Freed of the licensing system, the manufacturing sector began to grow faster, though in the longer run this sector has persisted in being a stumbling block for the nation. With the sharp lowering of import tariffs and easing up of

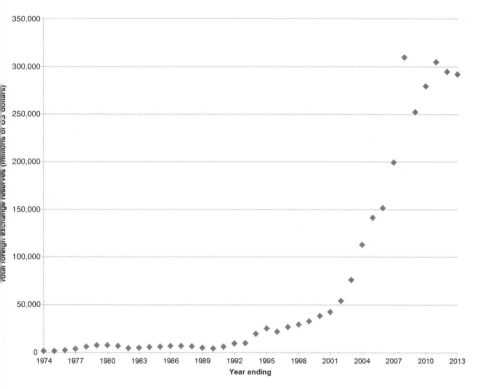

Figure 2.1
India's foreign exchange reserves

computer imports, India's information technology sector took off (Murthy 2004; Singh 2004; Chanda 2011). Other services sectors, such as finance and financial services, were also on the move and soon the service sector would take off like never before in India and nowhere in the world, for that matter. Over the next fifteen years India's services sector grew faster than in any other nation in the world.

All this was handsomely reflected in the country's overall growth rate. The nation's real national income, or GDP, grew by around 7 percent for three consecutive years, 1994–1995, 1995–1996, and 1996–1997. It is arguable that India had moved onto a higher growth path. There would be a disruption in the following year, 1997–1998, which had little to do with India. By early 1997 storm clouds were beginning to gather over the skies of East Asia. By the end of that year all the major East Asian nations were drawn into a kind of crisis they had not witnessed in the previous thirty years.

What happened was a complex story but it illustrates well how, in a globalized world, crisis in one segment can quickly infect others. In mid-1997
the Thai housing prices made a downward correction. Lots of companies
that had invested in property saw their balance sheets deteriorate. When
that happened people began to pull out some of their money invested in
the stocks of these companies, causing stock prices to travel south. This led
to a side effect that had rarely occurred earlier and therefore was not fully
anticipated. With the capitalization of global markets, we had for some
time been seeing savings from one country being invested in stocks and
shares in other countries. American pensioners, for instance, might put
their money in the Bangkok stock market. The way this is typically done is
to have U.S. savings, made in dollars, be sent to Bangkok, changed to Thai
bahts, and then invested in the local stock market.

In this setting, it is easy to see that a stock market collapse would have an
effect on exchange rates that would not have occurred in a nonglobalized
world, that is, one in which Thais invested in Thai stocks and Americans in
U.S. stocks with negligible cross holdings.

When the Thai stock market started doing poorly, people started taking
their money out of stocks. Unlike the locals, foreigners who had brought
their money into Thailand only to invest in the stock market clearly
wanted to take their money back out of the country. But as soon as large
numbers of people began to sell Thai bahts and buy dollars or pounds, the
Thai currency started to collapse. The exchange rate depreciated suddenly.
This happened across the board in East Asian countries at a speed that was
disquieting. Here are some depreciation rates of domestic currencies vis-
à-vis the dollar, between July 1, 1997, and February 16, 1998: Philippines
51 percent, Malaysia 55 percent, South Korea 83 percent, Thailand 87 percent, and Indonesia 231 percent. Such a sudden collapse left devastation
in its wake, affecting imports, causing foreign debts to shoot up (in terms
of domestic currency), savaging balance sheets, elevating unemployment
rates, and choking growth.[19]

India was not directly involved in this crisis but with the entire East
Asian region crashing, it was impossible not to feel the heat. India's growth
in 1997–1998 dropped to 4.8 percent. Over the next three or four years, the
situation in India improved but it did not immediately return to where it
had been in the three years prior to the crisis.

Growth Surge

Fortunately, the reforms of 1991–1993 had built up enough momentum that, with the other changes occurring during the first years of the new millennium, India could soon take another leap upward. This happened from 2003 onward, and even more markedly after 2005. It is interesting to study the factors behind this growth surge, which would have India join the club of the five or six fastest-growing nations of the world.

Old-fashioned economic theory taught us that one of the main drivers of growth in a developing country with surplus labor is the extent of saving and investment occurring in that nation: that is, the fraction of the nation's total income that is saved (the savings rate); and the fraction of the nation's total output that is investment goods such as factories, machines, and inventories that citizens do not consume immediately but that make higher future consumption possible (the investment rate). These two rates usually do not veer too far from each other. Early works by Roy Harrod in Britain and Evsey Domar in the United States had built models connecting a nation's savings rate to its growth rate. These models were later to be made much more sophisticated through the works of Robert Solow and Trevor Swan, and, later, Robert Lucas, John Roemer, and others; but the basic idea has stood its ground.[20]

India's savings rate story is an interesting one. In the 1960s and 1970s it used to be lamented that, in terms of savings behavior, India was like a Western or Latin American enclave in Asia. Indians saved too little and were not like the East Asian nations, which were saving at rates above 30 percent, and growing at breakneck speeds. This was true for Singapore, Korea, Taiwan, Malaysia, and, starting from earlier times, Japan; and a little later China too joined the club. What was not realized then was that change was already on its way in India as well.

Up to late 1960s India used to save just over 10 percent (of its national income). Over the next ten years this would rise to above 20 percent. It is not difficult to see what happened. This was the time when India took some major steps to make it easy for people to save, basically by creating places for people to park their savings. Most of this initial effort was state driven. In 1964, the government set up the Unit Trust of India (UTI), which allowed people to invest in mutual funds. This was run efficiently and also nicely sheltered by the state from the vagaries of the stock market. It is not in general a good idea to provide such artificial shelters, but that does not change the fact that the UTI became a safe haven for middle-class people to keep their money and earn a stable return. The returns were so stable that most Indians did not know that this was a mutual fund. They treated it like a fixed deposit scheme that gave excellent returns. This helped boost savings.

Another important change occurred in 1969. Indira Gandhi—recall this was her radical period—nationalized all Indian banks that year. The overall impact of this was questionable, but it had one good effect. The nationalization of banks made it possible for Indira Gandhi to give out orders to the banks to open branches in remote villages to make it easy for people to save money. Since all banks were now state run, profit was not a consideration and they generally complied (Basu and Maertens 2008). The number of bank branches rose sharply and, along with that, savings rose. By the late 1970s India's savings rate was at an all-time high of around 22 percent.

Thereafter, it remained roughly at this level until 2000. Then it began to rise once again and by 2003 had breached the 30 percent mark. This was unthinkable and India began, for the first time, to look like an Asian country. What caused this second step up is not well understood. First, it is arguable that when a nation begins to grow faster, people do not have the habit of consuming more and hence they see their savings rise. This hypothesis should be testable by studying all countries that have seen a sudden rise in the growth rate and checking if that is accompanied by a rise in the savings rate in the early years of the growth surge.

Second, this was a period of fiscal consolidation by the government, following some profligate years starting with 1998. This led to more government saving. Whatever the cause, savings and investment rates rose sharply, as sharply as in the early 1970s, and provided one more round of ballast for the Harrod–Domar and Solow–Swan type of growth.

Like the mysterious alignment of stars, various geopolitical factors moved into a favorable configuration around this time. Relations between India and the United States improved quite radically. It was evident to the United States that the world would not be the unipolar one with the United States at the helm, as may have appeared possible immediately after the collapse of the Soviet Union. China seemed almost certain to become one of the big powers of the world. For any nation, the ideal world is a unipolar one with that nation marking the pole; in some ways, the worst possible world is a bipolar one, where one big power faces off with a second big power, because that inevitably gives rise to risk and instability. When it is a fait accompli that a second big power is going to arrive on the scene, it is best to nurture a third and a fourth one. This is how India and some other large emerging economies came into prominent play in U.S. foreign policy.

The United States had some other important commonalities with India. Both nations, alongside several others, were battling terrorist threats. Both were deep-rooted secular democracies. In addition, the steady flow of professional Indians into the United States no doubt began to influence relations positively between the two countries. The sharp improvement in relations, founded in several long-term factors and not driven solely by short-term strategic considerations, was a boost to the Indian economy. Nicholas Burns (2014, 132) may well be right in arguing, "In the century ahead, US strategic interests will align more closely with India's than they will with any other continental power in Asia."

There have also been some advantages conferred on India, unwittingly. The U.S. presidential election in 2004, between George Bush and John Kerry, played an interesting role. From the beginning of this long drawn-out campaign, there was a lot of discussion and acrimony about outsourcing. India and Bangalore often figured in this. It is not clear that either of the presidential candidates believed that outsourcing did any harm to the U.S. economy, but for reasons of electoral politics they spoke as if it did. Thereafter, several conservative television commentators picked up on this theme. They criticized the lack of patriotism of U.S. entrepreneurs who outsourced their work to India and other emerging economies and claimed it was purely for the entrepreneurs' own profit.

Interestingly the main effect of these attacks was on U.S. entrepreneurs who had not outsourced their back-office work. Many of the smaller entrepreneurs, who did not even know that more profit could be made by outsourcing, woke up to this opportunity. Advertising on prime time television in the United States is phenomenally expensive. Small back-office firms in the Philippines, South Africa, and India would not be able to afford this on their own. In this instance, because of the commentators' attacks, they effectively got free advertisement. At least in the case of India there was a boom in outsourcing and back-office work following the period of television pundits battering the entrepreneurs.

All these forces lining up together helped India's growth climb in 2003 and again in 2005. From 2005 to 2008 for three consecutive years the Indian economy grew at over 9 percent per annum. The savings rate rose to over 35 percent, the investment rate to over 38 percent, and the consequences of this boom were visible even to the naked eye. India's infrastructure, ramshackle in the best of times, was palpably improving, the bazaars of the middle class were booming, and, as we would later learn from statistical studies, overall poverty in the nation, while still unconscionably high, was now declining faster than ever before since the nation's independence.

The most dramatic effect of this was that the popular narrative on India changed. Writing in the *Financial Times* of February 23, 2005, about China and India, Martin Wolf observed, "The economic rise of Asia's giants is, therefore, the most important story of our age. It heralds the end, in the not too distant a future, of as much as five centuries of domination by the Europeans and their colonial offshoots." In an interview for the *IMF Survey* (February 21, 2005, 40), Wanda Tseng, mission chief for India in the IMF, said, "India is one of the fastest growing economies in the world and is certainly looking to continue growing strongly." Stephen Cohen in his influential book on India (Cohen 2001, 34–35) writes, "India has long been counted among the have-nots. The situation is rapidly changing, which is what will make India such an interesting "great power" for the next dozen years."[21] Standard and Poor's *CreditWeek*, on January 5, 2005, credited China and India as "global success stories in reducing poverty and moving towards a prosperous market economy" (12) and noted that "since China initiated economic reform in 1978, its national income has more than quadrupled; since India began liberalizing its economy in 1991, its per capita income has almost doubled." On April 4, 2005, on the occasion of the founding of the Lee Kuan Yew School of Public Policy in Singapore, Lee Kuan Yew predicted in a speech crammed with statistics and deft analysis that India would be propelled into the "front ranks" of the global economy. He went on to say that "China and India will shake the world" and in some industries "have already leapfrogged the rest of Asia."

For me, the most notable incident affecting perception of India happened in Delhi. The only time I met former Secretary of State Henry Kissinger was at a small dinner hosted by Naresh Chandra in the Mountbatten Room at Oberoi Hotel in New Delhi on March 19, 2012. At the start of the meal, Chandra asked Kissinger if he would like to say a few words. Kissinger stood up a bit hesitantly, explaining that he had a damaged ligament, and he began speaking slowly. He said he had not been expecting to have to speak, but it was evident he enjoyed speaking, and he did so with complete fluency and at some length. The only slip in the talk was when at the start he said he was happy to be here and went on to add that he had been coming to "China" since 1961.

Keeping in mind that Kissinger had long been an India pessimist, placing all his bets on China, that day's dinnertime discourse was remarkable. Ranging over a diverse sweep of topics, from Afghanistan and Iran to the balance of power in Asia, he spoke with immense optimism about India and the role of India in promoting peace in the entire region. He spoke of world affairs with a certain deliberateness, with long pauses. We could have been listening to Metternich. But what stood out for all of us at the dinner was how optimistic he was about India.[22]

It will be argued in the pages that follow that the popular perception in the media and in Henry Kissinger's talk is valid. India is on a high-growth path and the next few decades are likely to raise the nation to the platform of industrialized countries. Of course, there will be challenges and pitfalls on the way; and there will be need for supportive policy. Indeed, the ride has been choppy since 2008, when the global economy hit a financial roadblock, and 2013 and 2014 especially have been difficult years.

I close this section with a digression on a topic that is likely to divide future historians. As the preceding account makes amply clear, the period from 1991 to 1993 represents a watershed in India's economic development and a large part of the credit for this goes to the then Finance Minister Manmohan Singh. Since I write this soon after the fall of a government led by Singh as prime minister, I am aware that most readers today will be in no mood to pay tribute to him, especially since there can be no doubt that the last days of his government were mired in indecision, even in the face of political scandals, including major corruption scandals, that made headlines and cut into the fabric of society.

How does one reconcile these two faces of the same government? My view is that while Manmohan Singh will in retrospect be regarded as a key figure in India's economic development and an exemplary leader in terms of personal integrity and human qualities, he lacked one skill that may have been his eventual undoing. He was a politician without a taste for politics. And in saying this, I should remind the reader that politics may well be the only profession in which not being good at it is a virtue.

Gathering Storm: The Global Financial Crisis and Its Fallout

I lived in the United States when the subprime mortgage crisis erupted in 2007 and 2008. The crisis soon spilled over into a full-blown financial recession. As the recession deepened and began hurting the real economy, its effects crossed the seas and engulfed other nations. Around the same time that this crisis spilled over from the United States to the rest of the world, I left the United States for "the rest of the world."[23] I moved to India in December 2009. In other words, I had a bird's eye view of the crisis as it coursed through the world, moving from industrialized countries to emerging economies, like few others did. There are meteorological enthusiasts who spend a lot of time and effort to go chasing the monsoon. I have been lucky as an economist; without intending to do so and with no special effort on my part, I went chasing the crisis.

The story has been told numerous times now. The crisis began innocuously, from a seemingly good effort in the United States to reach out to poorer people with cheap home loans, enabling them to own homes that they otherwise would not have been able to. This worked well for a while. Then, by late 2007, the cracks began to show. Many of these new homeowners belonged to a category that financiers used to refer to as "subprime," that is, borrowers whose financial situation is precarious enough that lending to them is not considered safe. Not surprisingly, many of these subprime borrowers ended up defaulting. In the beginning this seemed manageable and, at worst, a problem specific to the housing sector. When a default occurred, the lending bank or financial institution came and foreclosed the property and put it on sale to recover the loan. As more homes went on sale, housing prices began to fall.

This had a somewhat unexpected consequence. Home loans can be of two kinds—recourse and non-recourse. A recourse loan allows the lender to lay claims to more than the borrower's home, for instance, to the borrower's bank balance and car, to recover the loan. A non-recourse loan does not allow the borrower to lay claim to anything beyond what has been explicitly mortgaged, in this case, the home. Though the law varies across the states, in practice, the bulk of home lending in the United States is non-recourse.

Consider now a borrower who takes a loan of $100 and buys a house worth $110. Now suppose the prices of homes drop and houses of this kind drop to a price of $90. The rational thing for a borrower, who has taken a non-recourse loan, is to not repay the loan. The bank will come and foreclose the home (that is, take it away and sell it off on the market) but so what? He would have had to pay the bank $100 for a (now) $90 home. By walking away (and, if need be, picking up a similar home for $90), he saves money, since the loan was non-recourse and the lender would not be able to seize his other assets. This is exactly what happened. As house prices fell, more and more homebuyers walked away without paying.

As this problem increased another fault line showed up. Consider now a bank that gives a loan of $100 for a home worth $110. Its balance sheet will show that its asset is equal to $100 with a certain probability, namely, the probability of the loan being repaid, and $110 with the probability of the loan being defaulted, since $110 is the market price of the house.[24] In other words, the balance sheet shows a value of somewhere between $100 and $110. Now if the market price of homes drops, as described earlier, and the borrower defaults, the bank's balance sheet becomes $90, the price of the house. In other words, the bank's balance sheet deteriorates. And this too happened. As the mortgage market collapsed and house prices fell, the balance sheets of banks and financial institutions suddenly worsened. The mortgage crisis became a general financial crisis, with credit vanishing and corporations suddenly looking poorer[25] than they thought they were.

The link between the world of finance and the real world of goods and services—how exactly a change in the former transmits and affects the latter—is one of the least understood phenomena in economics. Some of the best-trained economists have struggled to get a full understanding of this but have failed to find one. (I would be remiss if I did not warn the reader that some ill-trained economists believe that they have found it.) The mathematics of this phenomenon is remarkably complex and has remained a research challenge. What we do know from past experience is that a credit collapse tends to quickly translate into lower production and trade.[26] Predictably, soon after this financial crisis, the U.S. output growth rate began to slow down and unemployment began to rise.

Though contenders are bound to appear, and arguably in the not-too-distant future, as of now the U.S. economy is the biggest driver of global growth.[27] As the U.S. economy slowed following the financial crisis of 2008, this was quickly transmitted to the rest of the world. India's GDP growth rate, which had been over 9 percent for three years, up to 2007–2008, came down suddenly to 6.7 percent in 2008–2009.

In 2008 and 2009 some commentators were predicting that India would have its own homegrown subprime crisis. India's mortgage market had also expanded and new borrowers had come on the scene. The indigenous crisis never happened, however. There were many important reasons for this including some shrewd cautionary moves by India's central bank, the Reserve Bank of India. But the reasons also included something that was and, unfortunately still is, special to India. A lot of the buying and selling of homes in India occurs with a part of the transaction being made in cash with no record kept of this in order to not leave a trail of evidence.[28] Let me explain. You want to buy a house valued at Rs. 100 from the private market. The chances are the seller will tell you that he will not take the full Rs. 100 in check but will ask for a part, maybe Rs. 50 or 60, in check with the rest paid in cash with no evidence of this payment. The latter is called a black money payment. This helps the seller not to have to pay a large capital gains tax. Even many buyers want to pay partly in cash and to show the value of the house to be less than it actually is in order to avoid having to pay too much property tax.

The upshot of the ubiquity of black money in the housing market is that the banks were never put in risk's way in the manner that happened in the United States. Since mortgage loans can only be taken on the "declared" part of the house price, a house valued at Rs. 100 would typically be bought with a mortgage of less than Rs. 50. This means that when house prices fell, unless the price drops were extraordinarily large, banks would not have the balance sheet problem of the kind that happened in the United States. Nor would it be worthwhile for borrowers to walk away from the home, allowing banks to foreclose.

Economics is not a moral subject. Often what is patently corrupt, like the pervasive use of black money, can turn out to be a bulwark against a crisis. Hence, the slowdown in growth that occurred in India was what came in as collateral damage from the global recession; India did not have a homegrown subprime crisis. This probably tempered the problem somewhat. This mildness of the crisis along with a carefully administered fiscal stimulus meant that by the very next year India began to pull out of the crisis. In 2009–2010 and 2010–2011, the Indian economy grew each year by nearly 8 percent.

But by 2011 the clouds darkened suddenly and more ominously than in 2008–2009. This time the problems were part global, part indigenous. A series of corruption scandals rocked the government, beginning with some big exposures related to the large construction and purchase orders that were given out in connection with the Commonwealth Games hosted by India in 2010. These scandals also galvanized India's already active civil society to be more alert to corruption and several movements picked up steam, most importantly, the one led by Anna Hazare, a former soldier who became a highly regarded grassroots worker and a celebrated social activist. It is difficult to say if the total volume of corruption in India has gone up in recent times. By its very nature, corruption is difficult to measure; and I have no conjectures on which way it is going. One thing however is evident; the magnitude of corruption is unpardonably large and this is eating into the fabric of society.

What has certainly happened with increasing awareness of corruption is that there is heightened vigilance and also a lot of finger pointing. This has had one unfortunate side effect. Bureaucrats, even those who are not corrupt (a vast majority, I can assure the reader, from my own experience in government), have become overcautious in making decisions. With every decision there is a risk that someone will point an accusing finger. One way of making sure that this does not happen is not to make a decision at all. It is arguable that there was been some drift toward this in 2012. In addition, the politics of coalition suddenly turned vile and important reforms got stalled.

This slowdown in decision making and reforms adversely affected the mood of business, and investments too slowed down. Also, the large fiscal deficit meant that the Indian government was borrowing heavily from the market (to finance the excess of expenditure over revenue collection) and this was edging out some private borrowing and, hence, investment.

Another domestic factor, which has no doubt had some adverse impact on growth, was the monetary tightening done by the Reserve Bank of India to combat the inflation. This was a deliberate decision by the RBI and the idea was that a little slowdown in the short term was worthwhile to get inflation under control and boost growth in the long run. India's central bank is one of the most impressive and impartial of institutions but the management of inflation is no settled science. There are many alternative theories and plenty of open questions. Hence, one can question the policies that we have followed. I believe India erred on the side of overcaution, tightening liquidity too much. Moreover, thanks to the changing landscape of the global economy, it is time to rethink the appropriateness of standard monetary and fiscal policies. I shall turn to some of this in chapters 3 and 4.

Finally, and most importantly, by 2011 Europe was rapidly sinking into a recession with several countries technically *in* recession, having registered negative growth in two successive quarters. To stave off the financial crisis of 2008, most nations had injected money into the economy to bolster demand and to prevent private banks and firms from going down under. As the sovereigns borrowed or printed money for this operation and leaned into the abyss to pull out private agents, it became clear that some of them were being sucked in instead. So three years later, in 2011, the world was back again in a crisis, this time a sovereign debt crisis, centered on the Eurozone nations.

While India's biggest trading partners are China, the United States, and UAE,[29] Europe is a significant partner. Over 18 percent of India's exports go to EU countries taken together. In 2010–2011 this was a value of over $50 billion. The slowdown in Europe has naturally had a massive impact on India. In addition, with banks in several Eurozone countries teetering on the edge, there is a certain nervousness in all financial markets, from stock markets to currencies. India's growth slowed in 2011–2012 to 6.7 percent and in 2012–2013, it slowed further to approximately 5 percent. By contemporary global standards this may not look bad but this is the slowest India had grown in nine years and it cast a pall of despondency over the nation.[30]

The Tea Leaves

Economic forecasting is a hazardous activity. While economics as a discipline has matured in leaps and bounds, yielding deep insights into markets, trade, and development, forecasting remains a nascent industry, with plenty of maturing still to occur. Those in the prediction business are not the most popular persons. At times the fault lies with them. One often hears statements from them, using their own forecasts, such as, "A year ago we were forecasting high growth and now the forecast is negative, which shows how sharply the economy has deteriorated," unmindful of the fact that, more than anything else, this shows how undependable their forecasts are. At times it is the genuine complexity of the subject that makes the margin of error large. In any case peering into the future is a risky activity at the best of times. All this is a preamble to warn the reader that I am about to peer into the future.

Before turning to India, it may be useful to do some crystal-ball gaz-
ing into Europe since this is a troubled region at this time and important
enough for its fate to be of consequence for all nations and certainly for
a rapidly globalizing country like India. As already mentioned in passing,
Europe got sucked into a crisis after its sovereigns leaned over to battle the
recession unleashed by the subprime crisis in the United States. Basically
what happened was that the fault lines in the construction of the Eurozone
began showing up under the strains. The construction of the Eurozone
with its new currency was arguably the world's second-largest deliberately
planned economic experiment, the first being Communism. The failure of
Communism shows how these artificial economic constructs, in contrast
to systems that evolve naturally, have a propensity to be fragile. Unantici-
pated fault lines show up, which may or may not be manageable. Fiscal and
banking autonomy, coupled with the lack of monetary autonomy, as was
inevitable with the creation of the euro, with several nations sharing one
central bank, gave rise to strains that no one had fully appreciated until the
symptoms were deep enough to be visible to the naked eye by 2009, soon
after the Lehman Brothers collapse.[31]

A crash was staved off by the injection of liquidity, the most significant being the Long Term Refinancing Operation (LTRO) that occurred
in December 2011 and February 2012, when the European Central Bank
infused a huge amount of money in two tranches, totaling approximately
$1.3 trillion, to banks. What was often forgotten is that these were basically
three-year loans given to European banks whether or not they had profitable investments to put their money in. This, in turn, meant that there was
a debt-repayment cliff that loomed up at the end of 2014 and early 2015.
Several measures have been taken to stave off this risk and there has been
a scramble to put the banking sector in order in Europe and to strengthen
mechanisms for resolution of banks that were on the verge of failure. The
steps that have been taken as this goes to press, such as the first moves
toward a 55 billion euro Single Resolution Mechanism, are still partial and
small compared to the size of the European economy.

It is evident that this will be a long-drawn process and so the struggles
of the Eurozone will continue to cast shadows on the global economy for
some time to come, creating headwinds for all nations in the world, including emerging and developing economies.

In addition, China, which is still growing very well, has seen an enormous growth in debt—well over 250 percent of its GDP at the time of completing this book. It is true that China's sovereign debt—approximately one-fifth of its aggregate debt—is not high; and its central bank has enormous foreign exchange reserves, which can be deployed in a crisis. Despite these strengths some turbulence from the large debt, and consequent short-term slowdown in growth, cannot be ruled out because in China, unlike in high-income countries, such as the Eurozone and Japan, a large intervention by the government and the People's Bank of China in terms of liquidity injection will have an inflation risk.

Given all this, it seems a reasonable judgment to make that the trajectory for the Indian economy over the short run will be strewn with impediments, some of global origins and some of its own making. Policy mistakes occur more easily when the economy begins to falter, thereby often exacerbating problems. However, over the last two decades India has built up strengths that are structural and so are likely to enable the economy to ride over the short-term tribulations. Thus, while growth will be slow in the immediate future, it ought to pick up in the medium term.

There is a huge popular anticipation of a growth upswing following the election victory of the Bharatiya Janata Party (BJP) in the Indian elections in April and May 2014, and the arrival of a new government in Delhi. This is rooted in the kind of hope that almost invariably accompanies a major electoral shift. During the election campaign the slowdown of India's economy over the previous year was being put down entirely to domestic policy failures, unmindful of the fact that there was a global slowdown and that in terms of growth-rate *ranking* India had slipped only marginally over the previous one or two years, and it still remained among the leading performers in the world.

The great global recession affected India badly, and in response to this there was some adverse reaction domestically, resulting in an unfortunate slowdown in economic reforms, negatively impacting the economy's performance.

Being free of the worries of an imminent election does create extra policy space, and the prospects for the Indian economy, which has grown very well over the last ten odd years, look excellent at this point of time. However, the new government has to work hard to skillfully utilize the space created by its overwhelming electoral victory. It clearly has the drive to do well but has to remember that the drive has to be combined with professional understanding of the complex machinery that is an economy.

In the medium to long run, the Indian economy is on firm grounds. Some deep structural strengths have accumulated over a long time, and the evolving global order places the country in the absolute frontline among the world's league of nations in terms of growth prospects. It is important for the nation to try to seize the moment.

Among the country's strengths are its savings and investment record in recent times. India saves and invests a substantial fraction of its national income. Savings and investment rates are not like stock market indicators. They do move up and down, but seldom wildly. Once in the 30 to 40 percent range, as is the case now in India, they can be expected to remain there. Indian entrepreneurs, plying their craft over a varied nation, have matured remarkably and over the last ten years have ventured out in the world, to both developed and developing countries. In recent years, for instance, more foreign direct investment has gone from India to Britain than the other way around. Governance remains sluggish and unremarkable but it has been that way since the 1950s and the system has learned to work around that to some extent. It must nevertheless be pointed out that creating an atmosphere in which it is easier to conduct business, one in which the creativity and enterprise of ordinary people are not thwarted by bureaucratic hurdles and transactions costs, will yield large benefits. As I shall argue later, this may well be the most important reform that India needs to make to unleash rapid, inclusive growth.

Fortunately, India invested early in democracy.[32] This should help usher in these and other reforms without political turbulence, which is the main challenge for more authoritarian nations. Further, and this is hard to establish with statistics and is based mainly on casual observation, the values and social norms that are prerequisites of a successful market economy are slowly beginning to fall into place.

Finally, and most importantly, between politics and economics, the one that can be more stubborn and harder to amend is politics. Luckily, the nation's founding fathers made a commitment to inclusiveness and democracy never before seen in a nation as poor as India. This was a costly investment at the start of a nation but in retrospect, a great advantage. If India had got this wrong, correcting it would entail painful upheavals and destructive realignments of society. Fortunately, that risk is minimal in India. Changes in economic policy are not gestalt matters and can be corrected as the nation trundles along, as long as the fundamental political foundation is sound; and that seems to be the case for India.

The current political situation has been troubled by the wranglings of coalitional democracy. But this seems to be the luck of the draw. It may create roadblocks for a year, maybe two, but, like the toss of a coin, can be expected to return to the average behavior soon. So for India to return to an average growth rate of 8.5 percent per annum as it has been recording since 2003 seems entirely feasible. With the population growing at roughly 1.4 percent per annum, this means that per capita income should be doubling every ten years.

Life, however, is strewn with uncertainties. Much will depend on resolve, passion, good dispassionate analysis, and luck. Since luck cannot be marshaled, it will be important for India to be on its toes, draw on the best of research and advice, no matter where it comes from, put it through the sieve of common sense and then put these ideas into practice. In a democracy, and ultimately in all nations, this can happen in a sustained way only if such ideas are conveyed to ordinary people and they are persuaded. As such, most of this book is written for laypersons to make up their own minds about what is good and what is not. Since, as I later argue, human beings in far-apart places are fundamentally similar, this book is meant for all developing and emerging economies. For readers in other countries, India, the focus of attention in this book, may be viewed as the case study that helps them understand some general principles of economics and economic policymaking.

In closing, it has to be kept in mind that while it is natural and to be welcomed that poor countries will strive to grow, economic growth is ultimately an instrument for better and happier lives and for the spoils of growth to be shared equitably in society. The free market has many strengths, but fairness and equity do not figure prominently among them.[33] That requires purposive action on the part of government, community, and society. Purposive action comes in part from passion and determination but it also needs clear analysis and an ability to ruthlessly dissect society and the forces that drive the economy. The chapters that follow are meant to be aids to such analysis and action.

3 Inflation: The Emperor of Economic Maladies

Understanding Inflation, Understanding Deflation

One thing that experts know and nonexperts do not is that experts know less than nonexperts think they do. Take, for instance, monetary and fiscal policies. Decades of careful data collection and mathematical and statistical research have given us important insights into these. But on many large questions we have little more than rules of thumb: if there is stagnation, lower interest rates and inject liquidity; if there is inflation, raise policy rates and the cash reserve ratio of banks. At times we use our judgment to give some new twist—Operation Twist[1]—or turn, for example, to blend interest rate action with open market operations. But the fact remains that our understanding of the mechanics of these matters is far from complete. The reason these rules of thumb nevertheless work, at least tolerably so, is evolution. Over time the wrong moves get penalized and their users either learn by watching others or disappear themselves. In brief, we get our monetary and fiscal policies right, partly, in the same way that birds get their nest building right.

As we venture into the difficult area of monetary and fiscal policies and especially the subject of inflation, it is important to keep this caveat in mind. Humility is in any case a good quality, but in this case it has the additional benefit of enabling us to analyze better by being candid about what we do not know. Understanding inflation in India, and, for that matter, in any democratic, emerging economy, is key because inflation is the most important economic variable that influences the mood of the electorate with virtually no time lag.

These remarks apply equally, though in the obverse, to deflation. As the Eurozone battles to stave off deflation and Japan strives to pull its economy out of a decades-old grip of falling or stalling prices, some of the same questions and policy puzzles that I discuss in this chapter apply. The fact that standard interventions are having so little effect in the Eurozone and Japan shows that some of the conundrums of inflation management apply with equal force to deflation management. Although I will not directly discuss policies for curing deflation, much of the analysis in this chapter and, in particular, the suggestions for alternative, experimental policies have relevance to the context of deflation.

Inflation affects everybody immediately. So, unlike a variable such as the fiscal deficit, which may be extremely important but is not something that people experience directly (most people would not even know the deficit has deteriorated unless the government puts out the data), inflation has an immediate, palpable impact. This in turn means the electorate's attitude toward the government depends critically on the level of inflation. As a consequence, politicians keep a closer watch on this economic variable than any other, and are willing to make other disproportionate sacrifices, say, to growth and employment, to keep inflation under control. This is what makes inflation such an important topic for all democratic developing nations.

A failure of a crop or a flash fashion trend involving a certain fabric can cause the price of that crop or of that fabric to rise, just as an unexpected glut in global crude oil can cause the price of crude to fall. These price movements are a signal to consumers that they should consume less of the commodity facing a shortage and more of the good in glut, and to producers to produce more of that which is in short supply and less of what is available in plenty. These relative price changes may annoy and anger people but usually we can see where they are coming from.

Inflation, however, has little to do with changes in *relative* prices. Inflation refers to a sustained rise in prices across the board, that is, a phenomenon where the average price of all goods is on the rise. It may or may not be accompanied by changes in relative prices. For laypersons there is something threatening about inflation because they cannot see where it comes from. What they do not know—and would be even more alarmed if they did—and is a closely guarded secret among experts is that the understanding of experts is also very incomplete. This is what makes inflation the emperor of economic maladies. It is not surprising that some of the world's highest inflation rates occurred in rich countries—Germany in 1923 and

Hungary in 1946, for instance—despite the fact that these were nations where there was easy access to economic expertise.

Admittedly, economists, unlike lay persons, have access to vast amounts of data on price movements and are privy to plenty of stylized facts. They have also developed rules of thumb about how to react to inflation and we see these in the relatively standard responses to inflation by central banks across the world. But when all is said and done, these are rules of thumb only; for the scientific community there is still a great distance to go in understanding inflation. That is what makes inflation such an exciting subject.

Starting from late 2009, India had nearly five unbroken years of inflation, ranging between 7 and 11 percent per annum. Inflation was very high when I joined office in Delhi in December 2009, and it breached the 10% mark in early 2010. I could see the frustration of people from the questions I would get—from irate relatives phoning me from Kolkata to complain about the high price of fish, to my ever-loyal official driver in Delhi echoing a commonly held opinion when he told me how inflation is caused by wicked shopkeepers. The oft-heard suggestion that a simple command from Delhi to hold prices down would be sufficient revealed a widespread misunderstanding of this phenomenon, as did my driver's hypothesis. The latter required, minimally, an explanation of why shopkeepers had become more wicked beginning in late 2009. There is an important methodological point here. I am not arguing that inflation is not caused by shopkeepers trying to raise prices, but simply pointing to the fact that since shopkeepers wanting to raise prices is always the case, picking this as the cause may be valid but not useful from a policy point of view. It is akin to someone arguing that the building that collapsed did so because of gravity. If this sounds too obviously flawed to expect anyone to make such an argument, I would urge the reader to listen to conversations carefully, including speeches by leading political figures.

For me, an alarming reminder that people thought prices were somehow directly controlled by government came from Sushma. Sushma—a tribal woman from the state of Jharkhand, of high intelligence but little formal education—was our cook during my stint in government. After joining our household, being a naturally warm and friendly person, she quickly got to know all the domestic staff of our neighbors. Once when the economy was going through some difficult months, with inflation over 10 percent per annum, and I was going through a very busy period, with other economic advisers and government officials dropping into our home frequently, one of the guests asked Sushma if she knew what work I did. She smiled broadly, and announced proudly that she had been chatting with our neighbors' household staff and had found out from them that I did a very important job and was the person "in charge of raising prices in India."

Inflation in India and the World

Inflation has been with humankind ever since barter gave way to the use of mediums of exchange, like paper money, precious metals, or even cigarettes, as happened in a prisoners of war camp during World War II (Radford 1945). And although we do not fully understand its origins, we have developed techniques and rules of policy intervention.[2]

Many of the policies that we use nowadays routinely and without thought are outcomes of the research of economists and policy experiments of earlier years. In this advance of fundamental ideas and policy practices, most of the contributions have come from Europe and the United States. This in itself should not bother emerging nations. Knowledge generated anywhere is knowledge. At the same time, the context matters. As has been pointed out for medical science, our knowledge of tropical illnesses has not progressed far enough because these are the concern of the tropics and not of the industrialized nations. Even in economics there are peculiarities that are specific to different regions and for nations at different stages of development. It is therefore important to do fundamental analytical research and policy experiments on inflation where the backdrop is an emerging market economy, such as India. This point actually carries over to rich nations as well. Thanks to the changing structure of the global economy, in particular the easy flow of goods, money, and even work across nations, the effects of within-country policy interventions have been changing and can explain why some of these nations have had to struggle with deflation.

It is useful to have the basic facts on the table. As I worked on this manuscript, India was in the midst of an inflationary episode that had gone on for over four years (there has been some easing in recent months). It began in December 2009, when inflation (measured in terms of the wholesale price index, WPI) climbed to 7.2 percent;[3] it continued to rise and peaked in April 2010, at just short of 11 percent. Thereafter, it was on a broadly downward trajectory, with occasional upswings.[4] Before this nearly five-year run,

India had one year of negligible inflation; but just prior to that there was another round from March 2008 to December 2008, when WPI inflation, that is, inflation measured in terms of the weighted average of the whole-sale prices indices of all goods, hovered at around 10 percent.

Prior to these two runs in quick succession, India had very little inflation for a dozen years. There were occasional months when inflation would exceed 8 percent, but not a single month when it was in double digits during these twelve years of relative price stability.[5]

To complete this account, it may be mentioned that independent India's worst inflationary episode was from November 1973 to December 1974, when inflation never dropped below 20 percent and was above 30 percent for four consecutive months starting June 1974. The highest inflation occurred in September 1974, when inflation reached 33.3 percent.

What is good performance and what is bad depends on the yardstick. Even during the dozen years of price stability we had more inflation than in virtually any industrialized country in recent times, but in comparison to most emerging market economies and developing nations in the world, India's performance was creditable. As for what is an "acceptable" level or "threshold" level of inflation for India, there is a lot of literature, most of it clustered around numbers ranging from 4 to 7 percent (see Rangarajan 2009, chapter 1).

One reason why the recent run of inflation seems so intolerable is the relative price stability of the previous twelve years. This is what led to talk of runaway inflation and hyperinflation. It is important to get the perspective right. While there can be no denial that an inflation ranging between 7 and 11 percent per annum is painful in a country like India, with so many precariously poor people, it is worth being clear that hyperinflation is usually defined as inflation over 50 percent per month (Cagan 1956). The world's biggest episodes of inflation occurred in Europe, once around 1923 and again around 1946. The all-time record is held by Hungary from August 1945 to July 1946. During these twelve months, prices rose by 3.8×10^{27}. That is, what cost 1 pengo on August 1, 1945, would cost 38000 . . . (a total of 26 such zeros) pengos on July 31, 1946. In August 1946 the pengo was replaced with the forint in an effort to shed the trillions of zeros that were needed to express prices. The second-highest inflation rate in recorded history was the celebrated one in Germany in 1923, even though Zimbabwe came close to it in 2008–2009.

Comparable high rates of inflation have occurred in Russia from December 1921 to January 1924, in Greece in 1943, and in many other instances. The German hyperinflation of 1923 may well be the most analyzed and diagnosed. It played havoc with the economy, created political tensions that contributed to the rise of Nazism, and also caused psychological disturbances. Doctors in Germany in 1923 identified a mental illness called "cipher stroke" with which many people were afflicted during the height of the hyperinflation. It referred to a person's neurotic urge to keep writing zeros and also to a propensity to meaninglessly add zeros when responding to routine questions, such as to saying "two trillion" when asked how many children the person had (Ahamed 2009).

Not quite as large as these European inflations but nevertheless staggeringly big ones occurred till two or three decades ago in many Latin American countries (see Garcia, Guillén, and Kehoe 2010). These being closer to our times may have greater relevance to us. Brazil is one country that has coped with mega-inflations, many times larger than that which India has had, and seems to have stabilized.

A study of the Brazilian economy shows that the nation did not have a single year where inflation was in single digits from 1962 to 1997. There were only two years (1973 and 1974) when inflation was below 20 percent. The worst period was 1988 to 1994. Prices were rising on average close to 2000 percent per annum during this time. Brazil's experience gives us a bit of an insight into what inflation does to growth. Eyeballing of the data suggests that, when inflation is below 10 percent, there is little correlation between the rate of inflation and the growth rate. But at higher levels, inflation is usually associated with lower growth; and especially when inflation starting at a high level rises even further, growth slows down. During the six hyperinflationary years mentioned previously, growth had a real setback with GDP growing at negative rates in three out of those six years. All this is not to deny that there are examples of nations sustaining over 10 percent inflation with very high growth over multiple years.

Asian countries have in general had more stable prices. South Korea, which grew at astonishingly high rates from the late 1960s to recently, did have high inflation but nowhere near the experience of Latin American economies like Brazil. The average inflation in South Korea in the 1970s and 1980s was virtually always well above 10 percent, with average annual inflation in the 1980s exceeding 28 percent. While this coincided with high growth for quite some time, it eventually seemed to have had a restraining effect on GDP growth. Tighter monetary and fiscal measures brought inflation down in the 1980s and, eventually, restored high growth.

This wide range of experience from around the world and prodigious amounts of research have enhanced our understanding of inflation. The relatively good inflation record among all industrialized nations and emerging market economies over the last two decades is testimony to this. However, this experience and research have also taught us that there is a lot that we do not understand and that the drivers of inflation, like those of bird flu, can change over time, rendering standard antidotes less effective and calling for fresh research and, maybe, new medicines.

For years, the U.S. Federal Reserve ("the Fed") kept a control on prices by selling and buying government bonds, in effect, absorbing money from and releasing money into the economy. However, money is not the only medium of exchange. There are "near monies" that can do some of the work for money. People can use all kinds of other commodities and papers to trade goods. If, for instance, government bonds were acceptable as a medium of exchange, then the central bank selling bonds and collecting money would have very little impact on the economy because people would use the bonds, in place of the money (that they would have given up to acquire the bonds), to buy and sell goods. It is the appearance of near monies that has compelled the Fed to change some of its strategies for maintaining stable prices.

Since these endogenous features of the economy can vary from one country to another, this calls for independent research in each nation. Over the last few years there has been a sense that the inflation faced by emerging economies is changing some of its characteristics, thereby demanding not just greater resolve but new ideas in order to have price stability.[6] In India there has been a lot of research and debate on the nature of inflation and its measurement. Should we measure inflation in terms of consumer prices or wholesale prices? If we decide to use consumer prices, who is the representative consumer in a nation as diverse as India? Is it the agricultural worker or the industrial worker? Is it the rich or the poor? After all, human consumption patterns differ a lot across these categories.

This is not the occasion to go into the details of this debate but consider this sampling of some tricky issues that can arise. The most popular among the consumer price indices in India is the consumer price index

for industrial workers or CPI(IW). Now for most bureaucrats and government workers, salaries in India are indexed by using the inflation rate as
measured by CPI(IW). Since it is government workers and bureaucrats who
collect the data for constructing the CPI(IW) index there is a potential conflict of interest, with the possibility of a tendency to record higher numbers
wherever the opportunity for this arises. A direct study of different inflation
indices shows that the CPI(IW) index has grown faster consistently since
around August 2008. This can of course happen for natural reasons because
all indices do not track the same commodities.

However, it so happens that the WPI and the CPI(IW) track several of the
same commodities. So one possibility is to take the goods common to the
two indices, and change the weights in one to match with the weights in
the other. If we make these and a few other technical changes[7] and plot the
two indices on the same graph we find a small but fairly systematic upward
bias in the CPI(IW), as compared to the WPI. This was a quick preliminary
exercise and will need more careful study but it does, interestingly, show an
upward bias in the price index that is used to compute the salary increases
of the people engaged in computing the numbers.

Before turning to policy challenges it is worth noting that while inflation, both for all goods and food items, has clearly been on the rise since
2000, it seems to be distinctly less volatile than it used to be, for instance,
before the mid-1980s. There is also a marked divergence between food
and nonfood inflation, since October 2008. Before 1982 India had some
stretches of very low inflation but also peaks of a kind that, fortunately,
we do not see any longer. This could be a sign of learning on the part of
government and the Reserve Bank of India, whereby they can manage price
instability better than they did in the past, but it could also be an indicator
of the changing character of inflation.

Another interesting pattern pertains to the comparative price movements
of perishable food items and nonperishable ones. Nonperishables can be
stored and so, with rational individuals, we would expect people to store in
times or plenty and draw on the stored food in times of shortage. This would
lead us to expect less volatility and also less inflation for nonperishables. The
data seem to bear this out, especially over the last decade. This underlines
one important policy lesson. It makes us realize that hoarding food should
not be castigated under all circumstances. It can lead to price stabilization.
Also, many big retail suppliers need to store food before they can take it

over to the retail outlets. There is an important law in India, the Essential Commodities Act, 1955, to ensure that ordinary consumers have easy access to certain essential goods and to protect them from unscrupulous traders. While exploitation of ordinary consumers does happen, as we know not just from India but even from rich, industrialized nations, and there is need for such a law, it is easy to misinterpret the spirit of such legislation and end up hurting consumers. Treating all storing and hoarding as illegal, as some do by citing the Essential Commodities Act, can do a lot of damage. The aim of the law should be to stop large traders from hoarding to deliberately manipulate prices. Reactive hoarding in response to price cycles, however, has much to commend it. This is the kind of idea that policymakers as well as ordinary citizens need to understand so that there is not a witch hunt against all forms of hoarding, as so often happens in India.

Some of the preceding discussion points to a newfound resilience of the Indian economy. It is arguable that earlier, overall inflation was powerfully driven by the agricultural sector. What happened to food prices affected everything else and so the two indices moved more or less in tandem. Over time, the share of agriculture in the total GDP has fallen and the growing strength of the economy means that food prices alone may not be in the driver's seat the way they were for the first several decades after independence.

This has an immediate policy implication that is worth noting here. In controlling overall inflation, food prices may not be as important as they were in the past. Of course, controlling food inflation is important in itself, since such a large segment of India continues to be poor and any inflation in food prices hurts them disproportionately. But in controlling overall inflation, we need to turn our attention much more to macro-demand management—fiscal and monetary—although, even here, there is need to look for newer channels of policy action.

Interest Rates and Liquidity

At the risk of oversimplification, inflation occurs when there is too much buying power chasing too few goods and services. It follows that an increase in demand or an insufficiency of supply can cause inflation. However, an economy is so complex and demand can come from so many sources that it is difficult to be sure what the source of inflation is. In some egregious cases we can put it down to reckless money creation by the central bank or overspending by government. But there are other subtle sources, such as changing banking behavior on the part of individuals, or the availability of new mediums of exchange, such as cryptocurrencies.

Fortunately inflation is one of those phenomena for which, even without our understanding its causes anywhere near fully, we have learned several techniques of control. Most of these pertain to demand management. When the price of one or two goods increases, we can respond by trying to supply more of those goods (by diverting effort from the production and supply of other goods). But if the prices of all or virtually all goods increase, as happens during any inflationary episode, there is little we can do in terms of supply, because there is no known way of suddenly providing more of all goods. If there were a way to do so, we should have done so already and made everybody better off. This is the reason why, when there is overall higher inflation, we have no choice but to turn to some form of demand management,[8] even while working on easing specific supply bottlenecks that may exist.

Relative price increases are, for the most part, best left alone, unless there is evidence that these are caused by sudden collusive behavior or the artificial manipulation of markets by large sellers. Such relative price movements are the market's way to equilibrate demand and supply.[9] There is plenty of evidence of adverse reactions from nations that tried to control relative price rises by government decree. The result was the encouragement of black markets. And from regular markets goods would often vanish, with consumers queuing up for long hours to get limited supplies of goods. Inflation, on the other hand, being a mismatch between overall supply and overall demand, deserves policy action, especially when it goes over a tolerable level of, for instance, 4 or 5 percent.[10] Overall demand in the economy comes from many sources—corporations, farmers, laborers, housewives, and government. This is what contributes to making inflation such a hard problem.

To see this, it is interesting to note a connection between the Indian government's financial inclusion program and inflation. In India, of the approximately 600,000 human habitations, only around 30,000 are fully serviced by commercial banks (Subbarao 2011). The government's financial inclusion policy is a plan to bring most of these habitations into the ambit of formal banking. We know that over 40 percent of rural savings are currently kept in rural households as cash, since so many villagers do not have bank accounts and are excluded from the nation's financial system. As the financial inclusion policy is implemented more and more people will put their money in bank accounts, post office savings schemes, and mutual funds. Note that this effectively brings into the financial system currency that was earlier lying dormant in the homes of village people. Hence, even with RBI holding money creation constant, the act of ordinary people pulling their money out from under their pillows and putting this in bank accounts will mean an increase in the "effective" money supply in the economy and can cause inflation.

To recognize that the policy of financial inclusion leads to inflation does not mean that we should abandon financial inclusion, just as to say that greater benefit directed to the poor will cause the price of essentials to rise does not mean that we should not direct greater benefit to the poor. Of course, even if it is people's action that causes the inflation, there are policies that the central bank and government can follow to control the inflation. Since inflation is caused by aggregate demand exceeding aggregate supply at a certain point of time, one blunt instrument is to redistribute some of the demand from that time to the future. This can be done by, for instance, confiscating from people a certain amount of their income for a certain duration of time. This can take the form of a 5 percent temporary income tax, which is then held by the government *without being put to use* (to use this would defeat the very purpose of withholding buying power) and eventually paid back to the taxpayers over the next four or five years, once the inflation eases out. This can have the side effect of output declining in case producers realize that demand will decline as a consequence of this move. But executed suddenly, it can curb the pressure on prices, though it is unlikely to make the government popular at the polls.

Before getting further into policy, we need to understand the causes of inflation at a more fundamental level. At an abstract, elemental level, inflation is the product of our ability to make contracts and deliver on promises. If we were a totally untrustworthy people, who never delivered on promises, we would not have inflation. Of course, we would also be crushingly poor, living in primitive conditions. But, if this is any comfort, there would be no inflation.

While we think of promises mostly in bilateral terms, the most important "economic" promise, one that has made modern civilization possible, is the mysterious promise represented by money—the note in your wallet or the bank balance in your account, which in itself is of no value but is a record of work you did for which you are yet to redeem goods and services. Money is nothing but a generic promise from society—government being the most important arbiter of that—that you will be able to change these bits of paper for goods and services in the future. This is why the worker who toils all day accepts money rather than insisting her employer hand over food, clothing, and shelter material as payment at the end of each day's hard work. Money is a kind of pledge to her by society at large. She can redeem that pledge at leisure and in small measures—buying food, shelter, education, as and when she needs these.

Money was not discovered one day in a moment of scientific triumph. It emerged gradually, in small measures and through little innovations. But in terms of human achievement it must stand right there at the pinnacle of inventions. Without it we would have very little of what we know today as civilized life.

By the seventeenth century, it was moreover clear that, unlike most other products, where we encourage multiple producers to get into business and to have competition, money is one area where competition is not desirable. Since money entails a generic promise, it creates scope for free riding in a way that does not happen for other goods. If there are many entities that can create money and the value of money is a public good, with competition we risk creating excess money, since at the time of creating money, the creator gets the value and the erosion of value in the future is borne by all. It was decided that this is one area where, far from boosting competition, what we want is a monopoly. Each economy must have at most one money-creating authority. It was with this principle in mind that the Bank of England was created in 1694, though its monopoly rights to creating money would be firmed up much more clearly only at the time of renewal of its Royal Charter in 1742.[11]

Inevitably, the central bank and the nation's treasury became the managers of a nation's liquidity and, through that, the value of money and the level of prices. In India, the major instruments for managing liquidity are the repo, reverse repo, and cash reserve ratio,[12] which refers to the minimum fraction of the total deposits with each commercial bank that the bank has to hold as reserves with the central bank. The repo rate is, essentially, the rate at which banks can borrow from the central bank to tide over their overnight liquidity shortfall and the reverse repo is the interest it receives when a bank parks its money with the central bank.[13]

It is interesting to check how well these policy instruments have succeeded in controlling inflation. In India, government does not control interest rates. In adjusting the repo and reverse repo rates it is expected that these changes influence the behavior of banks and cause the free market interest rates, for instance, on mortgages, fixed deposits, and other lending plans, to move in similar directions. Hence, through the adjustment of repo and reverse repo rates the RBI manages to influence interest rates in general.[14] The idea is that this in turn will influence liquidity and, through that, inflation.

A pretty picture emerges when we display the movement over time, as is done in figure 3.1, of the repo rate, the reverse repo rate, and inflation. What is evident much more than the connection between the repo rates and inflation is the noise in the system. It is not at all clear what drives what. There can be no doubt that the reckless fueling of demand by a nation's treasury or the central bank can fuel inflation. When in 1923 Rudolf von Havenstein, the president of the German Reichsbank (the predecessor of the Deutsche Bundesbank), acquiesced to the government's demand to spend more by recklessly printing money, it was all but inevitable that Germany would get embroiled in hyperinflation. On August 17, 1923, von Havenstein announced that he would soon be issuing new money in one day equal to two-thirds of the money in circulation. He kept his word and Germany paid for it. Yet, in the relation between liquidity, as controlled by the central bank, and prices there is a lot of white noise. It indicates that there is more to liquidity than what can be controlled through central bank action or the policies of the Ministry of Finance. What the corporates, the banks, the farmers, and ordinary individuals do can also effect liquidity and, through that, the level of inflation.[15]

The management of inflation and, for that matter, deflation, cannot be reduced to a mechanical exercise, where the formula connecting what is to be done by the government or the central bank and what will be achieved is written in stone.[16] It requires a combination of science, intuition, and experimentation, and we do too little of the latter.

It is assumed in popular discourse that if interest rates are raised, the demand for credit will go down; and hence the total amount of liquidity in the system will be less.[17] This is generally true. However, it can be shown that in certain contexts the opposite will occur. Consider the standard

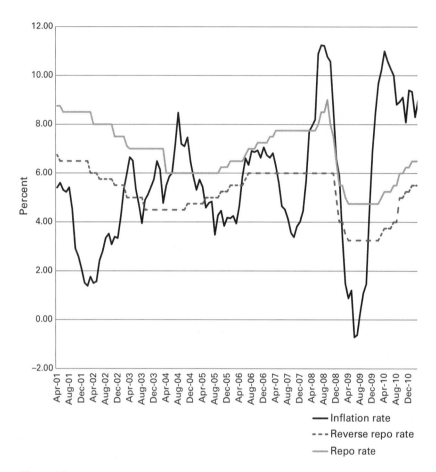

Figure 3.1
Policy rate changes and inflation

description of a credit market where the demand for credit is downward sloping while the supply of credit is upward rising. This simply means that, on the one hand, as the interest rate is raised, people will be prepared to save more and hence supply more credit. On the other hand, those seeking to borrow money, say, to invest in projects, will now want to borrow less. It is the latter that leads to the standard wisdom that you can curb liquidity by raising interest rates.

There is no reason why we should assume that the initial interest rate prevailing in the economy will always be at or above where the demand and supply curves intersect. Credit markets are subject to interventions by central banks and the government, and they also have other external rigidities, which can deflect the interest rate from the neoclassical market equilibrium rate, where demand always equals supply to a rate where demand exceeds supply, that is, to a zone where there is "liquidity deficiency."[18]

It is easy to see what would happen if that were the case. Begin with a case where demand for credit exceeds supply. Suppose now the interest rate is raised a little. This will typically cause the demand for credit to fall and supply to rise. However, since it was the supply that was the binding constraint (since there was an excess demand for credit), this rise in interest means that the total amount of money lent in the economy will increase. Hence, total credit in the economy goes up. Since there was excess demand for credit in the original equilibrium a small decline in demand is of no consequence. Hence, we get a paradoxical response to the interest rate tightening, whereby there is no reduction in liquidity and, in fact, a possible increase in liquidity, assuming that the supply curve of credit is upward sloping. Lilienfeld-Toal, Mookherjee, and Visaria (2012) have reported on some empirical corroboration of this and a similar line may also be found in a recent review in the *Economic and Political Weekly* (see EPW Research Foundation 2011, section 1.4). This has important policy implications. If we are in a predicament where raising interest rates has a feeble effect on inflation, we may consider using this policy more aggressively; but if we are in an economic context where interest rates have no effect on liquidity, or have a pathological reverse effect on liquidity, then we may have to desist from using this policy and look to other kinds of interventions.

It should be kept in mind that there is a difference between raising policy rates and raising the cap on the interest rate on ordinary bank savings.[19] There is also the question concerning the very concept of liquidity. Why should the fact that banks lend more mean greater liquidity? After all, greater lending simply means an altered portfolio of assets for people and not an increase or decrease in assets. This refers to some deep theoretical issues regarding the difference between money and various forms of near monies.

This is related to a fascinating question about the units into which a nation's aggregate money supply is divided. This is easy to see by considering the polar case. If the entire amount of currency in circulation in the nation consisted of one large-denomination note (the denomination being the size of aggregate currency in circulation), clearly this would be a very illiquid nation. And without some sophisticated substitute for signing contracts for exchange over time, most people would be starved of money at all times, since there is only one note in the hand of one agent. It immediately follows that not only do the monetary aggregates in the nation matter, but a lot also depends on how finely these aggregates are broken up—into notes of thousands, five-hundreds, hundreds, and so on. In fact, it is arguable that it is the granularity of the aggregate money that matters more than the aggregate money, when it comes to the measure of liquidity and inflationary pressure.

What the preceding analysis does is to warn us about possibilities. Economic theory simply alerts us to the need for empirical and statistical analysis to make sure that overall conditions in the economy are appropriate for us to use interest-rate tightening as a measure for controlling inflation. The theory also tells us where the empirical study ought to be focused. In this case, we are told to check out the prevailing conditions in the credit market, in particular, whether or not there is excess demand for credit, before we use interest-rate tightening to control inflation. It warns us that there exist situations where interest-rate tightening will have no effect and we will be paying the cost of such tightening without the attendant benefit of reduced inflation.

The unconventional moves by the central bank of Turkey and the subsequent response of the economy certainly add further weight to the need for out-of-the-box thinking. During 2009–2011 Turkey faced some periods of high inflation. In April 2010, its year-on-year inflation was at 10.2 percent. However, taking stock of the unusual global situation, where industrialized economies have near-zero interest rates, the central bank decided to move contrary to what is conventionally done. It began lowering its repo rate, in order to influence overall interest rates downward. This did cause some shock and confusion in the market initially but the central bank persisted with a gentle lowering of the interest rate during 2010 and 2011. Interestingly, its inflation rate was on a steady downward journey since April 2010 and stood at 6.30 in July 2011. And in terms of growth, in the first quarter of 2011, it topped the Group of 20 (better known as G20) chart, at 10.1 percent.

An economy is far too complex an entity for us to jump to making causal connections between policy moves and inflationary outcomes based on this experience. However, the obverse is also true. We must not remain rooted in the textbook doctrine; it is important to examine contrarian policy. It is interesting that in September 2011, Brazil's central bank followed Turkey and lowered interest rates, despite inflation being high. It is arguable that India erred in following the traditional policy of trying to control inflation by keeping central bank interest rates high. This reined in some of the growth, while having minimal effect on inflation.

While persisting with a policy it is worth remembering that the zone in which the economy is situated can change rapidly. Suppose that in India in early 2010 the economy was in the excess liquidity zone, that is, the prevailing interest rate was at or above where demand equals supply. In 2010 the Indian government conducted a very successful and well-designed auction of electromagnetic spectrum—the 3G auctions, enabling the government to raise billions of dollars. Once these auctions began, firms were scrambling to raise credit in order to be able to bid for spectrum. In other words, this auction caused the aggregate demand for credit to rise. This could easily mean that the economy shifted from the excess liquidity to the liquidity-deficient zone, even without any change in the interest rate. Did the 3G spectrum auction actually cause this? The answer is we do not know. But the direction of the demand curve's movement must have been exactly as I have reasoned. What I have tried to do here is to draw our attention to the kinds of questions that deserve empirical and theoretical investigation and to show how the efficacy of standard monetary policy could depend critically on the results that such an investigation yields.

Benefits for the Poor and Inflation

The reason why inflation is of particular concern to us is that the poor and the vulnerable may be hit adversely by it. If such people do not get wage increases that keep step with inflation, they can fall below the poverty line and even below survival income. Hence, the relation between inflation and the poor deserves special attention.

It has often been argued that the sharp rise in food prices in 2009 and the early months of 2010 were likely caused by the drought of 2009, which led to a decline in food grains production, but also by the fact that the government had considerably expanded income support to the poor, for instance, through the National Rural Employment Guarantee Scheme (NREGS) and loan waivers to poor farmers. This explanation has run into controversy: unfortunately so, because much of the controversy can be sorted out through pure reason.

It has been argued (Government of India 2011, chapter 2), that the greater benefits given to the poor may have caused some of the food price inflation in 2009 and 2010. Let me refer to this as the "benefits-based inflation hypothesis."

A common counterargument to this hypothesis is the following: If it were indeed true that it is the greater demand for food on the part of the poor that caused the inflation, then we would expect to see the poor consuming more. But there is no evidence for this. Hence, the benefits-based inflation hypothesis is invalid. For ease of reference, I will refer to this counterargument to the benefits-based inflation hypothesis as the "consumption-based challenge."

What is easy to see is that the consumption-based challenge, though interesting prima facie, does not stand up to scrutiny. So the benefits-based inflation hypothesis does have plausibility even though it may not be empirically established. To understand this, note that the poorest quintile of the rural population devotes approximately 67 percent of its consumption to food. We know this from National Sample Survey (NSS) household data (Government of India 2011) of 2004–2005. The rich spend nowhere near that proportion of their money on food. So, if money and financial benefits are diverted to the poor, it only stands to reason that the demand for food will rise in the nation. If that happens, the price of food will rise disproportionately. Since this is exactly what was happening in late 2009 and 2010, the benefits-based inflation hypothesis seems to have plausibility.

But what about the consumption-based challenge, which claims that there is no evidence that the poor are consuming more food and that this destroys the thesis that redistribution in favor of the poor has contributed to India's inflation? A little thought will show that there is no contradiction between the two. Even if we do not contest the claim that the poor have not been consuming more food, it is possible to maintain that their higher income is contributing to the higher inflation.

To see this, suppose that the poor get an income supplement that raises their demand for food, that is, they are willing to spend more to buy food. This however does not in itself mean that the poor will actually consume more. If the supply of food that is available is fixed, then the increased demand will not translate into greater consumption of food but merely to a greater competition to buy the (fixed) amount of food and thus result in a rise in food prices.

Interestingly, this phenomenon is also logically compatible with the poor becoming worse off, as we know from theoretical studies showing how the recipient of a benefit can end up worse off because his or her receiving that benefit causes such an adverse movement in the prices of goods that are consumed in large quantities by the recipient that the net benefit, in equilibrium, is negative (see also Basu 1997, chapter 5).[20]

This, of course, does not resolve the empirical question: Are the poor actually worse off? While the answer to this is not germane to the argument here, from the piecemeal evidence that we have, it is possible to claim that the answer is no. A recent round of NSS data shows that poverty in India has declined from around 37 percent in 2004 to approximately 32 percent in 2009 (using the Tendulkar measure of poverty in *both* cases). While 32 percent is still high and no reason for complacency, the sharp decline in poverty is commendable and suggests that the steps taken to transfer more buying power to the poor have had some effect.[21]

In conducting this analysis, I have stayed clear of deeper general equilibrium questions. If the larger benefits for the poor are made possible by transfers from the rich, then there must be a deflationary pressure on prices of goods consumed primarily by the rich. So, while the relative price of food may rise, why should overall inflation increase? Such questions take us to the heart of some of the most puzzling questions about the connection between the real and financial economies, examined by several economists (see, for instance, Hahn, 1982). A full discussion of these still-unresolved matters of "money in general equilibrium" is beyond the scope of this book.

Salad Bowl Stagflation

Another problem of using standard macroeconomic demand management for controlling inflation that we have to contend with in today's altered world has to do with globalization. In our increasingly flat world, there is need to worry about one's neighbor's money in a way that one never had to in the past. We get a sense of this by looking at the landscape of growth and inflation across the nations.[22] It is evident from such a study that the world in 2010–2012 was suffering from stagflation, albeit of an unusual kind. There was evidence of stagnation in virtually all industrialized nations, including the United States, the European countries, and Japan; and there was inflation in virtually all emerging market economies, including India,

Argentina, Brazil, Vietnam, and China. In other words, what we had was an unusual world economy, with some parts caught in the "stag" mode and some in "flation," giving rise to a kind of "salad bowl stagflation."

This points to an interesting challenge of globalization. Following the recession of 2008 and the painfully slow recovery in most industrialized nations, these nations resorted to liquidity easing and monetary expansion. However, instead of demand rising in those nations, as would happen pre-globalization, a large part of the extra liquidity flowed to emerging market economies that had growth potential and the ability to use the money. The resort to quantitative easing (QE) by the United States, whereby the U.S. Federal Reserve purchased prespecified amounts of securities from the market, thereby easing liquidity in the economy, is the most discussed such action. But there have been similar actions across the board in developed market economies.

There is not much evidence that this extra liquidity fueled growth in industrialized nations, even though bank profits rose soon after the start of the third round of Quantitative Easing or QE3. This is not to deny that this injection of liquidity was important. It went a long way in calming financial markets in developed countries. But, quite a lot of this liquidity has arguably gone over to the emerging economies that were growing at reasonable rates and fueled inflation. This is arguably what lies behind the salad bowl stagflation that we were seeing through much of 2010, 2011, and 2012.

What we could witness over the next few years is the reverse phenomenon, as the Fed continues with the QE tapering that began in December 2013; and, at some point, it will also begin to raise interest rates. This has already caused some strain for developing nations, with many of them facing currency depreciation, as some of the financial flows turn back toward the United States attracted by the rising interest rates. There will also be some strain felt by the United States, since much of its QE consisted of buying long-term securities, financed by short-term credit in the form of borrowing from the excess reserves with private banks. These reserves could be borrowed at very low interest rates, often 75 basis points. The long-term bonds, on the other hand, fetched the Fed much higher interest, resulting in its large profit and windfall gains. With tight money policy, its cost of borrowing will rise, causing deterioration in its balance sheet.

Another matter that will feed into this brew in the future is the expected revaluation of the renminbi. There are signs that China intends to do this, even though there have been wobbles on the way. China's exchange rate policy has been widely misunderstood. If it were true that China would perpetually keep its currency undervalued and so, effectively, sell its products to the world at below-cost prices that would be unmitigated good news for other nations. As I shall argue in a later chapter, this will change since it is in China's interest now to let the renminbi slowly appreciate. I will also argue that this will raise China's export profitability, for an interesting reason.

One consequence of this will be increased consumption by China. This will create an upward pressure on prices. Hence, the risk of salad bowl stagflation is likely to last for some time, and this makes the need for coordination of macro-demand management policies across nations that much more urgent. What the world is currently caught in is best understood by imagining an Indian economy in which we have high interest rates in Gujarat and low interest rates in Bihar. This would give rise to perverse capital flows from one region to another. The global economy being virtually a single economy, the current predicament of very different interest rates across nations creates a similar situation. All that this emphasizes is that, like so many other domains of policymaking in the modern world, there is now need to achieve a higher degree of coordination in policies pertaining to macroeconomic demand management across nations. Until this is achieved, we have to continue to use our somewhat impaired instruments of country-specific demand management to keep a control on inflation. This includes the challenge of prolonged deflation that tends to sap growth and is currently faced by many industrialized economies, including Japan and the Eurozone. In the long run, there is no escape from using multilateral organizations to work collectively to address problems such as those of inflation in emerging economies and stagnation and deflation in developed economies.

4 Fiscal and Other Macroeconomic Policies for an Emerging Economy

A "Repo" Mishap

Contrary to what many laypersons believe, there is no one who understands "the economy" of a nation. The big challenge of economic policy is that it entails coordination among experts, each of whom understands just a sliver of this enormously complex machine.

I heard this from an eminent economist friend of mine, who visited a small country. On his last evening there, the governor of the central bank came to see him and asked his opinion about the nation's repo rate being at 7.5 percent. The "repo rate," as we saw in chapter 3, is one of the most important instruments of monetary policy, through which inflation and unemployment can be influenced. Unfortunately, the eminent economist did not have the foggiest idea of what repo rates were. Not wanting to display his ignorance, he decided on the standard strategy in such situations: ask counter questions till you manage to glean enough information to break into an intelligent conversation. So he asked: "Why do you think you need to have the repo at that level?"

To his dismay, the governor's response was pithy: "You think 7.5 is too high? I suppose I could lower it by 25 basis points."

Alarmed and still ignorant about repos, he persisted: "What are your reasons for believing that such a small lowering would have a desirable effect?"

The governor looked worried: "If you think that is not enough, I could try lowering it by 50 basis points."

The conversation went on for a while. In the end, the eminent economist later admitted, he knew nothing about repo rates; all he knew was that he had, in all likelihood, lowered it by 100 basis points.

This story, apocryphal or not, tells us something important about the vastness and complexity of economics and how for an economic policy-maker not to recognize that can be a source of disaster. One mistake early Indian policymakers made was to try to micromanage the economy. While it is true that the government needs to attend to a range of policies, from shaping the quality of education in villages to managing the nation's international economic relations, it is imperative to realize that it is not feasible for the government to attend to all the varied and layered needs of society with equal diligence. An intelligent government recognizes that *no matter what kind of society it aims to build*, it is hopeless to try to deliver it all by itself. Instead, it has to create an ethos where people are incentivized to deliver what needs to be delivered. There is nothing ideological in this. No matter in what ideological direction you wish to pull the economy, this has to be achieved largely by creating incentives for ordinary people to do it.

It is important to realize that no single entity, not even one as large as the state, should try to deliver it all. Instead, its aim must be to create the right macroeconomic environment, where individuals with different talents, knowledge, and enterprise can flourish. This is not to deny that the state must provide public goods for its citizens, help build infrastructure, and also carry out redistributive functions in favor of the poor and the disadvantaged. But one of its central functions has to be to create a stable macroeconomic environment, where ordinary people's talent and enterprise can flourish. That is what this chapter is concerned with.

The most important kinds of macroeconomic policies that a government has to handle pertain to fiscal and monetary policies.[1] We have already encountered the logic of monetary policy in chapter 3 in the context of inflation management. In this chapter I introduce the reader to some of the fiscal and other macroeconomic policy dilemmas that India and many other emerging economies face. Attention will be confined to policies pertaining to investment, trade, and the management of the all-important exchange rate.

Fiscal Policy in the Emerging Economy

Fiscal policy is concerned with the management of the government's budget. A central focus of this policy is the fiscal deficit, that is, the gap between the total expenditure of the government and its total earnings.

Most governments spend more than they earn. Hence, the fiscal deficit is usually positive. We usually refer to the fiscal deficit as a percentage of the national income or GDP.

As with most budgeting exercises, the original aim was to heed the advice that grandmothers give of "don't live beyond your means," be responsible spenders, and keep the gap between what you spend and what you earn, basically, the fiscal deficit, as low as possible. As an aside on history, this advice actually goes much further back than our grandmothers. What is not always appreciated is that the ancient Indian classic, the *Arthashastra*, written by Kautilya approximately three hundred years B.C.[2] and famed as a brutally candid treatise on statecraft, is largely a treatise on fiscal policy, with detailed advice on how the emperor should manage the deficit of the state, acting both on the side of raising revenue and containing expenditure. True to Kautilya's reputation as a forebear of Machiavelli, some of the methods he describes to raise revenue are rather unnerving. Kautilya (1992, 272–273) observes how common people are extremely gullible and, should the state find itself in sufficiently dire fiscal state, it can exploit this gullibility. Thus, he points out, money can be collected by "exploiting an unnatural happening, such as an unseasonal flower or fruit, by making it into a divine phenomenon [or] using secret agents to frighten people into making offerings to drive away an evil spirit." And if there are people "not taken in so easily," "secret agents should give unbelievers an anesthetic in water and blame their condition on a curse of the gods." I had better stop here for fear that this book may fall into the hands of contemporary political leaders.

This view, held from ancient times, that deficits ought to be contained either by curbing expenditure or raising revenue, changed a little less than a hundred years ago, with the arrival of John Maynard Keynes and the Great Depression, when it was realized that overspending also had its virtues. During a depression, when private firms and ordinary individuals spend less, it was realized that the government could step in to compensate for this by overspending or, in other words, by running a larger fiscal deficit. This was the Keynesian prescription and President Roosevelt and his advisers in the United States stumbled upon this even before Keynes's classic book came out in 1936.

When the global financial crisis hit the world in 2008 and quickly spread to the entire world (with the possible exception of North Korea), we saw a virtual policy revolution. Almost all nations coordinated and used fiscal policy as a weapon. In other words, the fiscal deficit was expanded in most nations. India was in a very good position to do so, since its fiscal policy had been very tight until 2008. That meant there was scope for fiscal expansion. As we saw in chapter 2, this fiscal stimulus helped. The economy's growth, which had slumped to 6.7 percent in 2008–2009, shot up to nearly 9 percent in each of the two following years. However, growth began to come down again in 2011–2012 and now the options open to the government are much more limited. A fiscal stimulus is a bit like an antibiotic. It is very effective when used for a short period of time. But if used repeatedly and over long stretches of time, the side effects tend to outstrip the benefits. In India's case, a large deficit is likely to fuel the inflation rate.

Hence, choices have to be made very carefully. The first task to which more effort needs to be directed is raising tax revenue. In India, the gross tax revenue collected by the Union government as a percentage of GDP has hovered around 10.5 percent. It was 11.9 percent in 2007–2008, 10.8 percent in 2008–2009, 9.6 percent in 2009–2010, 10.2 percent in 2010–2011, and 10.7 percent in 2011–2012. So not only is India's tax-to-GDP ratio low, it went down over the last seven years. Global comparison suggests India can do much better. Industrialized countries usually cross 30 percent, with some of them going even higher. To quote from the recent paper by Besley and Persson (2014, 99): "Low-income countries typically collect taxes of between 10 and 20 percent of GDP, while the average for high-income countries is more like 40 percent." Hence, it is evident that there is scope for India to do better on this. India should aim to reach a tax revenue-to-GDP ratio of 15 percent within two or three years, and then set an even higher target of, for instance, 20 percent over the medium term.

This can be done almost entirely through plugging of loopholes and prevention of tax evasion, and the implementation of a more rational tax code, without having to raise tax rates.[3] Such an increase can make a large difference to the government's engagement with society. It can have a magical effect in terms of what the government can deliver to its citizens in terms of better infrastructure, energy, water, and general social welfare.

I shall comment on social welfare in a later chapter. Here I address the problem of infrastructure and growth. Raising the tax-to-GDP ratio is important for providing better infrastructure, but that is not the only instrument. Through skillful fiscal policy, it is possible to marshal the private sector to provide for infrastructure. Indeed, whether or not India manages to raise the tax-to-GDP ratio, it is important to recognize that government does not have the expertise for the multifarious demands of infrastructure. This is what was argued in the opening section of this chapter. Fiscal policy has a lot to do with infrastructure, the backbone of any economy, but in the manner suggested in the opening section, not by the state trying to provide it all but by creating appropriate incentives for private agents to deliver. Let me explain.

A major driver of economic growth in an emerging economy and especially one like India with plenty of surplus labor, is investment. The link between investment and growth in the case of India is quite visible to the naked eye, without need for fancy econometrics. The basic data for growth and investment over time was presented in table 2.1. We shall now translate these to a graph. Figure 4.1 plots India's investment rate, and the five-year moving average of annual GDP growth. As was discussed in chapter 2, it is evident that these two variables track each other well, bolstering our belief in what has come to be known as the neoclassical theory of economic growth.

We do know that once a country industrializes and labor becomes a binding constraint, this relationship no longer holds. Further, once the investment rate becomes very high, for instance, well over 40 percent, the

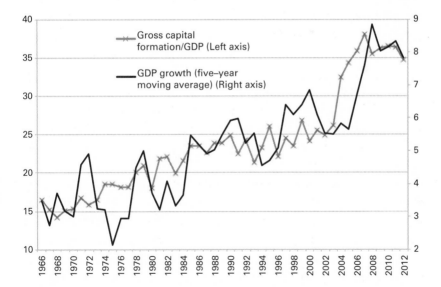

Figure 4.1
Growth and investment in India, 1966–2012
Source: Author's elaboration, based on data from the World Development Indicators.

returns to investment fall sharply. But clearly, India can still work on raising its investment rate by another four or five percentage points and expect to get a major boost to growth. The question must now turn to how India can boost investment and, in particular, infrastructure investment by another, say, five percentage points.

Infrastructural Investment and Government Guarantees

Recognizing that infrastructural investment is more a matter of finance than bricks and mortar, the Indian government talked about a target of $1 trillion of infrastructural investment during the twelfth Five-Year Plan, 2012–2017, with about half of this being raised from the private sector. It is clear however that the success of raising this will depend a lot on the government's policy. Should the government get involved in raising private sector money for this or should it follow a hands-off policy? Should the government give guarantees or "comfort letters,"[4] which are meant to act as an assurance without legal backing, to investors considering putting their money in infrastructure? We do know that such guarantees facilitate investment greatly but of course they also place responsibility on the government. This is a subject that has been heavily debated in India and abroad.

When trying to undertake large investment projects, reckless governments often give guarantees to investors, which, in effect, assert that in the event of the project going bankrupt the government will pay off the investors. Experience shows that when a government (with the ability to print money) gives a guarantee, investors are eager to put their money into projects. We have, however, come to learn now that this may not be such a good strategy for governments. Giving such a guarantee may do nothing to the government's fiscal arithmetic immediately, but it amounts to undertaking future fiscal expenditure. Since there is always the probability that such a guaranteed project will go belly up in the future, each such guarantee amounts to a certain additional expected expenditure by the government in the future. Hence, such guarantees, given recklessly, can lead to unsustainable fiscal deficits in the long run with all their attendant problems such as inflation, collapse in investment, and ultimately, economic recession.

India's fiscal history, originally noted for conservatism, became profligate in the late 1980s. Thereafter it has been on a path of consolidation with occasional lapses (for a brief account, see De 2012). One way in which these lapses occur is by giving future assurances, which do not show up on paper immediately but begin to weigh in when the future becomes the present.

For this reason, governments were warned by international standard bearers not to give guarantees to investors, especially for private sector initiatives. While this warning is a valid one and governments ought to heed it, there are circumstances where some strategic and well-designed guarantees or comfort letters from the government can be desirable in the overall interest of the nation. This can happen in a buoyant nation on the verge of an economic takeoff considering an expansion in a number of infrastructural projects.

The gist of the argument is simple. Among infrastructural projects there is typically a lot of positive externality (see Murphy, Shleifer, and Vishny 1989; Paternostro 1997; Oh 2011; Government of India 2012). The new road that will be operated by a tolling system is more likely to be successful if and when the residential township at the end of the road actually exists; and the residential township being contemplated by the developer is more likely to be successful if the road gets built. The government, by giving some carefully orchestrated guarantees to investors, can ensure that all these projects will develop, thereby raising the probability of success for all these projects without having to spend much money and without creating fiscal strain.

The idea is easy to illustrate. Let us suppose that there are two potential infrastructural projects. Each project is run by an independent private entrepreneur. To undertake the project entails an upfront cost of 10 (a very large sum). The project will yield results after a long time. If it succeeds, it gives a return of 16 and if it fails it gives 0. As just discussed the probability of each of these projects succeeding depends on whether or not the other is implemented. Suppose if only one of these two projects is implemented its probability of success is 1/2. If both are implemented, the probability of success of each project is 3/4.

As explained earlier, these are large projects and 10 is a very large sum of money. Entrepreneurs do not have this kind of money to invest. So they turn to private investors to seek angel funding or start-up money. However, 10 is sufficiently large that no single investor can invest in both projects. I shall assume that each private investor can invest in at most one project; and for simplicity assume that the investor can raise the money at zero interest cost. Hence, for an investor, it is worth investing money if the project yields more than 10.

The maximum that the investor can expect to earn when he alone makes the investment is given by 16/2–10 = -2. Hence, without a guarantee, no investor will, individually, choose to invest.

Now suppose the government gives a guarantee that, if the project fails, it will pay the investor 4 and, if it succeeds, it will charge a tax of 2. It is easy to see that it is now worthwhile for each investor to invest, and it is possible for all agents, including the government, to make a positive profit. In other words, by giving strategically designed guarantees to both investors, the government can actually guarantee itself against any increases in the total fiscal deficit.

Strategic government assurance is a powerful instrument but it has to be used with care. It must, by no means, be construed as justification for governments to rush into giving reckless guarantees. The government has to first check if the above claim is empirically valid and then select a careful cluster of complementary projects and give well-designed guarantees.

This is the kind of gamble that India has to consider, as it ponders how to make large infrastructural investments and push for a big leap to industrialization, as the new government that took office in Delhi in May 2014 is keen to do. This is the kind of big step that Deng Xiaoping's China undertook in the late 1970s with success. But it is sobering to recall that there were other policies like Mao Zedong's Cultural Revolution, which was launched in 1966 and saw the Chinese economy shrink by 5.7 percent in 1967 and by 4.1 percent in 1968. History makes suggestions but rarely gives a road map.

Exchange Rate Management

One area where China and India have followed very different policies, and therefore provides a natural experiment for learning, is in the management of exchange rates and trade. This has shaped the structure of development of the two nations. One of the major drivers of China's growth was exports. Not so, in the case of India. India's growth was much more domestically driven.

Now, as India tries to transition from a low-income agricultural nation to a growing industrial economy, and with Chinese wage rates rising and China beginning to concede space to other low-wage economies, India faces some important challenges concerning trade. The fact that India has been globalizing rapidly is evident from data. The change, in terms of presence in the global scene, came quite suddenly. In 1990, India's exports plus imports as a percentage of GDP was 14 percent. By 2010–2011 this had risen to 36.5 percent. During this same period, India's service exports rose from negligible to 12.5 percent of GDP. As we saw in chapter 2, up to 1991, for nearly two decades, India's foreign exchange reserves would hover around $5 billion. Over the next decade and a half they rose to over $300 billion. Equally remarkable, and not unconnected, was the rise of the Indian corporations, which have over the last decade been investing internationally, including in several industrialized nations. In many recent years there has been more foreign direct investment going from India to some rich countries than the other way around. This would have been unthinkable until a few years ago. While these are impressive achievements, a comparison with China suggests that India still has huge unexplored potential in the international sector.

Should the exchange rate be used as an active instrument in pursuing such a strategy? Many in India try to take a page out of China's experiments by which China kept its exchange rate fixed and devalued over a long stretch of time. I believe however that China's policy is poorly understood, even by the Chinese. Take, for instance, the policy of keeping the exchange rate artificially devalued in order to sell more to the world. This, in itself, has nothing to commend it. Such a policy basically means lowering your price to export more. It is like a store that decides to sell goods below the cost of production. This may enable the store to sell more and make the sales data (the equivalent of a nation's export data) look good but, overall, is poor policy, since the store has to make a loss to sustain it. For those who express China envy and recommend a policy of greater export, if need be by lowering the exchange rate, an alternative is to throw goods into the sea. That can mean a lot of export, at a massively devalued exchange rate, and we do not have to worry about adverse opinion from the importing nation. Clearly, this analogy shows that the argument of export at any cost is flawed.

How then did China benefit from this policy, if it did so? There is one situation where it is worthwhile to sell below cost of production for a certain stretch of time. This is so for "habit goods." Consider a good that is habit forming. One obvious example is a newspaper. Once we get used to a newspaper, we are loath to switch to another. Not surprisingly, when a new newspaper is started, a good strategy is to sell it at a low price, even if that means making a loss. The idea is that this loss will be more than made up for later by raising prices; and by then the reader will be so habituated to that newspaper that he or she would rather pay a little more for it than switch to another newspaper.

What people do not always realize is that buying from a nation is habit forming. This is understandable. Trade with another nation entails a lot of learning—the culture of the nation, the bureaucracy of the nation, the art of navigating its laws and rules. Once one has invested in it, there is an understandable proclivity to persist with that nation. The right policy for China, now that it has got a large customer base by virtue of having kept its prices low (through a depreciated currency) is to raise the price and capitalize on the buyer's habit. I believe, whether or not China pursued its exchange rate policy with this long-term strategy in mind, it will sooner or later realize this and raise prices.

All this opens up an interesting question for India and other emerging countries. Is it possible to mimic some of this policy? A direct policy imitation is not possible, since India is committed to a very different exchange rate regime. Beginning with some small moves in 1991, India has since been essentially on a floating exchange rate system. The first proper change in India's exchange rate policy happened because of the financial crisis of 1991. In 1992, a "dual exchange rate regime" was instituted. The 1991 *Report of the High Level Committee on Balance of Payments* by C. Rangarajan recommended the broad outlines of a market-determined exchange rate regime.[5] Current account convertibility was instituted in 1994, and a legal framework to assure such convertibility was put in place in June 2000. India now has limited but progressively increasing capital account convertibility.

There has been no effort to control the exchange rate by diktat. Instead, the system used is one in which there are some capital controls for foreign exchange sales and purchases, and on rare occasions the Reserve Bank of India has made market-based interventions that take the form of buying and selling dollars in order to keep the exchange rate stable. To quote from RBI's *Report on Foreign Exchange Reserves* (Reserve Bank of India 2008, 127): "India is classified under the 'managed float' exchange rate regime of the IMF. The Reserve Bank intervenes in the foreign exchange market to contain excessive volatility as and when necessary." Usually, the RBI stays behind the scene and the only visible action on the market is that of a public sector bank making a large purchase of dollars. Here is *Mint* newspaper's web edition, Livemint.com, August 20, 2008 (2:45 p.m.), speculating about central bank intervention in India: "State-run Indian banks were seen selling dollars to help the rupee recover from a 17-month low. . . . India's central bank uses state-run banks to intervene if it wants to slow a rupee decline or prevent it from rising too quickly, and private bank dealers said Wednesday's dollar selling looked like intervention."

Hence, if India is to use a deliberate policy of trying to get nations *habituated* to buying from India, this has to be through strategic central bank interventions in the exchange rate market. It is not evident to me that this is desirable strategy, even from the point of view of narrow economic benefit to the nation. Much depends on how it is executed and the nation's capacity for long-term planning. However, every nation, now and then, feels the need to intervene in the foreign exchange market. RBI's stated policy is not to try to buck the market trend in the exchange rate but to intervene to correct excessive fluctuations. So whether the aim is to depreciate the currency to boost exports or steady it against fluctuations, a central bank will feel the need to occasionally intervene in the foreign exchange market. This, in turn, raises a host of interesting analytical questions.

One consequence of using standard market intervention to try to hold the exchange rate below what market forces result in is that it leads to a buildup of foreign exchange reserves. This happened in China, which now has a staggering reserve of around $4 trillion. India also, over the last two decades, has seen a buildup of reserves.

As noted earlier, from 1977 to 1990, India's foreign exchange reserves hovered around $5 billion. In the early 1990s the rupee was put on a float, meaning banks, firms, and individuals were free to change currency at rates of their choosing without the government or the central bank exogenously fixing the rate. So from then onward, the way for the RBI to influence the exchange rate was essentially by buying and selling dollars. From 1993 to 2007 the rise in foreign exchange reserves was sharp, with a slowdown after that; though there has been a pickup again in recent months. Over the last few years the Reserve Bank's policy has been much more hands off. By and large, this has served India well, even though there have been dilemmas. Citing the depreciated exchange rate used by China, some advocates have proposed steady interventions in the form of buying up dollars and thereby shoring up the value of dollars and in the process lowering the value of the Indian rupee. This view was often heard, during much of 2009, 2010, and the first months of 2011, when the real exchange rate for the Indian rupee was appreciating (caused mainly by the fact that rupee inflation was greater than dollar inflation and the nominal rate was not changing enough to capture this). The argument was that there should be effort to keep the rupee value down by purchasing dollars, thereby enabling Indian exporters to be more competitive.[6]

The argument in the public space swung sharply over to the other side from mid-2011, when the rupee began to suddenly depreciate (see Rajwade 2012, for discussion). The trigger was Standard & Poor's downgrading, on August 5, 2011, of U.S. long-term sovereign credit from AAA to AA+. This caused widespread global uncertainty and, ironically, had investors run to the U.S. Treasury for cover. The exodus of foreign institutional investor money from India caused the rupee to depreciate sharply. Of course, this hurt a segment of traders, and the public debate lurched to the other side with statements of doom concerning the Indian rupee ruling the headlines. Indeed, in some ways a depreciation is harder to handle since it requires the central bank to sell its foreign exchange on the market and buy up rupees. Since there is a limit to how much foreign exchange the central bank has and so can release, there are natural upper bounds to what can be done to counter a currency depreciation. Countering an appreciation on the other hand requires using rupees to buy up dollars and euros. While this also, done in excess, has costs, there is no hard constraint on how much of this the central bank can indulge in.

Given India's commitment to a floating exchange rate, as in most industrialized nations, what can the Indian government and the RBI do in such situations? The commitment to the floating exchange rate is, in my view, the right one. As the economy grows and India takes its seat among global players, its decision makers must resist the temptation to fix the exchange rate, or at least desist from trying to buck the long-run trend.

Central banks, even of industrialized nations, wanting to devalue their currency, often intervene in the foreign exchange market by buying up foreign currency using domestic currency; conversely, if they want to revalue their currency they intervene by selling off foreign reserves. To quote from a textbook by Auerbach (1982, 414): "This method of influencing exchange rates is not always easy to detect. The central bank may have parties in the private sector intervene for them." In the United States, to effect an intervention in the foreign exchange market, the Federal Reserve will contact a dealing bank, such as Citibank and buy currency at Citibank's quoted rate. Moreover, a lot of the Fed's interventions, by some counts nearly half of them, are done secretly. And, often the explicit purpose of the Fed's intervention is to influence the exchange rate.

On September 6, 2011, the Swiss National Bank caused a stir by announcing a ceiling for the Swiss Franc vis-à-vis the euro; and stating that it "was prepared to buy foreign currencies in unlimited quantities" in order to maintain this ceiling.[7] Similar interventions by central banks to depreciate (and occasionally appreciate) currencies have been undertaken around the world. On September 15, 2010, the world felt the tremors when, following a sharp appreciation of the yen, the Bank of Japan sold yen and bought dollars. The immediate impact of this action was to weaken the yen vis-à-vis the U.S. dollar. India's RBI has also on occasion used similar action to smooth exchange rate fluctuations. One consequence of such action to depreciate the domestic currency is that it causes a buildup of foreign exchange reserves, such as happened with the People's Bank of China. This smoking-gun evidence of central bank action has been a source of global criticism. Also, some nations do not want to build up such costly reserves but are reconciled to them as a byproduct of exchange rate intervention.

It is, however, possible to argue that it is not necessary to have an impact on the reserves when trying to alter exchange rates. This requires us to use some innovatively designed interventions, the technical properties of which I have discussed elsewhere (Basu 2012). By using a suitable strategic technique—called "schedule intervention"—it is possible for the central bank to game the private foreign exchange dealers to influence the exchange rate without running up costly foreign currency reserves or running the risk of draining limited reserves. There was a lot of concern expressed in the Indian media about the sharp and sudden depreciation of the Indian rupee that occurred in the middle of 2013 and had occurred between August and October 2011,[8] as noted earlier. The standard way for the central bank to try to correct this (should it wish to) is to release dollars on the market and mop up rupees. Such action is, however, always laced with the concern that there are limits to how much foreign currency the central bank can off-load.

The argument is that (i) it is possible to remain on a system of floating exchange rates as an industrializing India would wish to do, (ii) exercise some influence on the exchange rate to appropriately boost trade and growth and effect restrictions on the nation's current account deficit and, at the same time, (iii) not build up reserves or run them down. By appropriately designing *the microstructure of intervention*, the acts of influencing the exchange rate and building up (or running down) foreign exchange reserves can be separated from each other. In particular, it is possible to depreciate your currency and leave no trail of large foreign reserves and equally to revalue your currency without running down your foreign exchange reserves.

It is questionable if the widely used quantity intervention, whereby the central bank (or some other bank acting as a front for the central bank) simply buys a certain quantity of foreign exchange, is the best kind of intervention. It is arguable that a "schedule intervention" does better. Broadly, a schedule intervention is one where the central bank or its agent bank enters the foreign exchange market not with a fixed quantity demand but with a demand that is conditional on price. In other words, it makes it clear that if the exchange rate is at a certain value it will buy (or sell) a certain amount of foreign exchange, if the exchange rate is at another level it will buy (or sell) another amount, and so on. Basically, a schedule intervention bends the demand or supply curve of foreign exchange (that private agents confront). Hence, a schedule intervention is a way for the central bank to game private players. By suitably "sloping" its demand for foreign currency, the central bank can fully immunize exchange rate interventions from a buildup or running down of reserves. What I am claiming is that exchange rate management and reserve management can be treated as two independent objectives. The secret is to choose a suitable schedule of intervention. If the currency market is fully competitive, there is no advantage from a schedule intervention; but if the market has big, strategic dealers and banks, then schedule interventions can be vastly more effective.

There is some interesting, indirect evidence supporting the real-life efficacy of schedule intervention. A cursory study of central banks around the world seems to provide no direct evidence of the use of a schedule intervention. However, Mexico's Currency Exchange Commission, which consists of members of Banco de Mexico and the Finance Ministry, has used a variant of conditional or schedule intervention in the foreign exchange market. On November 29, 2011, for instance, the Currency Exchange Commission announced it would release US$400 million per day *in case the peso declined by more than 2 percent in one day*. Similar interventions have been used by it in the past and there is some evidence that this kind of intervention has worked very effectively.

Despite this, it is admittedly the case that the argument I have provided is, at this stage, a theoretical construct. It will take time before it can be put to use. What will be important to check before it is put to use is its robustness against errors. Given that in reality we will never be able to estimate the precise form of the ideal schedule intervention, it will be important to work out the consequences of "small" mistakes in intervention. Even if this works perfectly if the correct schedule is implemented (this we already know will be the case, since it is theoretically verified), in case it turns out that errors can be hugely costly, we may have reason to be cautious about using it. In other words, there is still a lot of research to be done before schedule interventions can be used with certainty.

However, in a nation like India, which is committed to a floating exchange rate regime, to curb excessive exchange rate volatility, to steer the exchange rate minimally in certain directions when the need for that is felt, and to keep the real economy stable and the current account deficit within certain limits, central bank policy of the kind discussed will be worth considering.

Managing and Predicting Macro Parameters: A Conundrum

To close this chapter with an analytical digression, note that one problem that many policymakers have to contend with is balancing the art of managing an economy with making predictions about it. In India, thanks to a vibrant media, this is an ever-present problem. Getting in and out of my car at the North Block entrance, I often encountered journalists trying to get a word on what was expected to happen to the value of the rupee or the forecast for inflation or the outlook for the stock market. Since I had gotten to know many of these journalists well and some of them became friends, I often stopped to talk. But in addition there were the periodic formal media briefings, where invariably the main questions concerned the future and the responses to these were reported widely.

Such interactions give rise to an interesting phenomenon. Consider, for instance, the case of the rupee exchange rate. One troubling feature of the exchange rate is that it is partly determined by expectations. If it is expected that the rupee will lose value, it makes sense for ordinary people and firms to sell off some of the rupees they hold. But this in turn could cause the rupee to lose value even if it is true that in the absence of such action on the part of people the rupee would depreciate; it is likewise true for inflation. If there is expectation of inflation, it pays a seller of goods to hold back on supplying a little (especially with durable goods), since, by selling goods later, a higher price is fetched. But if goods are held back from being supplied, then prices indeed rise, thereby fulfilling the expectations.[9] For these reasons central bankers often justify certain policies in terms of dampening inflationary expectations. During times of inflation a higher benchmark interest rate, such as the repo rate, is often justified on such grounds. However, the formation of expectations and therefore the management of expectations remain a rather primitive science.

The link between managing macroeconomic variables and making predictions about them gives rise to an intriguing intellectual problem to which attention was drawn in Liaquat Ahamed's celebrated book on central banking. Discussing the efforts of the U.S. President Herbert Hoover to boost confidence in the U.S. economy in the aftermath of the Great Crash of 1929, Ahamed (2009, 363) observes, "To some extent he was caught in a dilemma that all political leaders face when they pronounce upon the economic situation. *What they have to say about the economy affects its outcome—an analogue to Heisenberg's principle.* As a consequence they have little choice but to restrict themselves to making fatuously positive statements which should never be taken seriously as forecasts" (my italics).

Thus, we hear about how a policymaker stoked inflation by saying in public that inflation would go up. Usually, behind such an observation is the critique that no one should be so irresponsible as to fuel inflation by making such statements. This immediately places a nation's Central Bank and the Treasury in the dilemma alluded to by Ahamed. This seems to suggest that it is impossible for the policymaker-analyst to both manage the macroeconomy and make forecasts—what Ahamed refers to as economics' Heisenberg challenge. This is an interesting observation. However, drawing on a theorem of mathematician-philosopher L. E. J. Brouwer, we can rescue ourselves, at least partly, from this challenge.

To understand this, suppose that, if no public forecast is made by the Treasury about future inflation, inflation will be 10 percent. Now suppose, if the Treasury forecasts an inflation number, that this will then influence human expectations and behavior so that the actual inflation will be partly shaped by it. Let me create an imaginary scenario or what economists call a "model" of how this happens. First define a "benchmark number" as follows. If the Treasury forecasts the inflation rate to be some number, let the benchmark number be defined as 10 plus half of that number. Thus, if the Treasury forecasts an inflation rate of 10, the benchmark number is 15. Now, assume that if the Treasury forecasts an inflation rate, the actual inflation turns out to be halfway between the forecast and the benchmark number. Thus if the Treasury forecasts 10, the actual inflation is going to be 12.5.

What is interesting to check now is that the fact that the actual inflation moves with the forecast does not mean that we can never make an accurate forecast. Let us ask what the Treasury should do if it is bent on making an accurate forecast. Basically, in this model, when the Treasury tries to forecast inflation it has to treat its own forecast as one of the determinants of the inflation. If, for instance, it makes a forecast of zero inflation, actual inflation will be 5 percent. If it forecasts inflation to be 10 percent, actual inflation will be 12.5 percent. It is now easy to see that if the Treasury wants to forecast inflation correctly, it has to make a forecast of 20 percent inflation. No other forecast will be borne out in practice. Basically, an accurate forecast is a search for a "fixed point" of the "forecast function," that is, a line that links each forecast to the corresponding actual inflation.[10] In this case, there is only one fixed point.

The policymaker's dilemma can be illustrated sharply with this model. Suppose the Treasury takes its job of holding inflation down seriously. Then, keeping in mind that its own forecast of inflation is one of the causes of inflation, and assuming for simplicity that it cannot make negative forecasts, what forecast should it make? Clearly, the answer is 0 percent. The forecast will turn out to be false but inflation will be as low as possible, to wit, at 5 percent. From the point of view of what the Treasury is tasked with achieving—namely to keep inflation down—this is worth it, since inflation would be 10 percent if the Treasury made no forecasts, and it would be higher than 5 percent if it forecast a number greater than zero.

So, the objective of accurate forecasting and the objective of inflation control pull in different directions; and therein lies the dilemma. It is not always possible to carry out both tasks the Treasury is entrusted with, namely, forecasting inflation as accurately as it can and minimizing inflation. There are situations, as I have illustrated, where an internal consistency problem arises between the two tasks. Do one task perfectly, the other gets thrown out of gear. Do the other task well, and the former gets out of control. This is not a problem specific to India or China or the United States. This is a problem with the way the world is. There is no way to resolve this; all policymakers in a position to make publicly observed forecasts have to live with this dilemma.

In case the forecast function is nonlinear and has more than one fixed point, then each fixed point would be an accurate forecast. In such a situation the task of predicting inflation accurately and trying to keep inflation low has some content. It means we should forecast the lowest value of inflation, which is a fixed point of the forecast function. Note, however, that this does not negate the fact that there may be other forecasts that will lower inflation further though by being wrong.

I do not know how to resolve this conundrum and so must leave that to others; what is certain is that, as things stand, virtually all policymakers, some time or the other, have to contend with it.

5 Globalization and the Challenge of Development

Tips to Industrialized Nations

On November 7, 2010, the Indian prime minister hosted a dinner at his residence, 7RCR, in honor of the visiting U.S. president, Barack Obama, and the first lady, Michelle Obama. Word had gone around for a while that there would be such a dinner and while it was clear that senior members of government would be there, there was speculation and gossip about who else would be present at the event, the chatter heightened by the understanding that there would be no more than eighty guests.

It turned out to be an interesting and diverse gathering, consisting of some well-known media personalities and journalists (Prannoy Roy, Shekhar Gupta), some prominent industrialists (Ratan Tata, Azim Premji), and, threatening to steal attention away not just from these people but also from prime ministers and presidents, some Bollywood personalities (Aamir Khan, Shabana Azmi). I was talking to Tim Geithner, then Treasury secretary in the United States, and Narayana Murthy of Infosys, when Manmohan Singh walked in with Barack Obama and began stopping at different clusters and introducing the guests. When he came to us he introduced Narayana Murthy and then turned to me, explaining to President Obama that I was brought in from academe in the United States to be the chief economic adviser to his government. India had just completed some years of remarkable sprint of over 9 percent growth per annum and was getting a lot of media attention globally. We exchanged a few words about the economy and its challenges and I said why, despite all the problems, I was optimistic. President Obama turned to me and pointing to Geithner said, "You should give this guy some tips."

Needless to say, we treated the remark as evidence of his dexterity with conversation and capacity for light banter, and, as they moved on, we turned to other topics. But with the world as interconnected as it is today, with emerging economies concerned about changes in the U.S. Federal Reserve's liquidity injection policy and withdrawal, and the structural reforms in the European Union countries, it seems appropriate to begin this chapter by giving some tips to the "guys" in charge of policymaking in industrialized nations.

How interconnected a world we live in was driven home to me dramatically on August 5, 2011, the day Standard & Poor's downgraded the long-term sovereign credit rating on the United States of America, from AAA to AA+. After a hard day's work, my wife and I had gone to the Chittaranjan Park fish market in Delhi to buy *hilsa*,[1] when my cell phone began to ring—once, twice, and more. I knew something had happened and decided to call back one of those numbers. It was a journalist—someone I knew a little, speaking hurriedly and saying that S&P's had just downgraded the United States. Soon there would be calls from colleagues and others in government and there was widespread concern about what would happen to the American economy and, in no time, the conversation shifted to what this would imply for us.

What happened over the next few weeks was quite baffling. With the United States' long-term sovereign credit rating having been downgraded, investors' money from around the world began to flow to the U.S. Treasury. That is, people began taking money out from around the world and especially developing and emerging market economies and buying bonds issued by the U.S. Treasury. As a consequence, with demand for Indian rupees down and demand for dollars up, the Indian rupee began to depreciate sharply. Similar developments were witnessed around the world.

Though this rush of money to the United States was quite baffling when it happened, in retrospect we can understand it. With the United States downgraded, there was concern that the entire global economy would be rocked. Where could investors put their money where it would be safe? With emerging economies there is always some anxiety of the sovereign defaulting, even though many such economies, India included, have never defaulted. In the event of such anxiety, the place to park your money is in a strong and powerful economy that has its own central bank and, as a last resort, can even print money and pay you back. The United States fit that bill. The only risk with the United States was that the dollar could lose value; so that when you are paid back your lending to the United States, the real value could be less. That risk, however, is less alarming than that of an outright default.

There are two additional factors that mitigated this risk. First, China holds around $4 trillion of foreign exchange reserves, a large part of this in U.S. dollars. A decline in the value of dollars will therefore hurt China badly. Hence, two of the largest economies in the world, the United States and China, will use their might to resist any substantial decline in the dollar. Second, if many others tried to buy U.S. dollars, then the price of dollars, instead of falling, would rise.

In the event, that is what happened. These structural strengths, coupled with—the less predictable part—herd behavior, led to money going to the U.S. Treasury, with a consequent sharp depreciation faced by a host of emerging market economies.

What happened to Eurozone countries during this time is important to understand for anyone trying to come to grips with today's global economy. The Eurozone economies are strong, rich economies and, under normal circumstances, money in search of safe haven would flow into them as well. But something important changed after 1999, when the euro was created. These countries had to give up their individual central banks when they joined the Eurozone. In the event of a Eurozone sovereign having repayment difficulty, there was no central bank that could come to its rescue. There was no reason why the European Central Bank would respond to any particular government and print money to rescue it. Indeed, there are provisions in the Treaty of Lisbon and in its predecessor, the Maastricht Treaty, which made a positive response to such an entreaty not possible.[2] This is what now set the otherwise strong European economies apart from the United States and gave an advantage to the latter. Hence, unlike in the older world, where the kind of news that came with Standard & Poor's downgrading of U.S. debt would have caused money to rush into European economies, that did not happen this time.[3]

This is a good moment to pause to understand the challenges faced by Europe since the creation of the Eurozone, which has had such important implications for the entire world.[4] The most cogent pictorial representation of what caused the Eurozone sovereign debt crisis is the graph in figure 5.1. It shows the borrowing costs of Eurozone countries from 1999 to recent

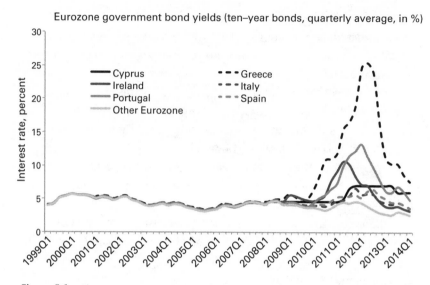

Figure 5.1

Borrowing costs in Eurozone nations. *Note*: "Other Eurozone" is a simple average of the bond yields of Austria, Belgium, Finland, France, Germany, Luxembourg, Malta, Netherlands, Slovak Republic, and Slovenia. Data for Estonia and Latvia are not available.

Source: International Financial Statistics.

times. As is obvious, eyeballing the graph, all Eurozone governments were borrowing at virtually the same rate. This reflected the great delusion that arose with the creation of the Eurozone: the presumption that now that these nations were part of a monetary union, lending money to one was as safe or unsafe as lending to any other.

However, this widely held presumption was wrong. The Eurozone was a monetary union and not a fiscal or banking union. When you lent money to a sovereign, it was the sovereign's responsibility to pay you back. Further, unlike earlier times, now the sovereign did not have a central bank of its own that could print money. Hence, the risk associated with lending to Spain was probably very different from the risk of lending to Germany since there was no collective EU or Eurozone responsibility for repayment.

This realization and the rupture of the great delusion occurred in 2008, amid the financial crisis unleashed by the subprime mortgage crisis in the United States. Once the realization of differential risk became clear, the borrowing costs of different countries within the Eurozone diverged as one can see in figure 5.1, where the overlapping lines suddenly open up like one of those Japanese hand-held fans. But during the long period of the great delusion, the damage had already been done. Countries borrowed at artificially low interest rates and piled up debts. For decades, the world had been accustomed to a map of fiscal behavior patterns, where the industrialized countries were models of responsible behavior, while emerging and developing countries had to be routinely reprimanded for reckless spending and fiscal profligacy. It was evident by 2011 that this pattern of behavior had been reversed. The debt-to-GDP ratios were soaring in European countries and their borrowing costs were spiraling out of control.

For emerging market economies there was another concern. The United States, in an effort to jump-start its economy, was injecting liquidity into its economy—popularly known as quantitative easing—and this was having a somewhat unusual effect. It had very little impact on the U.S. economy in terms of real growth and was not causing inflation in the United States. Instead, emerging economies were growing well but they had to contend with inflation. This was particularly true of India, as we saw in chapter 4. What the world seemed to be suffering from was what I referred to in an earlier chapter as global "salad bowl stagflation"—inflation and growth in some countries and no inflation and no growth in others. Since the United States has now ended QE, this pressure should lessen. Early in 2013, the chairman of the Fed indicated that the time might soon come when the United States will begin to taper off its program of quantitative easing, which at that time took the form of a monthly purchase of assets worth $85 billion by the Fed. In December 2013, the taper was formally announced.

The forces of globalization were on full display when the emerging market economies reacted as soon as the tapering was indicated as a possible strategy in May 2013. In anticipation of the cut back in credit in the United States, U.S. interest rates rose, and money started to flow out of emerging economies to the United States (Eichengreen and Gupta 2014).[5] There was sharp depreciation in exchange rates in India, Brazil, Indonesia, Mexico, Turkey, South Africa, and several other economies. Different measures were undertaken in each of these countries to counter this sudden outward flow. In the case of India, there was one clear saving grace. The sharp depreciation of the rupee boosted the country's exports and there was visible revival in sales abroad by the end of 2013. And the current account deficit, which had risen to alarming heights, decreased aided by the inflow of hard currencies as a consequence of the higher exports.

One thing has become evident to all governments and policymakers in the developing world by now: we are living in a more interconnected world than ever before. One must be ready to react to policies in other nations, especially the big and the powerful, and in crafting a policy one must be aware that its impact could turn out to be very different from what would happen in a more balkanized economy.

This changing structure of the global economy will cause enormous strains in the world and call upon nimbleness on the part of policymakers that may be hard to marshal.[6] In the remainder of this chapter, I want to illustrate some of the special policy challenges of our globalized world by delving into a welfare-related matter—the end of poverty and a better sharing of prosperity. These are usually treated as matters that are nation specific. However, with globalization, even this area has become one where interconnectivity of policies is critical.

Poverty, the Sharing of Prosperity, and Policy

In April 2013, the World Bank for the first time veered beyond its usual commitment to the mitigation of poverty to add the sharing of prosperity and promotion of greater equality among peoples as an explicit goal. This break from tradition has been long overdue since inequality has risen to intolerable levels. The total wealth of the ten richest persons in the world equals Nigeria's GDP; the wealth of the twenty richest people in the world is roughly equal to the entire foreign exchange reserves of South Korea, India, and Singapore, which are currently the eighth, ninth, and tenth largest foreign exchange reserve holding nations in the world. A recent study by OXFAM shows that the eighty-five wealthiest people in the world have the same amount of aggregate wealth among them as the bottom half of the world's population.[7]

A certain amount of inequality will always exist[8] and, in many ways, is welcome because it creates the tensions and incentives needed to propel society forward. But the kind of inequality that we see in the world today, with roughly a billion people living on less than $1.25 a day and a handful of people with incomes so high as to be difficult to comprehend, is surely unacceptable.[9] This need not be any individual's fault, because, if the opportunity arises, it is only natural that the ones who are able to exploit it will likely do so. But this is surely a policy failure. Luckily, there are individuals who, while they themselves have done well, including some billionaires, have been critical of policy regimes that make it possible to create such enormous disparities among human beings.

There are market fundamentalist thinkers who believe that this is in the nature of things and not a feature of society to fret about or to try to correct with policy interventions. All I will say in response is that at the height of U.S. slavery, when human beings were auctioned in public markets like livestock, there were plenty of people who saw nothing wrong with the practice and believed it was the most suitable fate for the "inferior" slaves. And during the high noon of caste practices in India, there were likewise many who argued that this is how society was meant to be. Fortunately, thanks to the phenomenal success of Piketty's (2014) magnum opus on inequality, and some scholarly documenting of the historical data on inequality (see, for instance, Bourguignon and Morrisson 2002; Milanović 2010), these matters have come to the fore of global debate.

Consider now the problem faced by a nation's policymakers who are keen to correct these extreme inequities and banish poverty from their land. This may not, however, be as easy as some laypersons and grassroots activists suppose. A part of the problem lies in the interconnectivity between countries and the heightened globalization of the last few decades. This is because effort to correct this within a country or within a region usually leads to a flight of capital and highly skilled people out of the country or the region, which could actually exacerbate the problem of poverty in the region or the state.

In India, this was the core of the mistake made by the Communist government that ruled in the state of West Bengal for nearly thirty years. This may well be a record of the longest-running elected Communist rule anywhere. For those unfamiliar with India, it may be pointed out that the Communist Party of India (Marxist), or CPI(M), that was repeatedly reelected and ruled in the state never went in for the extreme polices seen in Communist countries. It remains an enigma whether this was because the CPI(M) was ruling only in a part of a country where more draconian measures would not have been allowed by the constitution or by choice. But I knew some of the CPI(M) leaders and they seemed, by disposition, more in the mode of social democrats. I treat the period of the Communist rule largely as a failure for the state, which lost rank not only in terms of state GDP but also on other social and cultural measures. Right up to the 1960s and even 1970s, West Bengal was in the lead when it came to higher education and research. It has clearly lost rank on this. Even in terms of basic literacy and some health indicators it has lost out. Ironically, the failure of the state was an intellectual failure, consisting of a fatal mistake—it made policies unmindful of the fact that we live in a globalized world, people are largely self-interested and rational, and there are other governments waiting to lure capital and talent. What may have been good policy if instituted by a global government may not be so when implemented in a region or even a single nation.

Take one example. To ensure that rural people get good education, West Bengal made it compulsory for all teachers, including the best, to serve a term in rural areas. The biggest difference this made was it changed the catchment of "best" teachers, since many talented people preferred not to become teachers or, if they were already teachers, they preferred to move out to other places, where they would not be rotated; and this was an important factor in the decline of Kolkata as the leading hub of higher education.

All this means that nations and governments are often caught in a Prisoners' Dilemma type of trap. Rational governments realize this and are reconciled to it. Irrational governments try to unilaterally break out of it and do even worse. Let me illustrate this problem with the case of the new, shared prosperity goal of the World Bank.

Inequality and Taxation

The aim of this section is to illustrate how targets matter in shaping domestic policy and in laying out a global policy agenda. The second objective is relevant to multilateral development banks and international organizations. The discussion here is conducted in terms of fiscal policy and, in particular, taxation. This is purely for reasons of convenience, to illustrate in the simplest way the kinds of concerns that the goal of greater equity can give rise to.

The model, which draws on some of my earlier work (Basu 2006, 2010), is presented in a highly threadbare fashion, to show how shifting targets, from overall growth, through growth of the poorest people, to an exclusive focus on inequality mitigation, leads to different policies on the ground and also to raise some interesting questions pertaining to the challenges of policymaking in a globalized world.

In order to keep the arithmetic rudimentary, consider a society in which half the population is skilled and half unskilled. It will be assumed that the skilled people will be the rich ones and the unskilled the poor (I am aware that this is often not the case in reality). Hence, in this model the World Bank's goal of shared prosperity, focusing on the bottom 40 percent of the population, will translate to focusing on the income growth of the unskilled.

Suppose, if the tax rates are zero, each skilled or rich person earns a large sum and each unskilled or poor person earns a negligible amount. For the sake of argument one can think of this negligible amount as zero. Now, let me introduce a simple system of proportional income tax, which is used by the government as a mechanism for redistribution. The tax is imposed solely on the skilled people and the collection is transferred to all the unskilled people with each of them getting the same amount. Remember this is no more than an illustrative exercise and, as such, this is an economy with no public goods, no defense expenditure, no security challenges, no Ebola. So unlike in reality, the tax here is no more than an instrument of transfer. My aim here is simply to lay out the logic.

It seems reasonable to assume that as the government increases the tax rate, once it goes sufficiently high the skilled people choose to work less, and if the tax rate is 100 percent, they would rather not work. Now start from a tax rate of 0 percent and keep raising the tax rate. Clearly, for rich people, this will lower their post-tax income. As the tax rate keeps rising, beyond a point, the post-tax income of the rich will fall for two reasons. They will work less and so earn less, and on top of this, more will be taxed away from them, since the tax *rate* will have risen.

It is now easy to see that, as the tax rate goes from 0 to 100 percent, the total tax collection will first rise and then fall. After all, at a tax rate of 0, the tax collection is, by definition, 0. And at a rate of 100 percent, the collection is again 0, this time because people do not work and so there is nothing to impose the tax on. This has interesting implications for the poor, since in this abstract model they live entirely off tax transfers. As the tax rate rises, the poor will become better off, but as the tax moves toward 100 percent, they will again become worse off.

The relation between what we take to be our target or goal and the policy we choose (in this model, the only policy variable is the tax rate) is now easy to illustrate. If we are utilitarians, focused on aggregate income and overall growth, with no special attention to poverty eradication or inequality mitigation, we will be happy to have an income tax rate of 0. There will be no incentive for the skilled to cut down work, and so they will be very rich, and the unskilled will be abysmally poor, but the aggregate income in this society will be as large as it can be.

Next suppose we focus solely on the poor and want them to do as well as possible, in the spirit of the philosophy of Gandhi and Rawls (1971). Then we will raise the tax rate to exactly that level where the total tax collection is maximized. I am assuming for simplicity that at this point the skilled people are still better off than the poor.[10] Let me call this the Rawlsian tax rate.

If, however, we aim neither for aggregate income maximization, nor for the enhancement of the welfare of the poor, but solely on promoting equality, then we will have to raise the tax rate even more (given the preceding assumption), to the point where the post-tax income of the rich is the same as the income of the poor after they receive their transfer. Let me call this the equality tax.[11] This argument illustrates how there can be situations where the only way to achieve total equality is by hurting the poor. In this model, as we raise the tax rate from the Rawlsian one to the equality rate, we get greater equality but with the poor people (as well as the rich) having to be worse off.

Hence, the new goals announced by the World Bank would, in this model, suggest what I have called the Rawlsian tax rate, which is distinct from what would be recommended if our focus were solely on aggregate income (in which case the tax would be zero) or solely on equality (in which case the tax rate would be higher). The model illustrates this with the case of taxation policy but a similar logic would extend to other kinds of policies, from the provision of education, health services, and other benefits, to trade and monetary policy.

Also, for reasons of full disclosure, it should be pointed out that the argument was constructed without specifying the microfoundations. In a fully founded model, we would derive the behavior of people (who choose to work less when the tax rate goes up) from utility maximizing behavior. And in such a model we might want the policymaker to be attentive not just to people's incomes but to leisure as well.

Globalization and the Taxation Game

Globalization has conferred large benefits to society and created opportunities we could not foresee (Wolf 2004). But it has also given rise to new challenges. An example of this is the increased complexity of national policymaking today caused by the fact that decisions in one nation have positive or negative impact on others at a level rarely seen in history, thanks to new technology, easier transport, and expanding global institutions. This model can be used to illustrate a very interesting connection between policymaking in a single country and the interconnectedness of policymaking in a globalized world, thereby emphasizing the role of multilateral organizations like the World Bank, the International Labour Organization (ILO), and the World Trade Organization (WTO).

To see this, suppose there are several nations, each of which looks like the one described in the previous section. Assume also that each nation has decided to go along with the objective of shared prosperity. Hence, to start with, each government would be tempted to set the tax rate at what was called the Rawlsian rate, for the reasons discussed earlier. But it will soon strike a government that it can do better, in terms of the shared prosperity goal for its citizens, by the following maneuver: if it lowers the tax rate, unilaterally, a little, it will attract some of the skilled people from other nations. This will enable it to transfer more income to its own poor people, since despite the tax rate being lower there will be more people to tax. Hence, it would have furthered its shared prosperity target. I am implicitly assuming that there are some transactions costs involved with moving; and different people value this differently. Hence, as the tax rate is lowered some but not all skilled people will move to the low-tax economy.

If, however, all countries do this, they will all be worse off (in terms of their own goals). The only way to beat this is for the government to cut the tax rate further. But the same reasoning will prompt others to do the same. This reasoning used repeatedly would lead governments to a race-to-the-bottom exercise and they will end up setting their tax rates at zero. In other words, in a globalized world with skilled worker mobility, each government will end up behaving like a utilitarian who is interested only in overall income maximization (with no attention to poverty mitigation) even though that is not the real preference of any of these governments.

To illustrate this with numbers consider a world with two nations, A and B, where each government has to choose a tax rate and is interested in the welfare of its own poor. The game, described below, illustrates the problem. Suppose the two governments have to choose their respective tax rates and the welfare or payoff depends on the choice of both countries' tax rates. The payoff matrix of the Taxation Game describes the problem.

The Taxation Game

Country B (Tax rates)

		$\frac{1}{12}$	$\frac{1}{6}$	$\frac{1}{3}$
	$\frac{1}{12}$	1, 1	3, ½	3, 0
Country A (Tax rates)	$\frac{1}{6}$	½, 3	2, 2	4, 1
	$\frac{1}{3}$	0, 3	1, 4	3, 3

If both choose tax rate ⅓, each gets a welfare payoff of 3. If Country A chooses ⅙ and B chooses ⅓, A gets a payoff of 4, B gets 1. And so on. All this can be read off from the payoff matrix of the game.

In this game, the ideal outcome of (⅓, ⅓)—that is, each country choosing a tax rate of ⅓—cannot be sustained as an equilibrium because if the other country sets a tax rate of ⅓ you are better off lowering your tax rate to ⅙. Indeed the only equilibrium in this game is where the two governments choose the lowest tax option (1/12, 1/12). Even though both governments are committed to shared prosperity and this requires the tax rate to be set at ⅓, that outcome is not sustainable in equilibrium thanks to the pressures of globalization.

This underlines the need for a modicum of coordination in global fiscal policy. Unilateralism in terms of taxation and other fiscal policies was fine until a few decades ago when the global economy was largely balkanized, with respective national boundaries marking out each economy. As the February 16, 2013, *Economist* magazine cover story on global money laundering and tax havens illustrated, we no longer have that luxury.

In promoting shared prosperity and moving to end extreme and chronic poverty there is a lot that each country needs to do but, at the same time, there is a lot of cross-country coordination and global regulation that is needed (Stiglitz 2010, chapter 8). This is a relatively recent phenomenon, a feature of our new globalized world. The exact contours of how such coordination can be managed is still virgin territory (see Basu 2010a for discussion), but this places a special responsibility on international organizations and multilateral authorities that was not there earlier, certainly not in the urgent form it takes today.

Before moving on to other topics, I want to emphasize that global inequality, and the particularly extreme form it takes in some nations today, should be a matter of collective embarrassment as an important moral failure. Even if we are not concerned about this as an end in itself, we must not be unmindful of the fact that it can unleash political forces that are destabilizing for all citizens. In the context of India, I address the problem of food deprivation and the poor in chapter 6.

6 Food and Poverty

The Challenge of Poverty

In terms of growth, as we already saw, India has done well, especially since the mid-1990s. What remains a challenge for the nation is its unfortunate record in terms of the inclusiveness of the growth. Inequality in India has grown steadily over the last few decades (Ahluwalia 2002). While poverty, measured in terms of the percentage of population below the global poverty line of $1.25 (the dollar here refers to the purchasing power parity [ppp] adjusted U.S. dollar) per person, per day, has fallen since the 1970s, and the decline has been particularly sharp over the last ten years, it is still shockingly high. Even today, after nearly two decades of steady growth began, around 240 million Indians live below this low poverty line.

The data on poverty in India over time is presented in table 6.1 and the graph of India's head-count ratio of extreme poverty is illustrated in figure 6.1.[1] Needless to say, there are many different ways of measuring poverty, and many different ways of tracking poverty over time and across India's vast regions, and how these are done can influence policies in important ways.[2] But that is not germane to what I am about to discuss in this section and so I shall stay away from this contentious debate.

Given the strident rhetoric of pro-poor policies from 1947, the fact that India has such a high incidence of poverty is an embarrassment to the nation. This is clearly not for want of anti-poverty programs. India has run a slew of such programs—cheap food for the needy, employment for the poor, loans for the poor wanting to start up a small business, interest subventions for farmers, as well as subsidized fertilizer, kerosene, and diesel,[3] and this does not end the list. But the fact that all this has had a negligible impact on poverty tells us that inclusive growth is not just a matter of

Table 6.1
Percent of population in India living below the poverty line

Year	Headcount (%)
1977	65.9
1983	55.5
1987	53.6
1993	49.4
2004	41.6
2009	32.7
2012	21.9

Source: PovcalNet, Development Research Group of the World Bank, http://iresearch
.worldbank.org/PovcalNet/index.htm?2.

grit, determination, and the multiplication of programs. It needs an understanding of the causes and persistence of poverty.[4] Most of the programs
and interventions look good on paper, especially at first sight, but are often
deeply flawed.

In this chapter I examine India's anti-poverty programs through the lens
of one sector: food.[5] Providing cheap food and having a granary of stocks to
intervene in the event of a sudden food shortage has always been a central
part of the government's anti-poverty program. This has led to big success in
terms of averting famines and sudden distress; but in terms of battling chronic
poverty and malnutrition India's record is dismal (Drèze and Sen 2013).

As a consequence of this, the government brought in a new law, the
National Food Security Act, 2013.[6] Under this new law India will spend over
$4 billion each year and provide cheap food to 800 million people. But it
is one thing to make something the law and another to fulfill it. Why has
India done so poorly in this sector? That is what I try to answer in this section. Luckily, it is possible to design a vastly better system of food intervention than the one currently used by the government.

India's food policy is important also because it has been a part of global
discourse, with consequences for World Trade Organization (WTO) agreements. By some estimates India spends a whopping 18.5 billion dollars or
over a trillion rupees annually to subsidize food, with major implications
for the global economy.[7] This leads to some intercountry policy dynamics
of the kind discussed in chapter 5. What I want to examine here is not the

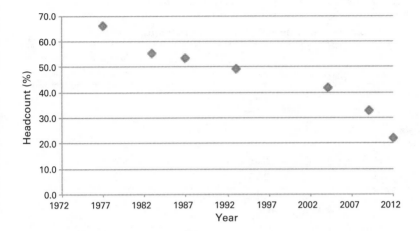

Figure 6.1
Headcount ratio: percent of population in India below the poverty line of $1.25

appropriateness of the size of this spending but its efficacy. To take the surprise away, if there were an index of efficacy, the current food policy system would not score well.

Food Buffers

Less than 14 percent of India's national income comes from agriculture and around 58 percent of India's labor force lives off agriculture. Hence, there is little surprise in the fact that people who live in rural India lead impoverished lives, and India's overall incidence of poverty is unconscionably high.

From October 2009 to March 2010, the year-on-year food-price inflation announced every week hovered around 20 percent. As discussed in chapter 3, it declined substantially after that, though it has persisted above any comfort level for a long time.

What is troubling is the amount of food stocks that the Indian government continued to hold during this period of high prices. As table 6.2 shows, India's grain procurement remains fairly steady from year to year and, furthermore, the reserves are almost always above the stated buffer norms, especially over the last five years. This should immediately make us suspect that the government may not have succeeded in the role of evening out fluctuations in food production as effectively as it could have. The strategy used for releasing food grains in India has scope for improvement.

Table 6.2
Aggregate food grain procurement, 2004–2010 (lakh tons)

Year	Rice	Wheat	Coarse grains	Total procurement (rice + wheat + coarsegrains)
2004–2005	246.9	168.0	8.3	423.1
2005–2006	276.6	147.9	11.5	435.9
2006–2007	251.1	92.3	0.0	343.3
2007–2008	287.4	111.1	2.0	400.7
2008–2009	336.9	226.9	13.8	577.5
2009–2010	297.1*	253.8	4.1*	555.1

Source: Ministry of Finance, Government of India.
Note: A "lakh" refers to 100,000.
*As of July 9, 2010. The reporting cycle for rice is from October 1 to September 30.

Around May–June 2010 the international price of wheat was approximately 30 percent lower than the price of wheat in India. In other words, Indian residents were paying more than what they would have if they could access the international market or, even better, if our own grain was released on the market. Though, as this chapter will clarify, the *mechanism* of the release is important and needs to be designed carefully to ensure that the impact on prices is substantial, there is no disputing that the *quantities* released have been quite inadequate.

The four observations in the four opening paragraphs of this section may appear at first sight to be disparate observations on the Indian economy. In reality, they have a common thread running through them. They illustrate a pervasive weakness that characterizes India's food grains policy. In the name of helping the farmer and the consumer and, likely, even with the intention of doing so, India ended up creating a food grains policy framework that has not done well in serving either of them. Many of India's poor households do not get adequate food and a large section of the nation's farmers remain impoverished, especially the small ones with no marketable surplus. While India does need to increase agricultural productivity, creating wrong incentives can stall the natural process of industrialization and the emergence of labor-intensive manufacturing activities in some regions, by keeping disproportionately large numbers of people engaged in agricultural activity.

We have rightly tried to put in place a mechanism for acquiring food so as to subsidize the poor and have ready reserves for hard times. Yet we need to work much harder to develop a good system to release the grain when those hard times come. This was a central lament in the much-cited Abhijit Sen Committee Report on food grain management (see Sen 2002), but the problem continues to persist even today.

Fortunately, there is now a new resolve to correct these defects. We can see this in the various right-to-food campaigns in the country and the Indian government's decision to enact a food security law, to enshrine people's right to a basic amount of food as a *legal* prerogative. The common person's right to food is well within the powers of the government to satisfy under most plausible scenarios and, moreover, this is a need that all civilized societies ought to try to fulfill. Hence, this is a move in the right direction and it provides an opportunity to improve India's food distribution system.

But it is critical to understand that it is not enough to throw money at the problem. The new law needs to be accompanied by a new mechanism for delivering support to the poor.[8] India needs to design the entire food grains policy skillfully in order to ensure that we can fulfill the right to food that has been conferred on our citizens, and at the same time ensure that India's fiscal system is able to withstand the expenditure. One has to understand the restrictions placed on the economic policymaker by the laws of the market, and then design mechanisms that can steer through and utilize those laws instead of being undone by them.

The popular view, understandably alluring, is that all the Indian government has to do to support poor consumers and poor farmers is to direct subsidies at them and make sure that anybody caught cheating the system and adulterating food is punished—but punished *by whom*? For that we have to rely on another layer of bureaucracy and police force, which will open another layer of opportunity for cheating the system. I shall return to this troubling issue of governance in chapters 8, 9, and 10.

It would be wonderful if people were innately honest and self-monitored their behavior; and government ought to educate the citizenry to develop these qualities. But to *assume* that they have these qualities when they do not is to risk designing a flawed mechanism that will be pilfered and adulterated. A comprehensive study by Khera (2010) showed that 67 percent of the wheat meant to be delivered to the poor misses the target. In other words, to get one kilogram of wheat to poor households we ended up directing three kilograms of wheat at them.[9]

In designing effective policy we have to recognize that the level of honesty varies from one group of agents to another and even one society to another, politically unpalatable though such a view may be.[10] We have to realistically assess the level of honesty among the enforcers of a society and then create systems that take account of this in laying out the mechanism through which the policy is to be administered.

The exasperation that the citizenry in India feels about food grain rotting in poorly maintained storage facilities is understandable.[11] However, the solution may not be as obvious as appears at first sight. Consider one popular demand, namely, that the government should simply open its granaries and let people take the food at very low prices. What is not always understood is that if food grain is given away at a low price to whoever comes to buy, it is likely that some of this grain will get picked up by traders and resold to the Indian government through the procurement window. In other words, the government will end up repeatedly subsidizing the same food grain.

My central argument is that in creating better food grains policy it is imperative that we look at the entire system of food production, food procurement, and the release and distribution of food. How we procure the food has an impact on how we release the food, and vice versa. Inspired by the sight of food grain going to waste, it is often made out to be that our central problem is that of poor food grain storage. I disagree with this popular view. While we no doubt should improve our storage facilities, it is important to be clear that this will not lower the price of food. To achieve that we need to redesign the mechanics of how we acquire and release food on the market.

This chapter does not go into the long-range problem of agricultural productivity and strategies for increasing this. This is indeed an important problem and much has been written on it.[12] It is assumed throughout that a modicum of self-sufficiency in food is desirable. This immediately means that the state will have the responsibility of maintaining a certain amount of food stocks. There are economists who believe that we should not do so, leaving it instead to private traders to maintain their own stocks and use imports and exports to even out fluctuations in endogenous prices. The position taken in this book is that it is politically risky, especially in a country as large as India, to rely entirely on private traders and international trade to iron out excessive price fluctuations. The state needs to provide some minimal insurance.

India's Food Grain Market: Description

There is a popular belief that India's inflation of the last few years was caused by poor food grain management. As is so often the case with complex economic matters, and as we saw in chapter 3, the reality of inflation is more complicated than popular perception suggests. In the case of recent Indian experience (in the second half of 2009), it was true both that food inflation was high and that India's food grain management left a lot to be desired. But it is not clear that the latter has caused the former. Poor management may keep the prices of some food grains higher than they need be, but inflation, defined as a sustained increase in price, is not caused by this, which would typically require a sustained deterioration in food grain management, for which there is no evidence.

This does not, however, change the fact that India needs to raise agricultural productivity and improve the management of the market for food grains. The flaw in the system is that while the government has steadily procured food grain, especially wheat and rice, it has not done well in releasing the grain when the need arises. Doing the former and not the latter has meant that the net effect has been to raise the average price of food. Also, a good market intervention, as discussed in greater detail in the sections that follow, entails buying up when prices are low and selling when prices are high. Comparing procurement and inflation data it is clear that little effort has gone into creating such a cycle. The years 2006–2007 and 2007–2008 were years of low inflation for both rice and wheat. There was no extra procurement in those years; in fact, wheat procurement actually fell. Given that 2009–2010 was an inflationary year, one would have expected lower procurement but that was not the case.

The theory of how India can improve its food grain management also will be discussed in the next sections. However, some simple lessons that will come out of this analysis can be stated in advance. First, the government needs to have a set of transparent rules concerning how and when to release food grain, a kind of standard operating procedure. There should be no need to have special cabinet committees, as is currently the practice, to take the decision. If prices are rising, there has to be a rule about the *automatic* release of food. Moreover, the release should be in small batches—the reason for this will become clear later.

Second, after the food is released, the government should not try to excessively monitor what the buyer of the food does with it. As per present practice, the food that is released through open market operations by the Food Corporation of India (FCI) is sold to millers, and only rarely to traders. These millers are then prohibited from selling the wheat to other buyers and making profit from this. However, if the aim in releasing food is to lower the price, it is not clear why there should be a prohibition on further reselling of the food. And the instinctive urge to prevent anybody from making a profit—and creating a bureaucracy to monitor this—does more harm than good (excepting maybe to the bureaucracy). What we should do instead is allow people to strive to make a profit but design a system that uses this striving to achieve social well-being.

The consequence of having such severe rules about what the buyer of food from FCI can do with the food means that the zest for buying FCI food will be low. At times when the price of food is high and we want to lower it, it is a mistake to curb the traders' and the millers' freedoms. This would result in poor distribution of food grains and prices remaining high. In general, the Indian government manages to release less food than it plans and, moreover, the release is even more inadequate when done through the Open Market Sale Scheme, which is a system for off-loading the food on the market.

The right policy is to place as little restriction on the buyers of food grains as we can and to permit them to make profits by selling the grain to the ultimate consumers. The profit of the trader and the miller is of course not the aim of the government but it is the instrument through which the government can direct food to the poor.

This does not mean that we should not have any strategy to limit the profit, but simply that this must not be done by creating disincentives for the trader or the miller for buying up grain and selling it to the ultimate consumer. The secret of keeping profits limited and delivering food to the ultimate consumer is to release the procured grain in small quantities to large numbers of traders and millers and to give them the freedom to make profits. Competition will drive prices down through natural market forces. Good policy consists of exploiting the laws of the market, not denying that they exist.

Theory of Food Market Intervention

In what follows, I use a simple structure to convey some of the central ideas of food grain management. We can focus on any particular grain. For the most part I will use wheat. In figure 6.2, I have drawn a demand and a supply curve for wheat represented by, respectively, D and S. As the price of wheat declines, the demand for wheat rises and the supply of wheat falls. This explains the slopes of the two curves. If the market is left free, with no government intervention, the price will settle at the point at which demand equals supply. This is referred to as the "free market equilibrium price" (identified as p_m in figure 6.2).

There are good reasons not to leave everything to the free market, even though there is a conservative school of thought that will advise you to do just that. We may feel that at the free market equilibrium price farmers get too low a price for their labor or that the equilibrium price is too high a price for the poor households. When I worked in India, we grappled with both these perceptions and they call for some carefully scripted government action.

Consider the case for supporting the farmers. One method that has actually been used in India is to announce a minimum support price (MSP). This is the procurement price at which the government offers to buy up as much as the farmers are willing to sell. If the MSP is set below the free market equilibrium price, a moment's inspection of figure 6.2 makes it clear, no one will sell to the government and the market price will continue to be

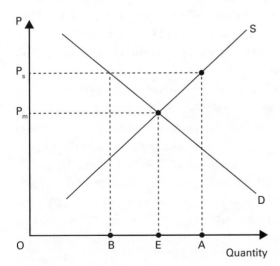

Figure 6.2
The demand and supply of food

p_m. Hence, for an MSP to have an impact, it has to be set above the market price, for instance, at the point marked p_s in the figure.

Before moving on, it is worth pointing out that it is not merely the need to support farmers that prompts an MSP policy. The valid perception that the state ought to keep a stock of food grain ready for bad times can also lead to the same kind of intervention.

Suppose now that the Indian government announces an MSP of p_s, as shown in figure 6.2. It is clear that the farmers' total supply is measured by OA marked on the horizontal axis, which means they will sell OB units of grain directly to ordinary households and BA units of grain to the government. In other words, the government buys up the supply in excess of the market demand. In India, in a typical year the government buys up a little less than one-third of the total production. Thus BA is typically close to one-third of OA. Contrary to a belief within the government bureaucracy, there is nothing sacrosanct about this ratio, except the force of habit. With this MSP policy the government will now have reserves equal to BA units of wheat in its storage facilities. The amount of money the government would have spent acquiring this grain is equal to BA multiplied by the MSP, in this case, p_s.

Now, consider the problem of off-loading this grain. If the government decides to sell this grain at a price above p_s in order not to incur a loss, there will be no buyers. This is because those willing to buy grain at a price above the MSP will have already got their grain (in this example, OB units of grain). If this is the pricing policy used by Food Corporation of India, there is no way the government will be able off-load the stocks on ordinary consumers. Observers often fret at reports of procured grain lying unattended to, rotting, and being eaten up by rats, and the belief is that this is the reason consumers do not get to buy this food. But that gets the causality wrong. Consumers do not get to buy the grain not because rats get at it but because of flaws in our food grains policy. In some ways, it is just as well that the rats get it.

It is often argued in official documents that unless the government sells food at a price above the purchase price (plus other sundry costs like that of storage and transport), this will add to the fiscal deficit. What this does not take into account is that if by trying to sell the food at such a price the government does not manage to sell the food at all and the fiscal burden is even greater. This is because the cost of procurement is a sunk cost. Therefore from a fiscal accounting point of view, not selling procured grain is equivalent to selling it at zero price.

It is important to recognize that the overall impact of the pricing policy just described is to raise the price of food grains, for at least a segment of consumers, to above the free-market equilibrium price (to wit, p_m) if there were no government intervention in the market for food. This is because an effective MSP is, by definition, a price higher than the free market equilibrium price. There is no getting away from the fact that having an MSP policy and selling some grain at or above the MSP (for instance, to households above the poverty line) means that we are selling grain to some consumers above the price they would have faced in a complete free-market equilibrium.

If all consumers are to get food below the equilibrium price, the only way to do this is for the government to buy up the entire food production at a price above p_m, for instance, at p_s, and off-load it on the market at some price, P, (not shown in the figure) which is below p_m. This by definition places a fiscal burden on the state. The government ends up spending (p_s - P) multiplied by the line segment OA, marked on the horizontal axis, which shows the units of food bought by the government to run this operation. And there is another problem—that it will be in the interest of people to buy the grain at P and sell it back again to the government at p_s and pocket the subsidy p_s – P per unit of grain. It is not impossible that this "revolving door strategy" of using the same grain to earn a subsidy multiple times from the government has been employed by traders. This was the problem with the Supreme Court order of July 2010.[13]

What the Indian government does in practice is to try to sell some grain at above the MSP (and this operation often has little success for the reasons already explained), and also to release some food grain below the market price to below poverty line (BPL) households and to some other special, vulnerable segments of the population. The net effect of this kind of government action is to give an upward push to the price of food grains that prevail in the open market. After government procurement, the "market" price is no longer p_m but p_s.

So for people who buy food grain at the market price, the price they face is above the price they would have had to pay in in the absence of government intervention. This is inevitable but it is important to remember that the buyers of food grain at market price in India includes millions of poor people who either do not have BPL cards or live in areas without easy access to outlets run by the nation's public distribution system (PDS).[14]

If we (1) want farmers to get a price above the free market price, and (2) want consumers to get as much or more food than they would have if the food market was left completely free, then it is inevitable that the government has to incur a fiscal cost. To ask for (1), (2), and (3), which requires that all government operations in the food market be commercially viable, is to ask for the impossible. Objectives (1) and (2) inevitably place a fiscal burden on the state and make (3) impossible. I labor this point because I sat in numerous government meetings that together aspired to achieve (1), (2), and (3).

Redesigning India's Food Grains Policy: Price Stabilization

An ideal food grains policy ought to have the following features:

• the government should maintain a buffer with the aim of using it to hold down prices during times of food shortage, and

• the government must make sure that the poor and the vulnerable have access to food at all times.

This second feature is connected to the general idea of food security.

If trade remained open at all times, holding a buffer would be considered a costly and largely unnecessary strategy; but this overlooks the politics of trade and the fact that nations can be held to ransom by threatened stoppage of trade. In 1974 when, facing a famine, Bangladesh needed to import food from the United States, it was denied this on the grounds that Bangladesh had trading relations with Cuba. It is therefore natural for most nations to want to be reasonably self-sufficient in food. India is no exception. Both these objectives are achievable for India but neither would be a trivial exercise. This explains why, despite pronouncements to the contrary, we still have so many gaps in our food policy.

To analyze food grains policy to achieve (1) and (2), we must begin by recognizing that agricultural production tends to be vulnerable to exogenous shocks, stemming from a variety of factors such as fluctuations in weather conditions, floods, pest attacks, and fluctuations in wage rates. For simplicity, assume that food grain supply can be high (good weather) or low (bad weather) with probability of half each.

If, as just discussed, the purpose of maintaining the food grains reserve with the government is to be self-sufficient in times of food shortage, we have to have a policy whereby food is acquired by the state when supply is plentiful (that is, the weather is good) and released when the supply is meager (that is, the weather is bad). To be a net buyer of food under all circumstances, as the government did, is the wrong strategy. The government must be prepared to switch the MSP window on and off or, as will be explained, set the MSP sufficiently low so that it will automatically switch itself on and off depending on market conditions.

There is one caveat worth stressing here. I am considering a procurement and release policy that is entirely concerned with self-sufficiency and price stabilization. I am at this time ignoring the objective of providing cheap food at all times for the poor and vulnerable, that is, objective (2), mentioned previously. This will be discussed later in the chapter. Note for now that if government was procuring for both objectives (1) and (2), then it would have to procure over and above what is needed to hold prices down in times of shortage. This can be a fairly substantial amount. Of the 33.6 million tons of rice procured in 2008–2009, 22 million tons were for the PDS. Under such circumstances, it is possible that the state would have to procure food grains in good and bad times, in order to have enough grains for price stabilization *and* support for the poor and vulnerable. However, the broad thrust of my argument would still be unchanged. We need to vary our procurement, taking in more when the weather is good, supply plentiful, and prices low, and less (maybe even nothing) when the weather is bad and prices high.

I should clarify that this does not mean that we actually close down the MSP window in periods of food shortage but simply not raise the MSP in such periods. It is fine to aim to acquire one-third—or whatever fraction we decide to settle on—of the aggregate food stock produced but the aim must be to do so *on average*, buying more in good times and less in bad times.

As is obvious, if there is no state intervention, in good weather the equilibrium food price will be low and, in bad weather, it will be high. The average food price will be a weighted average of the high and the low prices, where the weights are given by the probabilities of bad and good weather, respectively. We shall take the view that the bad-weather price is intolerably high, and so we need state action to hold down prices during bad weather. One way of achieving this is for the government to announce an MSP above the (low) good-weather price and below the (high) bad-weather price. This will allow government to buy up food grains during times of bounty and release them in times of shortage. This will mean that in good weather government will buy a certain amount of food grain and the market price of food grain in such times will be the MSP.

The procurement of food during times of bounty is just one side of the coin. To have a successful food management system it is equally important to have a method of food disbursement during times of food shortage. Interestingly, and this is a point that is not understood at all well in government, the amount of dampening effect we have on food price depends critically on "how" the food grain is released. The same total amount of grain off-loaded on the market through different mechanisms can have very different effects on the price.

Also note that if the government procures more than it releases, the average market price will be higher than what would have prevailed in the absence of government action. This is not surprising. If the government becomes a net hoarder, its effect has to be to raise the average price. A small increase in average price in order to stabilize excessive fluctuations may be worth it. But in the case of India the release has fallen well short of procurement. The statement by a senior member of this government that, when it comes to hoarding, it is the government of India that leads the pack is not off the mark.

It is worth emphasizing that to commit to holding a certain minimum reserve at all times is meaningless policy. It is equivalent to holding no reserves. If the reserves are never to be used, they may as well not be there. There is no advantage in holding reserves that must be held at all times. In fact, their only effect is on prices that increase as a consequence of the procurement of the reserves from the market. If we look at the Indian data concerning stocks and norms, what stands out is the fact that the government usually holds stocks way above the minimum buffer norm and the minimum buffer norm is virtually never violated. Ideally, when stating a minimum reserve requirement, there should be an explicit proviso about when it can and should be violated, so that administrators do not treat the minimum buffer as a stock that has to be held at all times.

Food Security for the Vulnerable

I have not yet addressed the subject of the government's special responsibility to the poor and vulnerable households, that is, objective (2), mentioned earlier in the chapter. The importance of this objective cannot be overstated. If we do not provide special support to the poor, small relative price changes or exchange entitlement shifts can lead to widespread suffering and even famines (Sen 1981; Basu 2009).[15]

The Indian government tries to meet a large part of objective (2) by releasing to BPL households a part of its acquired grain at a lower-than-market price, through the approximately 500,000 fair-price shops or ration shops scattered across the nation. The National Food Security Bill, which was debated during my tenure in government and was later enshrined as law, was motivated by this objective.

The right to a certain minimal amount of basic food is an achievable right, as long as some qualifications are carefully spelled out, and so, to that extent, is a move in the right direction for India.[16] The important qualification is that in the future there may be times when there simply is not enough food for everybody to achieve that minimal target—for instance, following a nuclear war or an environmental calamity. What would it mean, in such a situation, for the government to guarantee food security to all? This compels us to confront a common dictum of ethics, namely, that ought implies can.

One way to commit to food security while allowing for the possibility of the above kind of contingency is to assert that the government will ensure that as long as some people are able to get the basic minimal amount of food everybody should have the right to a certain basic amount of food. Stated in this manner, food security for all does not entail the false promise that there will be food for all at all times, but simply that government will ensure that everybody has access to a certain minimal amount of food and, in case there is an overall shortage of food in the nation (which cannot be corrected through imports), that everybody will share in the shortage.

With this clarification, let me turn to some practical policy matters. Basically a food security law should take the form of ensuring that the poorest and the most vulnerable people are given access to a certain minimal quantity of food. The better-off people, it will be assumed, have the ability to fend for themselves.

The important lesson to keep in mind is that to achieve this objective it is not enough to have the right intentions. One has to design a delivery mechanism which can work in the kind of world that we have. India's rationing system has not worked well enough not for lack of good intention but because of insufficient attention to the details of the delivery mechanism. The problem arises from the fact that in India the food subsidy is handed to poor households via the ration shops. The government delivers subsidized grain to the store owner and the owner is then instructed to hand this over at the prespecified price to BPL households and to some other categories of vulnerable households.

If the store owners were perfectly honest, this would work fine. But if they are not, then it is easy to see that many of them will give in to the temptation of making some easy money by selling off some of this subsidized grain on the open market where the price is higher, and turning away some of the deserving poor households or adulterating the grain that is to be sold to those households. In reality this is what happens. As noted earlier, a large share of the wheat meant to reach the poor never does because it is pilfered or sold on the open market en route.[17]

It is easy to respond to this by asking for better policing. But we have to be realistic. Trying to police such a large system by creating another layer of police and bureaucracy will come with its own problems of corruption and bureaucracy. This is where the question of systems design arises. It is with this in mind that the "Economic Survey 2009–2010" discussed the option of designing a better mechanism for delivering food grain to the poor (Government of India 2010, chapter 2).[18] The basic idea is that the subsidy should be handed over directly to the poor household instead of giving it to the PDS shop owner with the instruction that he or she transfer it to the poor. This can be done by handing over food coupons to BPL households, which they can use as money to buy food from any store. The store owner can then take the coupon to any bank and change it back for cash.[19] To allow for differences in preferences, we can allow individual households to buy any food items within a prespecified range with these coupons. The subsidy does not have to be a fixed amount for wheat and another for rice but a lump sum for a list of goods. In the parlance of economics, this can lead to a Pareto improvement.[20]

Note that since the stores get full price from the poor and, more importantly, the same price from the poor and the rich, they will have little incentive to turn the poor away. Further, the incentive to adulterate will also be greatly reduced since the poor will have the right to go to any store with their coupons. A system of coupons implies that private traders have a much larger part in the delivery system. Since buyers will have the right to go to any store to buy food using a combination of money and coupons, they will go to stores that charge the most competitive prices and assure quality.

Worries have been expressed about fake coupons. But this is not a problem unique to coupons. Even with regular currency we have to contend with this problem. There is indeed a certain amount of counterfeiting that occurs,[21] but that does not paralyze the system as a whole. It will be likewise for coupons.

Concerns are also expressed that with coupons some households may not buy food at all and will sell off the coupons and buy other goods. This is a legitimate concern but it is not a reason to jettison the coupons system. That would be like not offering poor workers a higher wage on the grounds that they may spend it on alcohol. My preference, in fact, is to make the selling of coupons legal. After all, even in programs like the one now in use in India, where actual food grains are given to the households, we do not monitor to make sure that the good grains actually go down the alimentary canals of the poor. We take the view that once we have delivered food to them, if they decide to exercise their individual freedom and not eat it that is their choice. We may not like their choice but trying to monitor it is likely to create greater problems.

It is the same with the coupons system. It empowers households to be able to have more food. If they then choose to spend the extra buying power on some other goods and services, it is not worth the bureaucracy trying to control this. It will be, after all, the poor households that will gain from the doling out of the coupons. If they choose not to take the benefit in the form of food and buy something else, it is not nearly so counterproductive as the benefit going to the owners of PDS stores as often happens in the current system.

Finally, what about the fact that, over time, with successive rounds of inflation, the coupons will tend to lose value in real terms? This is easily addressed by adjusting the value of coupons every year, taking account of the past and expected food inflation.

Once we are persuaded by this line of argument, it is possible to take the analysis further and argue not for a direct grain transfer, and not for a coupons transfer, but instead for a cash transfer to the poor. This is the concept of a negative income tax and it has been proposed time and again in the economics literature.[22]

This is a legitimate policy suggestion and a system with directed cash transfers would arguably be better than the current direct delivery of food grains to the poor through prespecified ration shops. Nevertheless, it could be argued that the best option is the intermediate arrangement of giving food coupons to the poor. This does create some incentive for poor households to spend their handout from the government actually on food, since all other uses will entail some transactions cost, because the coupons would have to be converted to cash and then spent.[23]

What we may wish to do is to hand over the cash or coupons to the adult woman in the household. There is ample evidence that when the same amount of transfer is handed to the woman instead of the man in the household, more is spent on goods that raise what would, by most observer criteria, be considered central to the well-being of the household (Desai and Jain 1994; Kanbur and Haddad 1994; Agarwal 1997). Moreover, the act of handing out coupons to women could lead to the benefit of empowering them and increasing their say in household decision making (Basu 2006; Jhabvala, Desai, and Dave 2010). This same effect has now been reported from the employment of women under the National Rural Employment Guarantee Scheme (Pankaj and Tankha 2010).

It should be pointed out that "coupons" do not have to literally mean paper coupons. We can take advantage of the age of electronics to use more foolproof substitutes such as the smart card or, even better, no cards or coupons but direct banking executed from one's hand-held cell phone.

Let me finally turn to the criticism that it will not be the genuine poor who get hold of the food coupons. Better-off households and corrupt intermediaries may corner a part of the coupons supplied by the government. All that can be said about this problem is that it is not unique to the coupons system. We currently face exactly the same problem whereby nonpoor households have cornered many of the BPL household certificates. If we dovetail the coupons system with the Unique Identification (UID) number or Aadhaar system, which uses a biometric method for identifying individuals that India has been developing, then some of this problem can be addressed. But even if we cannot do so, all that this criticism means is that the coupons or smart card or ration administered through the mobile banking system has several advantages over the current system but with some dimensions on which it is no better. But since a policy that is better in some dimensions and as good in others is an improvement in any case, the policy being recommended here seems superior.

Once one of the direct transfer systems, such as the smart card, comes into effect, the role of the PDS stores will diminish since they will come under competition from private traders. However, given the deep regional disparities in India and the fact that some parts of the nation are sufficiently poor and remote as to be not attractive to private traders, PDS stores will continue to play a significant role for many years to come.

To close on a methodological note, whenever a new policy intervention is proposed, there will be critics saying that if there is no evidence to show that the policy works, we must not implement it. This is an invalid argument, reflecting more than anything else our penchant for the status quo. If for policy X we do not have evidence whether or not it works, then for policy not-X we do not have evidence whether or not it works. Hence, if that is reason not to do X, that is reason not to do not-X. But not doing X and not-X is impossible, thereby establishing that the initial claim was false.

7   The Nuts and Bolts of the Economy

O-Rings

On January 28, 1986, seventy-three seconds after takeoff from Kennedy Space Center in Florida, the Space Shuttle *Challenger* broke apart in flame and smoke, killing its seven crew members. This caused a setback to the U.S. shuttle program for nearly three years. When the disaster occurred, the early speculation was all about big failures—something major seemed to have gone wrong. But it subsequently became clear that the entire disaster occurred because of the failure of an "O-ring" seal—the O-ring literally is a small ring meant to join and hold parts together. It was created and first patented in Sweden in 1896 by J. O. Lundberg. The O-ring played a quiet role in the applied sciences and shot into everyday parlance only after the *Challenger* disaster.

As for economists, the O-ring became a metaphor for how good and grand policies and plans can get foiled by the failure of matters of detail and what is often hardly visible, such as the nuts and bolts of the economy, and the plumbing beneath the surface.[1] *How* exactly are subsidies meant for the poor handed out to them? Is this done by the private sector or the government? Are subsidies given as cash or as goods? What is the regulatory structure within which credit markets work? Does the law permit one to pay "dividends," based on what is earned through the sale of new shares? How easy is it for a small entrepreneur to start up or close down a business and to have contracts enforced?

As it turns out, how well these nuts and bolts of the economy function and how well-oiled they are kept can make a large difference to development, both in facilitating and in strangling it. We saw this in the context of the architecture of food subsidies in chapter 6.

The grand themes with which this book has been concerned in the first five chapters—fiscal and monetary policies, trade and exchange rate management, the development of infrastructure, methods for navigating globalization—are those with which policymakers in government remain preoccupied most of the time. So was I during my years in government. One must not belittle these overarching topics, which span the expanse of the economy. Nevertheless, the clue to the success or failure of many a nation can also lie in the plumbing beneath the surface and the nuts and bolts that hold things together. During my time in the Indian government I experienced this when working on the food sector; I have discussed some of these challenges in chapter 6. What I plan to do in the next section is to present some of the basic welfare-theoretic arguments that underlie the microtheoretic, nuts-and-bolts matters of policymaking. This will also provide the groundwork for the remaining sections and chapters of this book.

This is too large a topic to attempt comprehensiveness. Instead, in this and the following chapters, I shall illustrate the main principles with some sectors that have played an important role in India and the world, where the heart of the problem lies in the minutiae of the economy's architecture. In this chapter I take on one sector as an example: finance. In an economy, finance is the classic analogue of plumbing in a house—something we remain unaware of until something goes wrong with it.[2] This sector shot into prominence the world over with the financial crisis of 2008. India also set up a commission to review the regulatory structure of this sector.

Similar issues arise in chapter 10, where I discuss some immediately implementable policy options to give the economy a boost. One example I will consider in that chapter is higher education, a sector where India has a natural advantage. In chapter 10 I present a full blueprint for the education sector, including some nuts-and-bolts policy reforms, which therefore also help reinforce the central idea behind this chapter.

After the *Challenger* disaster, the Rogers Commission was set up to investigate the proximate and distal cause of the disaster. The Commission recognized the fault of the O-ring, in particular its inability to withstand a sufficiently wide temperature range, and then went a step further to investigate why this flaw was not spotted and corrected earlier. In the process, the Commission unearthed problems in the organizational culture of NASA as the more foundational cause of the O-ring failure (Vaughan 1996). And that is the line I take here. I go through the microeconomic nuts-and-bolts

issues of several sectors—finance, education, food grains, and labor markets—in this and the next three chapters, but I also look beyond economics to law, culture and politics to try to understand the more distal factors
which cause our plumbing to falter and the O-rings to malfunction.

Soon after joining government in 2009, I tried to bring to the fore the
importance of these matters of microdesign by devoting a chapter of the
"Economic Survey of India" (see Government of India 2010, 2011) to the
"Micro-foundations of Inclusive Growth."[3] In the rough and tumble of
attending to the big macroeconomic questions, policymakers at the helm
often give short shrift to these nuts and bolts matters. The chapter stressed
the need to rectify this.

Contracts and Pareto

Before turning to finance, it is worth pausing to take stock of the most
important binding material for any modern economy—the common contract. A contract is in essence an agreement of the following kind: "You
will give me x today; in return, I will give you y tomorrow." The simplicity
is deceptive. It is true it can often take very simple forms: you give me a
taxi ride and I will give you money at the end of it. But depending on how
complex x and y are, the contract can be intricate, long, and stretched out
over time.

Consider two countries that have similar fiscal and monetary policies,
similar tax rates, similar expenditures on infrastructure, and so on in terms
of all the indicators that economists typically look at in forecasting how
well the economy will perform. If, however, between these two countries
one has the system in place to respect and efficiently enforce contracts
and the other does not, the performance of these two economies could be
vastly different. In the country where the respect for contract is weak, there
just will not be traction enough between individuals. People will not show
enough enterprise because they will know in advance that they will not be
able to rely on others. Superficially, some may call such people apathetic
and unenterprising, but the real cause for this could be the absence of this
one vital binding material, the contract, as vital as the O-ring.

The importance of contracts in a market economy cannot be overempha-
sized. A modern economy functions because we can rely on one another in
doing trade and exchange, either because society is imbued with the culture

of respecting promises or because there is a regulatory system with third-party enforcement that people can count on. This is an idea that will crop up several times later on.

India has scope for improvement in terms of the formal enforcement of contracts. *Doing Business*, the annual study of 189 countries by the World Bank (see World Bank 2014a), shows that in terms of the efficiency of formal contract fulfillment, India ranks 186th. One has to go through forty-six procedures, which usually takes 1,420 days, to enforce a contract on a reneging party. In Brazil it takes half that time, 731 days; in the United States, 420 days; in Korea, 230 days; and in Singapore, 150 days. The transactions' cost of bureaucracy is captured well by the finding that in India long-distance trucks carrying freight between cities spend close to 60 percent of the travel time parked at check posts to pay and negotiate various regional taxes.

It is true that all of these data pertain to the formal structure of regulation and not to informal arrangements, where, piecemeal evidence suggests, India does not do as poorly. It is also true that India has an independent justice system, which does not hesitate to give verdicts against the government and the political bosses. These are big advantages that have enabled the country to do well, as it has in recent years. Nevertheless, there can be no doubt that fixing this specific nuts-and-bolts matter—the speed and efficiency of bureaucratic transactions and the enforcement of legal contracts—can deliver a bounty to the Indian economy.

This is however a complex topic because while contract enforcement is the pivot for growth and enterprise, there are also situations where we have to place restriction on contracts. To get an understanding of this, note that the sanctity of the contract comes from the "principle of free contract," which says that when two or more consenting adults agree to some exchange or trade or contract, which does not adversely impact others, it is best not to interfere and stop them.

This immediately warns us of one restriction that comes from the fact that a contract between two persons may have negative "externalities" on uninvolved others. In such cases, as economists have long acknowledged, we have to place restrictions on the contracting individuals. But that is not all; there are greater complexities that go beyond this.

The "principle of free contract" follows from the compelling argument of the Italian economist Vilfredo Pareto that if there is a change which leaves some people better off and no one worse off, that change should be construed as desirable for a society.[4] So influential was Pareto's argument that such changes are referred to by economists as "Pareto improvements." I believe that in the absence of a compelling argument otherwise, the principle of free contract should be respected by governments and policymakers and that a lot of our woes are because of the propensity of governments to violate this principle. Creativity in economic life often requires unusual maneuvers, the creation of new innovative products, services, and activities.[5] If we have laws prohibiting these arbitrarily, simply because the bureaucrats at the top are not familiar with them, that will throttle creativity and, with that, growth and development.

Based on this, if we could leave it all to free contracts, with simply an eye on externalities, life would have been easy. Unfortunately, that is not the case. Regulation has a role to play and this needs reason and common sense. In short, the principle of free contract has exceptions. There are free contracts that even when they have no externalities seem to be "obnoxious" (Kanbur 2004). Popular examples consist of trade in body organs, where a poor person chooses to sell a body part to a person willing to buy it, and voluntary slavery, whereby people are given the right to opt to become a slave.[6] However, as I argue presently, it is not good enough to leave it to our instinct of what we find obnoxious; we must root it in certain principles.

In this same vein, I had considered (Basu 2003) the case of "voluntary" sexual harassment in the workplace. What I mean by this is the standard tenet of neoclassical economics, by which individual workers should have the freedom to sign away their right not to be harassed in the workplace. That is, if they feel that that pain is worth the extra money, it is their right to make that decision. I like to believe most human beings feel uneasy with these libertarian rules.

However, faced with these uncomfortable dilemmas, people often resort to hand waving and try to rule out these kinds of contracts by saying that they are obnoxious. Unfortunately, that plays either into the hands of neoconservative thinkers who dismiss the reaction as emotional and not founded in reason or into the hands of policymakers looking for alibis to overregulate. In the city of Kolkata, there are apartments and small plots of land that were sold by the government to the relatively less well-off, with the proviso that they could not sell these flats and land. The argument was that the rich would buy up these properties and leave the poor, once more, without land and home. But such restrictions are completely unproductive and fly in the face of the Pareto principle and the principle of free contract. There may be a person needing to sell his home and a person wanting to buy it, but government will not allow that to happen. This is the kind of restriction that hurts development.

So what is the principle by which we may want to allow people to sell their homes but not give up their right not to be sexually harassed in the workplace? I developed what I called the "large numbers argument," echoing some earlier work by the philosopher Parfit (Parfit 1984; Basu 2007).[7] Note that allowing an individual to sign away the right not to be harassed may be a Pareto improvement—that person is better off (because he or she manages to bargain for a higher wage by giving up this right), the employer is better off, and no one else is affected. However, it is arguable that if lots of people sign such contracts, individuals who are very strongly averse to trading this right for extra money may then be worse off. It is possible to show that the wages received by those signing no-harassment contracts will be lower if others are allowed to sign contracts whereby they waive their rights. This means that we can no longer evoke the Pareto principle to justify voluntary harassment contracts or voluntary slavery. Once we are freed from this, we have the scope for bringing in other normative principles to decide why we may want to not allow certain kinds of voluntary contracts (warranteeism, for instance) and allow some others (such as home buying). The large numbers argument does not lead us to a unique prescription but simply shows how all free contracts do not have to be in the same normative basket.[8]

In brief, we should try to respect free contracting in general, but put each case through the large-numbers argument test. What would lots of people signing such contracts do to those who do not want to give away these rights? This argument could carry over to other important cases like the practice of making workers give up some basic rights in order to be allowed to work in export processing zones. We could develop a principle-based argument to disallow such practices.

With these somewhat philosophical (but no less important for that reason, as popular imagination often leads people to believe) matters in the background, let me now turn to some examples that have cropped up in recent policy debates, in some detail.

Finance and Development

One of the least understood sectors of an economy, in rich and poor countries, is finance. One pervasive misunderstanding is that this sector is largely irrelevant, especially for the common person. One of course hears of the rich and the famous, who rise and fall with financial booms and busts, one hears of celebrated Ponzi and pyramid schemes—such as Bernie Madoff's—which create some millionaires and leaves wreckage in the wake of their collapse. For most people, the poor and even some of the middle classes, this has the appeal of soap operas on television. This is what leads to the belief that it does not affect their real lives. Such belief however has no basis.

As was remarked earlier, finance is to an economy what plumbing is to your home life. Most of the time, it is invisible. But once one thinks carefully, it becomes evident that normal functioning would be impossible without finance. Modern economic life is highly specialized. Individuals spend all their lives doing things for which they themselves have no direct use. Researchers spend all their adult lives writing papers, which they cannot eat, wear, or live under; and likewise, for most professions. Moreover, unlike in ancient times, people do not get paid in terms of food, clothing, and housing. Their payment, in money, is simply a long-term contract for being able to later acquire food and clothing, go to the theater and travel, in exchange for the work they once did. It is finance that makes possible these transactions over vast expanses of geography and time. Most people become aware of the role of finance only when it begins to break down, as happened in the financial crisis of 2008 that originated in the United States and quickly spread to the world, and ordinary people suddenly found themselves out of jobs and with shrinking consumption.

The 2008 crisis led many countries to do some soul searching and reassessing of their regulatory systems. It was no different in India. India's Ministry of Finance set up the Financial Sector Legislative Reforms Commission in March 2011 to examine the institutional structure of India's financial sector that had built up over many centuries—a multilayered palimpsest of rules, customs, and laws. This was important for India because, contrary to popular opinion, the poor are as much or more affected by financial scams as the rich. Their troubles do not make headlines, but exploitation by moneylenders and ensnarement in Ponzi schemes is part and parcel of their lives too.

The trouble with finance, unlike some other areas of the economy, is that there is very little by way of formulaic advice to be given. This is one area where it is critical for policymakers to be conversant with some principles of economics because the challenges will keep evolving and they will have to modify policies and enact laws to rise to the new challenges. This is the reason why in this area both our failures and our successes are often inadvertent.

The first stirring for the takeoff of the Indian economy was an unintended byproduct of financial sector reform. In 1969 Indira Gandhi, with her early radical vision, nationalized the banking sector in India. The nationalized banks were then asked to open branches in rural India and remote areas, even though some of those branches would clearly make a loss. But being nationalized meant they could persist despite the losses.

A few years before, in 1964, India began its state-owned mutual fund scheme, the Unit Trust of India, which became a popular place for parking the savings of middle-class Indians. These initiatives had an implication that was not a part of the plan. India's savings rate, which until the mid-1960s had remained woefully low, around 12 percent of GDP, began to rise from the early 1970s. And by the late 1970s a savings rate that had remained stationary for decades moved up to over 20 percent. This is almost certainly a consequence of the two big financial sector initiatives just mentioned.

We can see evidence of this in the statistics of bank branches. As table 7.1, taken from Basu and Maertens (2008), shows the number of bank branches in India rose sharply from the early 1960s to 1986. In 1961, there was a total of just over five thousand branches. By 1986 this had risen to well over fifty thousand. By the mid-1970s and certainly by the early 1980s it was clear that India had broken out of the clutches of the so-called Hindu rate of growth discussed earlier in this book. There are strong grounds for believing that it was the rising savings and investment rates that boosted India's growth rate, pretty much in keeping with what theory would predict.[9] Not only did overall savings rise sharply during this period, but household savings rose from approximately 10 to 25 percent over three decades starting in the mid-1970s (Bosworth, Collins, and Virmani 2007). Interestingly, half of this took the form of financial savings, which could be easily channeled into actual investment.

But one cannot live in the past. Even with these gains in savings rates, too large a fraction of India's population continues to be unbanked. More space needs to be created for private banking. Also evident is the need for

Table 7.1
Number of bank branches in India (scheduled and nonscheduled commercial banks)

Year	Number
1941	2,074*
1951	4,119
1961	5,113
1969	9,051
1971	12,985
1976	23,656
1981	38,047
1986	53,397
1991	62,740
1996	64,937
2001	67,856
2005	70,324

Source: Reserve Bank of India, Statistical Tables Related to Banks in India, 2005–2006 and previous issues.
*1941 data includes Burma (officially now Myanmar).

further reform and bold initiatives in India's finance and banking sector. The whole financial regulatory system is old and creaking. There are more than sixty separate laws that regulate India's financial sector. These have been on the books, unchanged, for a very long time. The preamble of the Reserve Bank of India Act, 1934, points to the "temporary" nature of the law. The Securities Contract Regulation Act came into existence in 1956 at a time when derivatives did not exist, nor did a host of complex financial products. Some of these laws act at cross purposes, some ignore the basic laws of economics, and many need to be amended because of evolving norms and practices of behavior and the arrival of new products in this sector. The Financial Sector Legislative Reforms Commission, set up with the intention of modernizing India's financial system and creating space for greater inventiveness and entrepreneurship, is a desirable move.

In moving toward this, it is important to be aware—and this is what makes financial policy so hard—that one has to balance this with intelligent regulation to protect the weak and marginalized. Finance is a notorious area where the poor and the vulnerable get trapped in contracts they do not fully understand.[10] This happened in the U.S. mortgage market; it happens routinely in rural India. Also, this is one area where behavioral economics is very relevant because there is evidence that systematic deviations from rationality occur when people make financial decisions especially pertaining to investment and savings.[11]

For knowledge of specific human irrationalities and, in particular, to spot patterns in these, there is much that one can learn simply by being observant in everyday life. Through the late 1980s and early 1990s, I used to go with groups of students and some faculty to the village of Nawadih in the state of Bihar. While the students gathered data, I spent the bulk of my time chatting with the poor villagers and occasionally with the not-so-poor moneylenders, in their homes or at the local teashop. Even from those cursory interactions it was clear that the most profitable profession in the village was moneylending. This was because most poor villagers so obviously displayed hyperbolic discounting, whereby they underestimated their cost burdens of the future. In addition, they misread interest burdens, depending on how the information was given to them by the lender. It was fairly routine to find poor villagers taking loans that were described to them as "10 percent per month." There was no misinformation in this. But few borrowers realized they were paying an effective annual interest of over 200 percent.

Banerjee and Duflo (2011, 157–158) describe fruit sellers on the streets of Chennai who get fruits and vegetables from the wholesaler in the morning, on credit, sell them during the day, and pay back the credit with interest to the wholesaler at night or the next morning. The interest they paid for the one-day loan was 4.69 percent. As Banerjee and Duflo point out, if a fruit seller took 100 rupees one morning and paid back after a month, she would have to pay 400 rupees. And if she kept it for a year the repayment burden would be 1,842 million rupees.

There are few activities in life profitable enough to make such expensive borrowing viable. And, in Nawadih certainly they were not. The poor were perpetually indebted, living lives on the edge. I came away convinced that to think of these transactions in terms of standard economics textbook categories was wrong. These were "semi-feudal" relationships, where the poor lived off the "kindness" of the lenders who had an interest in keeping them close to subsistence, not above and, most of the time, not below. The poor in that village were reconciled to the fact that no matter what they did, they would end up on that borderline.[12]

This experience convinced me of the need for usury laws that place restrictions on the terms of credit contracts. I say this with some caution because most governments have a propensity to overregulate markets. The line between regulation and the space for free contracting is a tricky one; and the success or failure of an economy often depends on where that is drawn. There is no cookbook for how and where to draw this line. What is important is for senior policymakers to have a modicum of understanding of the *principles* which should guide us in creating an appropriate setting for doing business, developing regulation, and getting the plumbing right for economic life to flourish.

Ponzis

Let me turn to another area, this one specific to finance, where we may need regulation to prevent contracts, despite the fact that they may be fully voluntary. In finance, as we have already seen, people often fail to take full rational account of their own long-term interest. This was on full display during the U.S. subprime crisis, when it became evident that household after household had signed mortgage contracts without fully understanding the terms. This is what has motivated new legislative initiatives in several countries, such as the Dodd-Frank legislation in the United States and the Financial Sector Legislative Reforms Commission in India.

One area where free contracting may have to be regulated or even stopped is Ponzis. In its elemental form a Ponzi is easy to understand. Put yourself in the shoes of a Ponzi entrepreneur. You announce a wealth management scheme which will give investors a phenomenal return of 10 percent per month. Persuade one person to put in 100 rupees. Keep that money for yourself and next month persuade two persons to invest 100 rupees each. Give the investor from the previous period 10 rupees as interest as promised and keep 190 rupees for yourself. In the third month persuade four persons (double the previous period's customers) to invest 100 rupees each. Use 30 rupees from this to pay interest to the three investors you have and keep 370 rupees for yourself.

In the fourth month get eight persons (double the previous period's customers) to invest in your scheme. Of the 800 rupees you get from them, you pay out interest to all the investors you have from the previous periods, to wit 7 (=1 + 2 + 4) of them. You get to keep 730 rupees. If you stick to this schedule diligently, your reputation for paying a fabulous interest will spread and new customers will flock to you. The money you get to make for yourself will also grow at a phenomenal pace, as must be evident from the above arithmetic. Indeed it is easy to check from a back-of-the-envelope calculation that, starting from the 100 rupees in the first month, your income in the tenth month will be 46,090 rupees.[13] It is not surprising that people who have run successful Ponzi schemes have amassed phenomenal wealth.

The catch lies in the fact that there is no stopping point. Since old investors get paid with the deposits made by the new investors, you need an ever-growing pool of investors. This cannot happen endlessly in our finite world. So the tragedy of the Ponzi scheme is that it has to crash and what compounds the challenge of regulation is that there is no fixed point where it crashes.

Ponzi schemes acquired their name and notoriety from Carlo Pietro Giovanni Ponzi, later known as Charles Ponzi (1882–1949). Carlo Pietro was born March 3, 1882 in Lugo, Italy. After squandering four years in the name of university education in Rome, which he treated as a vacation, paid for by his parents, Ponzi migrated to America, landing in Boston in November 1903. His lack of scruples as well as his high intelligence soon became evident—the former when he landed in a Canadian prison for forging a signature, and the latter when he wrote to his beloved mother from the prison explaining his new address as part of his wonderful job as "special assistant" to a prison warden. Returning to Boston after his release, he went on to create one ingenious financial scheme after another to lure the vulnerable middle classes and to give financial fraud a proper name. The crash of one of his big schemes not only ruined many families but brought down six Boston banks. In and out of prison, he was finally deported to Italy, from where he migrated to Brazil. Broken in spirit and health, and nearly blind, he died in poverty in Rio de Janeiro on January 18, 1949, but not before bequeathing to the world one of the most troubling financial products, the Ponzi scheme.

The reason why this is such a dangerous idea is not the pure Ponzi just described but because a Ponzi can wear a thousand camouflages. I develop a very simple example here to make the mechanics of camouflaged Ponzis clear. Suppose an entrepreneur manufactures a car that is costly to produce so that it has to be "overpriced" to make sure its sales generate profit. Let us suppose he sets a price such that each car sold earns him a profit of r dollars, where r is a positive number.

The question is: if the car is overpriced, why will people buy it? This is where the Ponzi comes in. Here is a selling strategy which will make this car popular and will earn the entrepreneur an unconscionably large profit. In period 1, offer 1 car for sale and to whoever buys this announce a share option. In particular, the buyer gets (for no additional charge) shares for half of all future profits of this company (starting from period 1). The entrepreneur keeps the remaining shares. In the next period (period 2), sell 2 cars and to each buyer offer the stock option for $\frac{1}{8}$ (or a share of $\frac{1}{2}^3$) of all future profit of the company. In period 3, sell 2^2 or 4 cars, and to each buyer offer shares worth $\frac{1}{2}^5$ or $\frac{1}{32}$ of all future profit of the company. In other words, sales grow exponentially over time.[14]

If everybody expects this company to survive, the offer made by the company is excellent and people should pick up these overpriced cars because the value of the car actually matters little. A person who buys this car earns a small share of the profit in the period in which she buys the car, but from then on, the profit income keeps doubling each year. It is this exponential increase in earnings over time that makes this an attractive purchase. Certain standard criteria for choosing among aggregate streams, such as Rubinstein's (1979) overtaking criterion, make it compelling for individuals to buy such a car (assuming that others will buy the car in the future). As for the entrepreneur, it is easy to check that he or she earns a regular income in each period and so this is clearly worthwhile for the entrepreneur.

This project is actually a camouflaged Ponzi. It relies on there being an ever-larger number of people buying into the scheme or people going in for their second, third, and endlessly more cars. That being not possible in any realistic scenario, the scheme has to crash at some point, inflicting losses on a large number of buyers and assured profit only for the entrepreneur. This use of an ever-larger number of participants is the reason these schemes are often referred to as pyramids.

There are many other schemes that can be run as a camouflaged Ponzi. Consider the widespread and perfectly legal practice of giving stock options to the employees of a company. This can generate profit even though the company may create little value. A company that has labor productivity below the prevailing wage rate can generate profit by setting the salary of each employee below the market wage rate and making it attractive for workers to nevertheless join this company by offering stock options in cleverly worked out proportions. As the firm grows by employing more workers, it can earn very high profits, even though, like all Ponzis, it will eventually crash, hurting, in this case, the workers.

Reality is, of course, messier. A firm that indulges in such practices may, somewhere along the way, end up innovating and creating more valuable products which makes the employment of workers possible even without the stock options. It can then slow down on its expansion and gradually become viable, without the need for endless expansion. But given the large number of firms that get created each year and the large number that go bust, it is evident that not all firms manage to break out of the grip of the Ponzi. Therefore, the role of stock options in camouflaging Ponzis ought to come under greater scrutiny from the government than it has. This can have an important role to play in understanding why financial markets end up going bust periodically.

In all such cases, it is the intertwining of malignant practices with perfectly legitimate and, in themselves, benign practices that makes the regulation of these operations and, more generally, of financial markets so hard. There is, however, a reason to do with government policy that compounds the problem. Many governments have made it a point to step in and rescue very large corporations when they are about to fail. This practice of "Too Big to Fail" (ubiquitous enough to have acquired the unpleasant acronym TBTF) can make it rational for people to invest in firms that are scams in the belief that once the firm becomes sufficiently large, the government will step in at the time of collapse with taxpayer money, thereby protecting investors fully or at least in part. As should be evident from this, the principle of TBTF is in many instances the legalistic name for crony capitalism.

Thanks to years of accumulated data and analysis, there are now many laws to prevent financial fraud. In the United States, the Securities and Exchange Commission is the body that tries to enforce action against Ponzis. Ever more sophisticated laws, such as the Dodd-Frank Act in the United States, are meant to tackle the myriad forms that these pyramid schemes can take. The spate of Ponzi-like scams has led to recent discussions in India to amend the 1992 Securities and Exchange Board of India Act to make it more effective in controlling financial scams. Despite all this effort there is still a great distance to cover. The broad problem is with finance itself. Financial markets are strange because they are created by us but not fully understood by us.[15]

Fortunately, there are areas where our understanding is gradually improving. Consider the policy TBTF, referred to earlier. This is founded on the belief that if a big investment company fails, the collateral damage on ordinary citizens is so large that governments have reason to step in to save the company. It has now become evident that the well-meaning (or ill-meaning but well-disguised) TBTF policy exacerbated the recent global crisis by assuring financial honchos that if they made a profit it would be theirs to keep and if they made a loss that would be for taxpayers to bear.

This led to reckless risk taking and irresponsible financial ventures. It is clear that what we need is a policy that may, on special occasions, entail government stepping in to save a private company from ruin, but it must not save the people who run the company and make the decisions. Saving the company must not be equated with saving the people who head the company. With this realization there has been effort in most nations to create guidelines to ring-fence financial companies to ensure that taxpayer money will not have to be spent to save large companies from collapsing.

Among other new ideas prompted by the last decade of scams and financial crises is a system of prescription for financial products. As in the case of dangerous drugs, this will entail getting a financial professional or authority to sign off on a new financial product, like a complex home mortgage, as safe for the person buying it before he or she can sign on to such a product.

These are still early days identifying and clearing up the weeds in the thicket of our complex world of finance. Finance is an essential part of the modern world. Blanket prohibitions and excessive regulation can do damage. But the obverse of leaving it all to the market is no panacea either. We have to live in a world of continuous research and evolving regulation. According to some schools of thought life will always be a battle between good and evil. There may be reason to doubt the metaphysics of this; but what is nearly certain is that the economy will be an unending battle between new financial products and practices and ever-evolving regulation to sift the good from the bad. Hence, it is not possible to design laws that are optimal forever. As society evolves, its laws will need to evolve. So from the point of view of an economy, it is important to understand the principles that underlie the law, so that we can modify and adapt with our needs. The subject of law and economics has deep conceptual flaws, which handicap economic growth and development, especially in emerging economies, such as India, and that is what I turn to in the next chapter.

8   Law and Economics

Preamble

A poorly implemented law or, for that matter, a well-implemented one can do devastating damage to an economy. In the minds of most people the law is about crime, retribution, justice, and fairness. The fact that the law can be critical in determining the rate of growth of the GDP, the length of the queue for buying some essential commodity, or the level of unemployment is not something that is widely appreciated. This is especially true in developing nations.

In industrialized countries, the discipline of law and economics came to acquire some importance because of the early recognition that the law plays a significant role in promoting competition. The enactment of the Sherman Act in the United States in 1890, which placed restrictions on monopolistic and collusive practices by industry, was a landmark event. Subsequently, it came to be recognized, if grudgingly, that, quite apart from what the law does to crime and punishment, it can do a lot to the economy, good and bad. This recognition is not quite there yet in most developing and emerging economies. If the chief economic adviser of such a nation comments on some legislative matter it is usually treated as an intrusion. But the fact remains that many a developing nation has brought great harm upon its economy and development prospects by not enacting a law or by failing to implement a law that has been enacted or by enacting and implementing a faulty law. This is one area where there is a lot yet to be understood and much to be gained from such an understanding.

Corruption and the Law

How contentious the law can be, I learned by fire, when I was chief economic adviser in India. Corruption has been a long-standing problem in India that successive regimes and governments have battled or given the impression of battling and mostly failed. One can sense the despair in the classical master of statecraft, Kautilya, when in his magnum opus, *Arthashastra*, written nearly three centuries before the Christian era, he observed: "Just as it is impossible to know when a fish moving in water is drinking it, so it is impossible to find out when government servants in charge of undertakings misappropriate money" (1992, 281).

Some two thousand three hundred years after those lines were penned the nation was being traumatized by one corruption scandal breaking after another. As briefly mentioned in chapter 2, Anna Hazare's call to eradicate corruption struck a chord and brought thousands out to protest. As some well-intentioned individuals in government looked at the vastness of the problem in despair, I spent a lot of time thinking about what we, sitting in the North Block, could do to curb this dreadful menace that inflicts harm on people and, in my view, damages economic development.[1] A simple idea struck me about one particular kind of corruption, which I went on to call "harassment bribery," and how it could be reduced. I felt convinced that the idea was morally and theoretically well founded enough to at least merit debate and discussion.

Let me present the gist of this idea. In India ordinary citizens and, at times, even large corporations are asked to pay a bribe for something to which they have legal entitlement. I had called these "harassment bribes." Say a woman has filed her tax return properly and it turns out that the Income Tax Department owes her some money. It is not uncommon for a critical employee of the department to ask for some money before he releases the reimbursement. To give another example: a person has imported some cargo, done all the required paper work, and paid the requisite taxes; he is nevertheless asked to pay some money in cash before he can get all the papers that he needs to take the cargo out. These are examples of harassment bribes.

One advantage of getting a senior government job is that one is never asked to pay a harassment bribe. So it is genuinely easy for those high up in government to forget that the crime of bribery is ubiquitous. Plaintive calls for help from relatives and friends being harassed for bribes act as a reminder that all is well in the underworld and not all is well for the common citizen. This also raises a question: are these ordinary folks who pay bribes culpable given they are virtually *compelled* to do so?

According to India's main anti-bribery law, the Prevention of Corruption Act, 1988, bribe taking and bribe giving are equally wrong. In the event of conviction, both the taker (usually a public servant) and the giver are equally punishable. As section 12 of the law states, "Whoever abets any offence [pertaining to bribery], whether or not that offence is committed in consequence of the abetment, shall be punishable with imprisonment for a term which shall be not less than six months but which may extend up to five years and shall also be liable to fine." It may be added here that the giving of a bribe is treated under the Indian law as abetment to the crime of bribery, and so bribe giving is covered under this section.

I want to point out that there is, allegedly, an exception to the law on bribe giving in the form of section 24 of the Prevention of Corruption Act, 1988, which says: "Notwithstanding anything contained in any law for the time being in force, a statement made by a person in any proceeding against a public servant for an offence under sections 7 to 11 or under section 13 or section 15, that he offered or agreed to offer any gratification (other than legal remuneration) or any valuable thing to the public servant, shall not subject such person to a prosecution under section 12."

However, section 24 has a lot of ambiguity. In a 2008 case, *Bhupinder Singh Patel v. CBI*, 2008 (3) CCR 247 at p. 261 (Del): 2008 Cri LJ 4396, it was ruled that this exemption would apply only if the bribe giver could establish that the bribe was given unwillingly and in order to trap the public servant. The word "unwillingly" is so ambiguous that the use of this judgment as precedence is not easy. As a consequence, section 24 has effectively become a clause meant exclusively for those wanting to carry out a sting operation to trap a public servant in the act of bribe taking, and seeking protection from the law.[2] Consequently, section 12, which suggests that bribe giving and taking should both be treated as equally punishable, has come to dominate the Indian anti-bribery legal system.

This, in the case of harassment bribes, seemed to me to be wrong. In situations where a civil servant asks for a bribe from a person who is legally entitled to a particular service, it is important to distinguish between the perpetrator of a crime and the victim. But over and above this moral position, there is an interesting strategic argument that one can put forward to distinguish between the giver and the taker.

Note that under the current law, once a bribe has been paid, the interests of the bribe giver and the taker become fully aligned. If this criminal act gets exposed, both will be in trouble. Hence, they tend to collude to keep the act of bribery hidden. And even if they do not actively collude, each has a level of comfort in the knowledge that it is not in the interest of the other to reveal any information. It is not surprising that while all Indians know of the widespread prevalence of bribery and, behind closed doors, people will tell you how they had to pay a bribe, this is seldom revealed in the courts and a vast majority of bribery incidents go unpunished.

It seemed to me that this could be changed by making the following simple amendment to the Prevention of Corruption Act. In all cases of this kind of bribery, declare the act of giving a bribe legal while continuing to hold the act of taking a bribe illegal. If need be, we could double up the punishment for taking a bribe, so that the total magnitude of punishment remains the same. Further, once the bribery has been proven, the bribe taker will be required to return the bribe to the giver.

Now think of a civil servant trying to take a bribe. He will know that, once he has taken the bribe, he can no longer rely on help from the giver in keeping this fact a secret. Unlike under the existing law, *after the bribery*, the interests of the giver and the taker are diametrically opposed to each other. Knowing that this will happen, the bribe taker will be much more hesitant to take the bribe in the first place. Hence, if the law were amended, as is being suggested here, the incidence of bribery would drop sharply.

The argument that I just spelled out is rooted in game theory. It is called a subgame perfect equilibrium and was an idea that was published by Reinhart Selten in 1975, and David Kreps and Robert Wilson in 1982, building on the fundamental work of the celebrated economist and subject of a popular biography and film, John Nash.[3] Subgame perfection can be a complex idea in situations of complicated interaction between individuals over time, but in this case, its use is so commonsensical that one needs no prior training to understand its use.

The idea seemed sufficiently compelling and of practical value that I quickly wrote and put it up on the website of the Ministry of Finance as a working paper. There was a rancorous debate going on in India on corruption at that time. Much of the debate, while founded in genuine passion and concern, generated few practical ideas of what could be done. Most of the popular talk was of creating a layer of special bureaucracy to catch and punish corruption. Little thought was given to what David Hume recognized some 250 years ago—that with each such layer of bureaucracy, there would be a tendency for a new layer of corruption to arise. This was the fundamental question of who would police the policeman. Indeed, one factor behind the high incidence of corruption in India was the complex layers of laws and inspectorates that we had built up over time in order to curb corruption.

I felt pleased with the idea. I knew I was addressing only a segment of the problem—namely, corruption that took the form of harassment bribery—but this segment was not negligible by any means. If we could bring this down drastically through a small change in the law without adding to the size of the bureaucracy, that seemed to be worthwhile.

What I did not anticipate was the level of anger (and misreporting) that my note would generate. It began with small mentions of my paper in the newspapers, followed by lacerating editorials and op-eds.[4] Some of them stemmed from the mistaken view that I was somehow condoning corruption and saying that bribery should be made legal. I may add that I myself would be upset if someone made such an argument (even though I must admit I could never quite follow what making bribery legal means). Soon there were some members of parliament (MPs) writing to various leaders in government protesting against the floating of this idea. Two MPs, members of the Communist Party of India, wrote letters to the prime minister and the finance minister, asking that action be taken against such an immoral idea on a government website and insisting that it be taken down. Then the television channels picked this up and there were some screaming matches debating the idea.

Some individuals including some prominent industrialists called me up to support this kind of an amendment to the law. Narayana Murthy, the founder of Infosys and one of the pivotal figures in India's takeoff in the information technology sector, publicly stated that it deserved serious consideration and was roundly subjected to criticism himself.[5] I knew that, at least for the next two or three years, my idea was dead. No politician would want to be associated with it. Not openly. Yet, curiously, it revealed a side of Indian politics which gave me hope.

At the peak of this debate, when protest letters were sent to the finance minister and others and the political leaders had to write back and explain the government's position on this, I thought I would be asked to take the working paper down from the Ministry of Finance website. That did not happen. Moreover, no politician in the ruling party, not one, asked me either to relent or told me off for causing embarrassment to the government. On April 23, 2011, a Saturday evening, the prominent TV journalist Barkha Dutt phoned me requesting me to appear on her show *We the People* the following evening. Having an instinctive taste for such discussions but not knowing whether this would churn up the debate more or dampen it, I decided to do something which I rarely did—ask the finance minister or the prime minister whether I should risk stoking the fires by participating in the debate. The finance minister was away in Vietnam so I phoned the prime minister at his residence. When he called me back, I told him I enjoyed these debates and, left to myself, I would love to explain my idea to the public, but since I had caused grief enough to the government, I was wondering whether or not I should go on the Barkha Dutt show.

This was the first time I was speaking to Prime Minister Singh on this subject. There was a moment's pause, and then the prime minister said that he had heard about my idea on how to control corruption, but he had to say he did not agree with me on this. Fearing that he had heard one of the many misstatements that were floating around, I explained briefly what my argument was. I doubt I would have succeeded in persuading him so quickly. But anyway, what he went on to say was very heartening to me. He said he was leaving the decision on whether or not to appear on this particular program to me, but since it was my job as chief economic adviser to bring ideas to the table, I should feel free to articulate my ideas in public and discuss them.

Eventually, I, on my own, decided not to appear on *We the People*, but I participated in many subsequent debates and felt strangely good about India. There are not too many developing countries, and not that many industrialized nations either, that would give this kind of space not just to the nation's writers, intellectuals, and journalists, but also to its professional and technical advisers to air new ideas that may be unpopular and perhaps not even in keeping with the government's own position, but are potentially useful in the long run. This strategy creates short-term turbulence, but by enriching the quality of a nation's public discourse it contributes to a more robust development.

I had a similar experience in Washington, D.C., after a lecture I gave at the Carnegie Institute, where I admitted that economic reforms in India had slowed down. This got picked up by the Indian media, which gave it wide publicity, with some condiments tossed in for good measure. The opposition parties joined in, and there was a lot of controversy. This time it was the finance minister who reminded me that my task was to bring ideas to the table. It is this openness that is India's long-standing strength,[6] and I hope that we will continue to protect this space for reasoned debate. In the long run, the nation's progress will depend on this.

I believe that my public airing of ideas concerning corruption served an important role, even though the immediate negative reaction to my proposed amendment made it impossible to implement it. I have hope that my proposal will gradually gather momentum as more people mull it over and think through the argument carefully. I also got subsequent reactions that were heartening. Some feminists wrote to me supportively since my suggestion struck a chord with them: they have argued that just because dowry is illegal must not mean that the dowry giver and the taker should be treated as equally culpable. In the Indian context, the dowry giver was the bride's family who almost invariably agreed to pay because of social pressures to get a daughter married; so we must distinguish between the victim and the perpetrator.

The strategic side of my argument for an amendment was also bolstered by an incident from history. The Indian practice of *sati*, whereby when a man died his wife was expected to die on his pyre, was prevalent for hundreds of years, mainly in eastern and north-western India, and has been written about extensively. The British rulers of India did declare *sati* criminal and then, as additional deterrent for those who abetted and encouraged *sati*, declared the witnessing of *sati* also a crime. This tragic ritual flourished during the British period. There were many sociopolitical reasons for this, but one factor cannot be ignored. Every time a case of *sati* came up in the courts, somehow it was impossible to find witnesses. Clearly the law had created a catch-22.

Harassment bribes, which are ubiquitous and the source of much pain for ordinary citizens, can also be put to a virtual end. And for this we do not need to create a large layer of bureaucracy to catch the corrupt. Nor do we need to build complex enforcement structures. We simply need to make laws to keep the strategic aspect of human behavior in the fore. I expect this to happen eventually.

Law's Responsibility

The argument for handling harassment bribes is just one example of what is possible by crafting laws imaginatively. The scope for such changes is huge once we recognize that the fate of an economy is closely intertwined with the nature of the laws that govern the nation. The laws have the responsibility of bringing about justice and fairness, but they also have the charge, not wholly but in good measure, of promoting development and economic well-being. One can see evidence of this in the experience of Bihar, one of India's poorest states. Bihar's economy saw a puzzling growth sprint from 2006 to 2012, registering a per capita income growth of 10.4 percent per annum. This was remarkable because it came after a decade and a half of 0.9 percent growth. What caused this? In retrospect it is clear that the proximate cause was investment in health, education, and infrastructure. But all this was made possible by the far-sightedness of the chief minister of the state, Nitish Kumar, who took office in 2005, and devoted a large amount of effort to improving law, order, and governance (see Singh and Stern 2013, xxiv–xxv). It is not possible in a slender book to spell out all that needs to be done, but one can sketch the broad principles that would have to guide such an exercise.

From the perspective of the economy, the fundamental principle to be kept in mind in crafting legislation is the centrality of the contract. An economy progresses by facilitating trade and exchange. If there were no exchange, we would be abysmally poor. Each of us would then have to produce or hunt for the food we eat, stitch or steal the clothes we wear, and build or try to build the homes we intend to occupy. We would be so inefficient trying to do so many things that life would be "solitary, poor, nasty, brutish and short," to steal a phrase from Thomas Hobbes's *Leviathan*. To break away from this we need to specialize and with that comes the need to trade and exchange. I produce the food, you the clothing, and we trade; I work on your home, you give me money, your neighbor produces food, and I buy it from him.

But with trade and exchange come the need to respect contracts, for rarely are trade and exchange instantaneous. The New York store pays the apparel firm located outside Delhi, and after fifteen days, the firm sends a consignment of clothes to the New York store; or the firm sends the clothes to the New York store, which pays the money after that. The bank gives me money to buy a house and I pay back the bank in small installments over the next thirty years.

The heart of such transactions is the ability to feel assured that these millions of implicit or explicit contracts will be respected by the parties involved. If that expectation is not there or is deficient in a society, that society is destined to stagnate and be poor. One major function of the law is to facilitate such contracts and exchanges. As society progresses, these contracts and exchanges tend to become more complex and the law needs to be nimble enough to allow for this.[7]

Faults in the law that make trade and exchange difficult can stall development. Consider a rental law of the kind to be found in parts of New York City and many Indian metropolises, which grants tenants the right to stay on in an apartment and pay an unchanging rent. This kind of "rent control regime"—where the initial rent can be freely chosen by the landlord and the tenant but once that is fixed the tenant can stay on and continue to pay the same rent—can do damage to the housing market and can often, ironically, hurt tenants.

A common fact of economic life is that average prices tend to rise or, more correctly, they seldom fall over a protracted length of time. If this increase is large, say above 5 or 6 percent, we worry that it is an inflationary situation; but if the increase is less than 2 percent it is considered pretty normal in most countries. What would be abnormal is if prices fell, even by 1 or 2 percent per annum over a sustained period. This is something that rarely happens. This typically means that house rentals over time will also tend to rise. In such a scenario, the rent control law seems to be a nice protection for tenants since, once a tenant moves in, she does not have to worry about rentals increasing from one year to the next. But that logic is flawed. Since the landlord also knows that he will not be able to raise the rent on a sitting tenant, even when the market rental (for new tenants) rises, the landlord in a city with rent control will ask for a higher rent knowing that once fixed, the rent will be unchanged for as long as the tenant wishes to stay. Hence, the starting rental will tend to be higher in a rent-controlled regime to insure the landlord against the fact that, even if inflation occurs, he will not be able to raise the rent on his sitting tenant.

But there is another problem, which is closely associated with the pioneering work of Akerlof (1970), Spence (1973), and Stiglitz and Weiss (1981) on asymmetric information. Suppose you want to rent a home for two years (maybe because you plan to go off to another city after that). You will clearly want to tell your landlord this, perhaps sign a contract to this effect, and ask him to let you pay a smaller rent because you will leave after two years. The landlord then will have the option of renting the place again and at a higher rate. The problem is, given your right by law to stay on, no matter what you may have assured the landlord, the contract to leave in two years is useless. Moreover, if such an assurance worked, every tenant would pretend to come in for two years, get a lower rent, and then stay on for longer. Of course, there are tenants of different kinds—those who genuinely want to stay for a short term and those who want to stay much longer. But while the tenant herself knows this, there is no way for the landlord to tell which tenant is of which kind. This is the famous problem of "asymmetric information." As a consequence, even those tenants who are genuinely interested in short stays get penalized. Moreover, this problem can result in unraveling of markets, with few homes being put out on rental and house construction activity slowing down.

In general, it is best to give two or more adults the freedom to sign contracts in situations where there is no negative fallout on outsiders, that is, on those who were not party to the deal. In addition, the state and the judiciary should provide the machinery to enforce these contracts. What a rent control law does is to overrule contracts because it says that, whether or not a tenant assured a landlord to the contrary when taking on the tenancy, she has the right to stay on and not have her rent raised.[8]

Another area where the Indian law overrules the freedom of adults to sign contracts as they see fit pertains to labor. This is a controversial topic but it is arguable that, overall, workers have been hurt by this. A large number of rules and laws guide and control the labor market. That in itself is not surprising. Every modern labor market has to work within some parameters set by the law. The one law that is the source of a lot of controversy in India is the Industrial Disputes Act, 1947. Given that this became law in 1947, the month matters. As it happens, this became the law in April 1947, a few months before India's independence. So both India and Pakistan inherited this law. The Industrial Disputes Act basically requires firms that employ fifty or more workers pay a compensation, which is specified in the Act, to any worker who is retrenched (fired). In addition, an amendment to the Act, which became effective in 1984, requires firms that employ more than a hundred workers to actually seek prior permission from the government before retrenching workers. And, as is well known, the government seldom grants such permission and, in general, places a lot of a priori restrictions on the terms for hiring and firing workers. In 1992 in a case involving a bankrupt private firm, Justice S. K. Hazari of the Calcutta High Court argued that if another private firm took over the firm, there would be no guaranteeing that that firm would not, in turn, go bankrupt and cause workers to be laid off. He therefore directed the government of West Bengal to take over the firm and run it with its existing workers.

For reasons that must be evident from the earlier argument concerning rent control, since the fundamental logic is the same, it can be argued that far from helping workers this law has hurt them. People have argued that this kind of a law, which basically protects workers only in the organized sector, could disadvantage those who work in the informal sector and are often self-employed. While that is correct, I would go further and argue that it has probably hurt the very workers it was meant to help.[9] By making it hard for firms to retrench workers it has created disincentives for firms to employ workers in the first place. This has encouraged firms in India to use more capital-intensive technology than they might have otherwise. This has lowered the demand for organized sector labor and has kept wages low.

From all accounts it is embarrassing how small India's organized labor sector is. In 2010, overall employment in the organized sector of India was 28.7 million. Moreover, 17.9 million of these workers were in the public sector. So organized private sector employment of workers in India, a country with a population of approximately 1.2 billion, was 10.8 million. Interestingly, there is evidence that the number of workers in firms employing more than one hundred workers dropped sharply between 1980 and 1985. This was arguably a response to the amendment of the Industrial Disputes Act, which became effective in 1984, and required all firms employing more than 100 workers to receive government permission before retrenching workers. It is arguable that this law has harmed Indian workers by keeping demand for labor small.

This takes us back to the basic point made in chapter 7 on the importance of the principle of free contract. This principle has important caveats, some of which were discussed in chapter 7 and some I will get to later, but the wanton violation of this principle has done harm.

This principle has a long intellectual history. Here is John Stuart Mill making the case: "As soon as any part of a person's conduct affects prejudicially the interests of others, society has jurisdiction over it. . . . But there is no room for entertaining any such question when a person's conduct affects the interests of no persons besides himself, or needs not affect them unless they like (all the persons concerned being of full age, and the ordinary amount of understanding). In all such cases, there should be perfect freedom, legal and social, to do the action and stand the consequences" (Mill 1859, 132).

Returning to the subject of labor, what I recommend is not that we should give firms the right to dismiss workers at will, but that we open up more space for firms and workers to strike contracts as they see fit—some may opt for contracts in which firms pay a higher wage and retain the right to retrench workers, while others may go for contracts where wages are low but workers cannot be dismissed—and to have a judicial system that helps enforce these contracts efficiently.

Consider a textile and garments firm in India that supplies fashion garments to American stores. This is a volatile sector. Suppose there is suddenly a rush of demand for a product for which India has a relative advantage. What this firm would like to do is to employ more workers and meet this sudden demand. But, if it knows that once it has done so, it will not be able to retrench the workers, it may well decide to let the opportunity pass. The employer will lose out of course but so will the workers who could have found jobs and even other workers who would gain from the rise in wages that this would bring about. I have just virtually paraphrased my conversation with a producer of garments in Gurgaon, just outside Delhi. He lamented how he must let so many expansion opportunities go because he knows his contraction opportunities are limited.[10]

Without going all the way to allowing *any* contracts (and there are good reasons not to go to that extreme, as we shall see), what the law should do minimally is to explicitly allow two kinds of contracts—the first, in which wages may be low but workers cannot be retrenched; and the second, in which wages may be high but firms retain the right to dismiss workers with very little notice. Once this is allowed it is possible that many firms will employ both kinds of workers and there should be a great increase in the demand for labor and growth of the manufacturing sector of a kind not seen thus far in India.

More generally, it is critically important for India's lawmakers to examine the body of legislation that pertains to or impinges upon economic activities and make sure that the laws do not place arbitrary restrictions on individuals that prevent them from trading, exchanging, creating new businesses, and innovating. To compel individuals to take permission from the government or uninvolved third parties is to slow down these activities and by default to slow down development and, unless there are compelling reasons to do so, we must not.

Let me make a brief ideological digression here. The argument for more flexible labor laws as put forward earlier is typically met with strong opposition from radicals and progressives. This troubles me since my own sympathy lies with the progressives. The world today is an unfair place where the poor and the dispossessed are duped into complacency by being persuaded that what they get is what they deserve. We do need to alter this fundamental and by no means necessary unfairness in modern economic life. Having said this, the radical agenda is often marred by poor analysis. Since (a certain kind of) flexible labor laws have been argued for by neoconservative thinkers, progressives refuse to distinguish between those and what is being proposed here. Also, the fact that we ought to aspire to a radically better world does not mean that every traditional idea of mainstream economics is wrong. To make such an assumption and design policies that ignore current incentives is to court failure.

With this let me return to the main argument. I mentioned that the principle of free contract has important exceptions. Indeed, I would be remiss if I did not warn the reader that this is not as simple and uncomplicated as may appear at first sight. To treat this as a call for unmitigated space for free contracting and the free market is to err on the other side—that of market fundamentalism. While it has been argued in several places in this book that India needs to work on removing bureaucratic roadblocks and the culture of "permissionism," we will do ourselves injustice if we do not recognize that virtually all simple rules have exceptions. Policymaking cannot be reduced to one-liner basic principles. Common sense and reason must be allowed to impinge on our textbook rules. Even the "principle of free contract" has its limitations.

For one, contracts can get so complex that it is not possible for ordinary individuals to fully comprehend what they are signing on to. In such cases the state has the responsibility to make sure that individuals do not get cheated by virtue of this. In some complex areas, the government may have to limit the domain from within which the contract has to be chosen. Over and above this, there are other problems to do with competitive price and wage formation as discussed in chapter 7.

John Stuart Mill, having argued strongly for the principle of free contract had been troubled by the possibility that by this argument it is possible to justify voluntary slavery or warranteeism, that is, giving workers the freedom to sign away all their freedom. If one ponders the matter sufficiently one will reach the conclusion that the principle of free contract should have exceptions. As noted in the previous chapter, there are situations where each contract between two persons may be fully voluntary but the collectivity of many such contracts affect market wages in a way that some workers become worse off. This has major implications for a variety of labor-related matters. Some countries have decreed that workers in an export-processing zone have to forego certain rights, such as the right to bargain collectively and the right to strike. At one level it seems possible to justify this by appealing to the principle of free contract. After all, no one is forced to work in an export-processing zone. However, if several such export-processing zones are allowed then workers who wish to retain their right to bargain collectively may get lower wages than they would have got otherwise, proving the point that the collective effect of free contracts may result in some segments of society ending up worse off.[11]

What this illustrates above anything else is the need to have individuals with a modicum of professional training in economics, a capacity to conduct deductive reasoning, and certain basic moral commitments to draft the laws that define the boundaries of the workplace and all economic activities. In a nation like India, the overall direction to pursue is the creation of more space for contracts among consenting individuals. At the same time, there have to be boundaries to limit these to prevent people from being unwittingly exploited. But these boundaries must not be set arbitrarily for that can hurt the very constituencies meant to be helped, as happens so often. There is a need to develop metaprinciples, along the lines discussed earlier, to demarcate the limits of the principle of free contract.

Law as Focal Point

The big problem with the use of law to direct the economy in developing countries and emerging economies is the propensity of citizens and inhabitants in many of these nations to collectively overlook the law. In such cases good laws may get drafted but often they sit on the shelves gathering dust, while people wantonly violate them. From child labor laws to minimum wage laws, I can think of laws that are better known for their violation than adherence to them. The common complaint in India, repeated to the point of boredom in umpteen parlors and coffee houses is that "India's problem is not in the laws but in their implementation."

Those making this observation tend to view this as a simple matter of grit and determination on the part of leaders. In reality, this complaint points to a deep fault line underlying the subject of law and economics and the way in which it has been described and developed in the literature. I believe that our traditional wisdom on this topic is deeply flawed; and this intellectual failing has spilled over and hurt actual policymaking.

According to the standard paradigm of law and economics, the law influences the behavior of individuals by allowing or disallowing certain actions, or by altering the returns individuals earn from certain actions. In the language of game theory, the same thing can be asserted by saying that a law affects behavior by altering the game people are playing.

Consider a new speed limit law that imposes a penalty on drivers for driving above a certain speed, say, 60 miles an hour. Prior to this law when a man considered driving above 60 miles per hour, he would think of the benefit of driving time saved, the expected cost of an accident, and so on. However, once the new law is announced, he will have to factor in the additional expected cost of being caught by a traffic police officer and having to pay a fine. So, at first sight, the traditional view of law, just outlined, seems to be valid.

But think again. Why should the law alter the payoffs of people? After all, a new law is nothing but some "ink on paper"—just some new words written on paper. Clearly, that cannot change the game that people are playing.[12] If everybody continued to behave the way they did before the new law was enacted, the new law would have no effect on anybody. In other words, the fresh ink on the paper surely cannot change the game of life being played out.

The traditional approach to law and economics is flawed because it is predicated on the assumption that the enforcers of the law will do their job mechanically, in a preprogrammed way. They are treated as being "outside" the economy or the game of life. So the traditional model looks only at a part of the economy, taking the enforcers of the law as robots. But once we treat all human beings as having agency and making choices, it is not clear that the law can be thought of as a game-changer. If all human beings—the citizens, the police, and the judges—decide to ignore the law, the law will make no difference. The returns people got from the actions they undertook before the law would be the same after the law. The law cannot change that. There is nothing quite as concrete about the law as the traditional view supposes. Though this approach seems novel today, as I pointed out in Basu 2010, it is rooted in ideas quite explicitly outlined by David Hume in his essay on government (Hume 1858).

This critique, however, opens up another question. Given that the law is nothing but some ink on paper, how then *does* it affect anything? If players' feasible actions are unchanged and payoffs are unchanged (and indeed the fact that some new law is written down on paper is no reason why these should change), why should the outcome in terms of actual human behavior be any different?

At the same time, we can see all around us examples of how laws often do alter behavior. A ban on smoking in public spaces frequently leads to a reduction in smoking in public spaces. New speed limit laws may not be obeyed fully but they do impact the speeds people drive their vehicles at in many countries. Moreover, at least in industrialized countries, laws do alter what the police do. When there was no speed limit, policemen did not stop cars driving at 70 mph and ask the driver to pay a fine. But they do so once there is a new law prohibiting driving above 60 mph.

These are valid questions. And trying to answer them leads to a different perspective on how and why the law affects behavior. According to this view, the law changes people's behavior, to the extent that it does, by altering their expectations of what others will do. In the language of game theory, when the law changes behavior it does so by creating a new focal point in the game.[13]

I shall briefly pause here to introduce the reader to the fascinating concept of "focal point" first developed by Thomas Schelling (1963). That, in turn, will entail a short primer on the concept of "Nash equilibrium," developed by John Nash. Consider a situation, like so many in life, where each person has to make a choice from an available set of possible actions, but where each person's welfare depends not only on what he or she chooses but, possibly, also on the choices of others. Such a situation, following the classic work of John von Neumann and Oskar Morgenstern in 1944, is called a "game." A Nash equilibrium of a game is simply a choice of action on the part of each person (or player) such that, given other people's choices, no one wants to change his or her own choice. Hence, it is also often called a "self-enforcing" outcome.

Consider an example. There is a highway where the law puts no restrictions on which side of the road you drive. Two persons coming from opposite directions have to decide which side of the road to drive on. It is easy to see that if both choose the right side that is a Nash equilibrium. Clearly, if person B chooses to drive on the right it is best for A to drive on the right. It is worthwhile for the reader untutored in this field to check that A driving on the left and B driving on the right is not an equilibrium because, given B's choice, A would do better switching to the right.

One problem with the idea of the Nash equilibrium is that in many situations there can be more than one Nash equilibrium. In such a situation even if both players wish to converge on to a Nash equilibrium, they may fail to do so simply because each targets a different Nash equilibrium.

It is easy to see that in the driving example, there is another Nash equilibrium—one in which both choose to drive on the left. In such games it is entirely possible that despite wanting to be in a Nash equilibrium the two players will end up with a mismatch. This is where the concept of focal point comes into play. A focal point is a Nash equilibrium that is salient and so everybody knows it is the one each of them is rooting for.

Focal points arise somewhat mysteriously from human psychology and enable people to correctly guess what others are planning to do. It does not always work but the surprise is that it often does. Try this out for yourself. Suppose you and another person, with no communication between you have to choose one number from among 7, 18, 93, and 100. If both of you choose the same number, you will each be given $1,000. Otherwise you get nothing. Clearly, this game has four Nash equilibria—both choosing 7, both choosing 18, both choosing 93, and both choosing 100. Hence, when playing this game there is a huge uncertainty about which Nash equilibrium to aim for. But somehow individuals manage to do very well in terms of coordination when they play this game. They typically choose 100. There is something salient about this outcome.[14]

Now one can see the connection between the law and focal point. In some simple situations, the law does not really need policing. The mere announcement of the law creates salience and influences behavior. In the driving game, if the government publicly announces that the law is you drive on the left, then even if it is known that this government does not have the money to police the streets, it is very likely that people will begin to drive on the left. The law creates a focal point—that is, it gives salience to one Nash equilibrium.

The idea is more complicated where the law needs to motivate the police, the bureaucrat, and the judge, alongside ordinary citizens and inhabitants, to behave appropriately, but in essence it is the same idea. It is the propensity to look away from this complexity that handicapped the traditional discipline of law and economics and rendered it fundamentally flawed. It is essential to confront the complexity if we want to create laws that are more effective.

For anybody who has worked in a developing country, it is obvious that the focal point approach to law and economics is not an esoteric academic exercise but is critical to understanding how the law works or, for that matter, does not work. In India, there are examples galore of laws that exist merely on paper. They fail to create salience and are overlooked by all, including the enforcers of the law. The focal point approach helps us understand why this may happen.

Note first of all that a focal point has to be a Nash equilibrium, that is, a self-enforcing outcome,[15] meaning a choice of action on the part of individuals from which no one has the incentive to unilaterally deviate. If we try to direct society to behave in a way that is not self-enforcing, then it is doomed to fail, since, by definition, it is in the interest of someone to deviate. Traditional policy has often floundered on this. It paid too little attention to individual incentives, and especially the incentives of the civil servants and enforcers of the law, treating them as robotic followers of the law. This is a mistake and the poor enforcement of the law is a consequence.

Also, if the law is internally inconsistent or too cluttered or unclear, people learn to ignore it. Once this happens with several laws, this damages the focal point role of all laws. People then do not treat laws as signals to be taken seriously. In this way even a good law fails to be effective, since people may have learned not to take law itself as a signal. This is a focal point problem. A focal point influences behavior only if all players treat it as focal. In many emerging economies the law may not have acquired that status. When a new law is announced we do not assume that others will treat it as focal and hence there is no reason for anybody to treat it as focal. In India, one can easily list laws that exist only in their violation. This used to be true of our child labor laws, and still is to a considerable degree. No one bothered about these laws. There are also laws about the treatment of household servants, about minimum wages, about the decibels of music one can play on public systems, and about the prescriptions one must show before one buys certain drugs from chemists. All of these laws are wantonly violated. Some of these violations may well be welfare enhancing.[16] But in general, not being able to rely on laws is a huge handicap for society. We face this handicap in India in collecting taxes, enforcing safety rules, preventing road accidents, and many other ways.

The traditional view of the law tries to correct this by creating more laws and developing additional layers of bureaucracy. The focal point view of the law sounds a warning bell about these traditional remedies. It says that since the law works for no other reason than through its influence on our minds and expectations, we need to work on education, culture, and social norms to create the prerequisite for more effective law. As already pointed out, one standard mistake is to create a surfeit of laws. By enacting excessive laws, which we know will be violated, we destroy the law's focal point properties.

Let me explain this with a real-life example. Meeting up with people at large airports can be a challenging task. Suppose Xavier (X) and Yogesh (Y) decide to meet at Heathrow's terminal 3 at noon but forget to specify where. When they arrive at Heathrow, they confront a classic game-theoretic problem. Each person has to choose a place where to wait at noon for the other person. In the olden days X would try hard to guess where Y might wait for you. Y loves books and so may choose to wait at W. H. Smith, a bookstore. But then it strikes X that Y knows that X does not care for books and so may go elsewhere. And so on.

Some years ago the authorities at Heathrow tried to solve this problem by putting up a sign at some arbitrary place saying "Meeting Point." This is a clever use of the idea of focal point and has worked wonders. The place marked Meeting Point has become a focal point for people playing the game of trying to meet each other. X goes to the Meeting Point because he knows that Y will go to the Meeting Point. And Y does so because she knows that X will.

Suppose now that, seeing the success of putting up the Meeting Point sign, and in the light of the airport terminal being large, someone in the airport authority gets the bright idea of putting up several Meeting Point signs in several places; and, as he is a senior bureaucrat, no one dares object to his plan. It is easy to see that this could render the whole project useless. The whole idea of a focal point is everybody has the same expectation. Having multiple identical signs destroys this focus. Each Meeting Point sign is then at risk of being ignored by virtue of the fact that there are other Meeting Point signs, and so it is unclear where anyone being met will go.

Similarly, if we have a clutter of laws and especially if there are contradictions among them so that following one means violating another, the legal system will fail to play the role of coordinator for human behavior. In short, the law ceases to be a signal for the focal point. Once that happens, a new law that is well drafted and could have been effective ceases to be so because the very culture of taking guidance from the law has been damaged. This is the reason why elsewhere in the book I advise against conferring too many legal rights on the people, without being clear that they can actually be enforced. This does more damage than simply having those rights unenforced.

To have a society where the law is effective, we need to have simple, easy-to-follow, noncontradictory laws; and we have to also gradually nurture the norm of following the law, through education and through the leaders setting an example. Of course, each of these raises further questions. The reason I have delved into this topic in some detail is to precisely provoke such a quest; and to move on from merely wringing our hands and repeating the cliché that the problem is not with the law but with its implementation, and saying that the government should do this or government should do that, unmindful of the fact that there is no individual called government, and to the extent that government can be associated with a group of individuals, those individuals also have desires and motives, like you and I do, that cannot ignored.

The entire subject of social norms has a close connection to the law and, hence, to economic development and the performance of the economy. In books on economic policy and economic development, we generally tend to ignore the role of norms and political institutions. But they are crucial determinants of growth and efficiency. Getting these right is as important as getting our trade and monetary policies right. Too little attention has been paid to these by economists, though, fortunately, there is a now a small and growing literature on the subject.[17] I try to make amends for this in chapter 9.

Postscript

My one chilling encounter with corruption occurred not in India but in Russia, in 1992. Corruption in India, as I have argued, is rampant; yet it is nowhere as ubiquitous as it was in Russia in the early 1990s. In India it is not an everyday affair but something one encounters in major dealings with the government. Many tourists and visitors may not even realize that corruption is widespread. But in 1992 even during my five-day visit to Moscow, I recall several bribery encounters.[18]

Most of the bribery and corruption incidents I encountered were innocuous but not the one at Moscow's Sheremetyevo Airport as I prepared to leave the country. A liveried immigration officer examined my passport and said, "There's a problem. Your visa expired yesterday so you have overstayed." I could not fault his logic but decided against giving verbal expression to that. I checked the passport and that was indeed the case. I had not realized that when I applied for a five-day visa in New Delhi and got my passport back, the officer had actually given me a visa for four days.

USSR was still recent history and I wondered if I would at last get to see Siberia. Sensing my nervousness he said I did not need to worry. If I slipped a $50 bill to him, he would stamp my passport and let me go. If I had been living in the United States then I would have been tempted to take that option quickly. But reminding myself of my paltry salary at the Delhi School of Economics, I picked up courage and said he would have to make do with less. He bargained hard but he stood little chance faced with a person whose skills were honed in the bazaars of Delhi. We settled on $5.

Then there was another argument about whether I would have to give him the $5 first or he would stamp and return my passport first. I got my way again. He handed over my passport and I began to reach for my wallet. But the thought suddenly crossed my mind that in case this was all planned and someone came and caught me for bribing an official, I would not only get to see Siberia but see no place else thereafter. Then I did something I did not know I had it in me to do. I reneged after making a full commitment to this transaction.

I did not pay the bribe; with passport in hand I ran for the Air India Boeing, which by then had its doors open and was boarding passengers.

To date, I am not totally sure if what I did was morally right or wrong. It is not right to pay a bribe but not right to renege either. It is true that my decision was prompted entirely by considerations of flight to safety and had nothing to do with morals. If I had to make a choice, purely based on morals, I would, on balance, take the same option I took. But it is a stern reminder of some of the blurred lines of morality in deciding about these matters.

Seeing the chaos that prevailed in Russia then, it was also evident that an economy's success depends on many more things than good economic policy. Sociology and politics matter, as do the values and beliefs that people have and the social norms that are shared by the people. Chapter 9 is a short introduction to this important subject in the context of India, its brevity a reflection of my inadequacy rather than the relative unimportance of the subject.

9 The Social and Organizational Foundations of Economic Development

A Critical Flaw

In searching for factors that lead to economic development, policymakers focus on economic policy—having the right monetary targets, keeping the fiscal deficit under control, setting trade tariffs right, having an effective regulatory system for banks, and so on. This is only to be expected. However, the presumption that that is all there is to development is deeply flawed. Economic development depends critically on the presence of appropriate social norms, mindsets, and institutions. These social and psychological conditions are often fundamental in the sense that if they are not in place, standard economic policies are likely to have little traction. Once the facilitating norms are in place, they begin to play a relatively dormant role and, hence, it is easy to forget about their critical importance. In rich and industrialized countries, by definition, the "right" norms are in place; and since much of economic theory has been developed in industrialized nations, there has been a tendency to relegate social norms to the background. While this is relatively inconsequential for rich nations, for developing countries trying to grow and achieve a higher standard of living, to ignore these social and institutional drivers can be ruinous. This is why many conventional policy prescriptions given to developing economies, which emanate from industrialized nations, such as the Washington Consensus, had little positive impact and often actually backfired.

It is, however, one thing to recognize a shortcoming and another to rectify it. While there is enough evidence about the importance of noneconomic drivers of economic development, our understanding of how exactly they work, how we can change these sociopolitical variables, is still rudimentary. Yet, thanks to research, initially in new institutional economics and more recently in behavioral and social economics, there is a literature, small but growing steadily, that can give us some guidance on policy.[1] It has to be admitted that it is a bit of an indictment of mainstream economics that economists needed large amounts of laboratory experiments and randomized trials to recognize that human beings are not always rational. But, given that that is now sunk cost, we should put it to use. The most exciting venture, here on, is not the cataloguing of human irrationalities but the use of analytic thinking to draw out the implications of systematic human irrationalities for the functioning of economies and the construction of better policies.

The relatively little space devoted to this topic in this book must not be construed as signaling its insignificance. I have written on the importance of social norms and culture in economic theory and in everyday Indian life elsewhere (Basu 2000, 2011a, chapter 6). Cultural norms permeate all aspects of life and mostly go unnoticed by those who live by them. However, an understanding of such "local knowledge" is important for successful business, policy, and the avoidance of grief in everyday life. I still remember gratefully the tip Sanjay Subrahmanyam, historian and one-time economics student of mine, had given me in my early days in Delhi, when I used to commute to work by public transport. In Delhi buses when someone says "I am requesting you," that indicates the last effort on the part of that person to resolve differences in words, before resorting to physical force.

The recent initiative I have been closely associated with at the World Bank to bring these neighboring disciplines—especially sociology, psychology, and anthropology—to bear on questions of development policy (World Bank 2014b) is intended to draw attention to the important and neglected drivers of economic development. The subject is in its nascency and the knowledge that we have for concrete policy action is still limited, even though the potential is large. What I hope to do in this chapter is to set the ball rolling in the context of Indian policymaking, with a few pointed examples, and broad indications of directions that we have to pursue in the future.

Guarding the Jewelry and Stealing in the Bazaar

A fundamental mistake that political leaders and early policymakers committed in India was to design delivery systems for various subsidies intended for the poor assuming that the agents meant to deliver the subsidies were robotic creatures who would do as asked. Thus it was taken for granted that ration shop owners, who are supposed to deliver the subsidized food grains they receive from the Food Corporation of India to households below the poverty line at specified below-market prices, would do so like preprogrammed robots. That these agents are also human and might try to make a profit where opportunity knocks was overlooked. This has led to massive leakages in the distribution of subsidies. These agents turned out to be neither robots nor saints. They realized that selling off some of this food on the open market and turning the poor away on the pretext that they had not received the food supplies from government or giving them grain adulterated with stone chips was not such a bad idea from their own point of view. As we saw in chapter 6, large quantities of the food grain meant for the poor were siphoned off and sold on the open market for a profit.

To correct this, the economist's response is to try to design delivery systems which are fully incentive-compatible with the self-interest of all agents involved, including the ration shop owners. An incentive-compatible system is one in which each agent is asked to do what is in the agent's self-interest anyway.

While this may work well in situations where such designs are available, what I am arguing is that this approach of the economist, with little regard for society and culture, can be wrong as well and extremely costly. This is because it is possible that, in one society, in one context, agents are self-seeking, whereas in another they are programmed to be dutiful and to carry out what they are supposed to do heedless of their own financial gains. Thus it may well be the case that it is fine to rely on the ration shop owners to do their job irrespective of their self-interest in Japan but not so in India. I suspect, in fact, that this is the case. Where one uses self-interest and where one uses some social norm to guide one's behavior will vary from one society to another.

In short, culture and custom can program us to desist from profit-maximizing behavior in certain situations and to endow us with certain norms of behavior, for instance, those exhibiting altruism and regard for others.[2] Hence, it is important to understand each society's social norms and customs in designing policies successfully.

When we handle horses, we do not, typically, worry about being bitten; but we try not to stand behind a horse because it could kick us. With dogs we do not hesitate to stand behind them, but we take precaution against being bitten. This is because, while horses can bite, we know they do not; and while dogs can kick, we know they do not. In dealing with any creature successfully it is important to know what they are preprogrammed to do or not to do. Likewise, human beings have certain deeply embedded social norms and in designing policies it is important to have an understanding of these.

My mother, in her last years in Kolkata, had long-standing domestic help in the form of a cook who doubled as a driver. He was a wonderful and caring person. You could leave watches and other valuables lying around, as my mother so often did in her old age; he would not touch them and, in fact, kept guard over them. But whenever you sent him out with money to do some shopping, he would inflate the prices of what he bought and pocket the balance. My calculation was that he would easily skim off 40–60 percent of the actual cost in this manner. The reason he was such a valuable person in my mother's home was that we—my sisters, my wife, and I—knew these "normative" aspects of his personality. We seldom sent him shopping but gave him a free hand in managing the household in every other way.

If, on the one hand, we had instead behaved the way Indian policymakers did with India's food rationing system, described in chapter 6, and assumed that he would do what he was supposed to do with robotic precision, we would have given him tasks (like shopping) where he would fleece us. If, on the other hand, we acted like the mainstream economist and assumed that he would make money wherever he saw an opportunity, we would spend a lot in setting up expensive vigilance systems and keeping watches and other valuables locked up.

What I am arguing is that this same applies to the world of policymaking. We need to do careful mechanism design but with a difference, by keeping in mind the social norms and customs of the people we are dealing with. We could then operate the system much more efficiently. This is what good management is all about. Good managers get to know who can be trusted with what and apportion work accordingly. Yet in the crafting and execution of development policy, this approach is seldom used.

Utilizing Norms and Modifying Norms

Once we recognize the existence of noneconomic drivers of economic development, two new avenues of action open up. To understand these, it is useful to step back for a moment. Psychologists have long recognized that human beings face so many choices in life that it is not feasible for them to deliberate and exert thought before every choice. Kahneman (2011) notes how when people are given a four-digit number and asked what number they would get if they added 3 to each digit, their pupils expand by 50 percent and heartbeat increases by seven beats per minute. Examples like this explain why on many matters people think "automatically" and desist from "analytic" thinking. Rubinstein (2014) refers to these, more aptly, as "instinctive" behavior and "contemplative" behavior.[3]

What the discussion in the previous section alerts us to is that to run an economy effectively, we need a sense of where the people of that economy choose instinctively and where they choose contemplatively. This can then be used to design programs and policies more effectively. In Japan, we may be able to distribute subsidized food to the poor by the government handing it over to thousands of shops and asking the shop owners to give it to the poor at below-market price, because the Japanese, it is believed, carry out such instructions automatically. To try the same in India may be folly because whether to give the food to the poor as instructed or sell it off at the higher market price usually falls within the domain of analytic choice here, and on contemplation shopkeepers discover they can do better by violating the government's instruction. Hence, if this system is followed in India, you will have to set up a system of spot checks on the shops and provision for serious punishment if they are found violating the government's rules. However, even then you would have to worry about the supervisors sent to do the spot checks and to fine erring shopkeepers; they may strike side deals. Alas for societies with too many rational people!

However, *utilizing* our knowledge of people's norms is not the only way to go. Norms can be changed. Our behavior norms are shaped by our history, recent experience, and also as an equilibrium response to how others behave. There is evidence that many human behaviors that we take to be built into or inherent in societies change and at times do so quite dramatically. Consider the behavior norm of punctuality. We know that this norm varies across societies. The Japanese are very punctual, Americans are quite punctual, and Brazilians are—to use politically correct language—not too fussy about time. An interesting study by Levine, West, and Reis (1980, 542) found that one reason Brazilians are less punctual is that "public clocks and personal watches [are] less accurate in Brazil than in the United States."

When I was doing research on punctuality with Jorgen Weibull (Basu and Weibull 2003), I looked for evidence whether in India, like in Brazil, the time shown on watches varied from one person's wrist to another's. I could not find any *data*, but, during a visit to Delhi at that time, a man strode up to me at the airport and asked for the time using a sentence which is common in India: "Excuse me sir, what is the time by your watch?" The implicit recognition of time's watch-dependence built into the construction of that question made me realize I did not need data.

This research convinced me that norms typically do not reflect inherent differences between societies but a response to one's environment, and the behavior of others.

One piece of evidence of the early battles with punctuality came from the ubiquitous folders with important and unimportant documents that shuttled back and forth between offices in the Ministry of Finance. To help build the linguistic skills of bureaucrats the space in the inside covers of the folders was crammed with a helpful list of more than eighty widely used phrases in bureaucratese, in Hindi, and, next to it, in English. It was interesting how many of these pertained to time and punctuality. Here are some examples: "Expedite action" (*sheeghra karwai karen*); "Delay cannot be waived" (*vilambh ko maaf nahi kiya ja sakta*); continuing in the same vein, "Delay should be avoided"; "Delay may be explained"; "Pending case to be disposed of early"; "Reply today/early/immediately without delay"; and, most alarmingly, "On return from tour/leave."

The recognition that social norms and culture play an important role in economic outcomes goes back to the works of at least Polanyi (1944) and Granovetter (1985). This is at times viewed as a politically retrograde idea that implies that norms are hardwired into societies. There is, however, plenty of reason to reject such a suggestion. There is enough evidence from around the world that norms are malleable. My impression during my years in the Indian government was that India's punctuality norms were changing, with distinctly greater punctuality than in the olden days.

There are many examples of the malleability of norms from around the world. Let me present a striking example of the lack of punctuality in a certain country by suppressing the name of the country in the quotation that follows, so that the reader can try to guess which country this refers to:

In his published memoir, Kattendyke (an European visiting "this country") cited a series of events to illustrate the frustrating slowness of "the nation." For example,

the supplies necessary to make repairs, which he had specifically ordered to be delivered at high tide, did not arrive on time; one worker showed up just once and never
returned. . . . Kattendyke's frustrations were in fact shared by most of the foreign
engineers in the country. . . . They often found themselves vexed by the work habits
of the "locals," and the main reason for their vexation was the apparent lack of any
sense of time. To these foreigners, the "locals" worked with an apparent indifference
to the clock. (Hashimoto 2008)

The country that this passage is referring to is Japan at the start of the
twentieth century. It shows that barely a hundred years ago, Japan was as
tardy as the tardiest nations today. The fact that Japan today is arguably the
most punctual society shows that norms that appear built into the DNA of
a society are not so. Likewise, we can find descriptions of Koreans by American and British visitors sixty years ago recounting how lazy and lacking in
industry the Koreans are. In 1950, the British Charge d'Affaire, Alec Adams,
noted this lack of hard work, and went on to opine that he found it "hard
to believe that they will ever be able to successfully govern themselves"
(Clifford 1994, 29). That Koreans are among the hardest working people
today and have built their nation into a fully industrialized, rich nation is
again testimony to the fact that norms change.

Once it is recognized that norms can be changed, it is immediately obvious that there is a huge agenda ahead of any economy, especially emerging
ones, to try to build norms that promote development and help create a
better society. This means that when we distribute subsidized food or health
benefits via bureaucrats and government workers, we will, in the short run,
have to try to create a system which does not provide scope for cheating
on the part of these bureaucrats. But in the long run we can try to change
the norms whereby government workers do not even try to cheat and take
advantage of the system. Not cheating should be part of their instinctive
behavior. The scope for what the government can do would open up hugely
once these behavior patterns become instinctive in the people.

Teacher Absenteeism in India

One serious problem that has dogged India is that of teacher absenteeism
in government schools. Anecdotal evidence on this had been coming in
for a long time. But it often got brushed aside, with casual comments such
asthis happens in all countries, the so-called evidence is loose talk, it is

just a campaign to give teachers a bad name. Then there was a controlled study in early 2000, when a team of researchers from the World Bank and Harvard sent inspectors, with no prior notice, to a random selection of nearly three thousand government-run primary schools (Kremer et al. 2005; Chaudhury et al. 2006).

The findings were devastating. Twenty-five percent of the teachers were found to be missing from the school premises at the time of inspection. And among those who were in school, 40 percent were not teaching. Among the six developing nations for which similar data were collected, only Uganda had a slightly higher rate of absenteeism, 27 percent. Performance was much better than India and Uganda in the other countries: Peru, Ecuador, and Bangladesh had absenteeism rates of, respectively, 11 percent, 14 percent, and 16 percent. There are other studies that confirm that Indian teacher absenteeism in government-run schools is reaching epidemic proportions and this problem is representative of much that is wrong with the bureaucracy (PROBE 1999; Rana, Rafique, and Sengupta 2002).[4] It is not surprising that while in terms of higher education India compares well even with industrialized nations many times richer, in terms of basic literacy India is at the bottom end of global charts, trailing behind several much poorer sub-Saharan African nations.

What should be done about this? Economists have typically been concerned with creating the right incentives. This at one level is right. We have to institute a system of penalty for being absent, including dismissal from service for repeat violators, and maybe institute some reward for being present and doing the work one is supposed to do with diligence. But this approach taken by economists is at times too mechanistic; and, used on its own, is unlikely to resolve the problem. To have this kind of a system of punishment, the government has to appoint inspectors to check on the teachers and issue certificates of absenteeism and diligence. But who will make sure that the inspectors are doing *their* job? One way to ensure this is to create a cadre of super inspectors. But the same question arises in their case. This simply means that while we have to pay attention to narrow incentives—punishments and rewards—we have to be aware that there are other drivers of human behavior. Behavioral norms often exhibit multiple equilibria. If everybody behaves in a certain way, each person feels it is fine to behave in that way and the behavior settles into an equilibrium (Bowles, Durlauf, and Hoff 2006; Gintis 2009; Ferguson 2013).

One can see a hint of this in the fact that there is great variation in teacher absenteeism across Indian states. Maharashtra had the lowest absenteeism with a rate of 15 percent, Kerala 22 percent, West Bengal 25 percent, Punjab 34 percent, Bihar 37 percent, and Jharkhand was in the lead with 42 percent (Kremer et al. 2005). Given that India's pay and punishment norms are virtually the same across the nation, these widely varied rates clearly suggest that behavior has noneconomic drivers.[5] At the Delhi School of Economics where I taught for a decade and a half, there was no system of monitoring teachers and rewarding and punishing them for failure to take classes. But absenteeism was negligible. The standards of diligence were comparable to what one would find in the United States and other industrialized nations.

There are many reasons for the existence of multiple equilibria, ranging from ones rooted in competitive market-based explanations[6] to ones founded in more sociological explanations such as social stigma[7] or one's own social norms.[8] Different methods have to be used to deflect an economy to a better equilibrium. In some cases the simple use of the law can do it, as we saw in chapter 8. It is also possible to think of ordinary citizens or private groups deliberately shifting their own behavior to a superior self-fulfilling one. Avinash Dixit (2015) has recently proposed an ingenious scheme for controlling corruption, which has nothing to do with governments. The idea is that in a nation where there is a lot of corruption, one group hurt by this is the business community. It may not be in the interest of each private business to be noncorrupt but by giving into their individual interests the businesses are all collectively worse off. What Dixit shows is that it is possible to create rules of boycotting corrupt firms by other firms that enables them all to shift to a corruption-free equilibrium, that is, a situation where it is no longer in a firm's self-interest to be corrupt.

If this sounds like an abstract, academic idea, consider that the Jewish Maghribi traders in the eleventh century used self-enforcing institutions to ensure that the group's reputation for contract fulfillment would be upheld (Greif 1993). Likewise, in her biography of the Indian business doyen G. D. Birla, Kudaisya (1993, 37–38) recounts how individual acts of corruption among the Marwari traders of Kolkata caused the elders of the Marwari community to worry that such acts were "endangering the interests of the entire community." The Marwari Association decided to take it upon itself to punish recalcitrant members of its community. Later, following some food adulteration scandals, the association raided the godowns of its members and made sure that those found guilty were fined and "ex-communicated from the community." What I am stressing is that instead of leaving the task of corruption control invariably to government, it is possible for business leaders and chambers of commerce to take some of the initiative upon themselves. The collective benefit for society, including the business leaders, can be large.

There are other illustrations of equilibrium shifting from diverse fields such as child labor and restrictions on hours of work. Some of these phenomena that we want to either usher out or in may be amenable to well-crafted laws and appropriate penalties and rewards; and this can be so effective in shifting to the superior equilibrium that after a while the law will be merely something on paper with little occasion to actually use it.

In other cases, we could use social persuasion; the rise of behavioral economics has given us a plethora of tools for this. But in all this an important part is played by how the leaders behave, what the policymakers who confer behind doors in various ministries on Raisina Hill do, and what the political leaders and the bureaucrats at the helm say and how they conduct themselves.

The Sociology of Bureaucracy

India has one of the most talented and most obstructive bureaucracies in the world. Small enterprises going about the daily chore of business; ordinary citizens trying to pay their taxes, their electricity dues, and get their designated food rations; tourists trying to acquire a visa to come to India—all complain about the slow and almost instinctively unhelpful bureaucracy that they have to navigate. In terms of the World Bank's *Doing Business* rankings India currently ranks at 142 of 189 countries. Since *Doing Business* tries to capture the ease with which a small business can function—start a business, get electrical service, export goods, seek damages from someone reneging on a contract—it is not surprising that India ranks so low in the *Doing Business* ranking.

If the nation is to grow at rates it is innately capable of, it is important to have administrative reforms to change this individually talented bureaucracy into a collective-supportive force instead of the obstructive body it currently is.[9] To do this, it is important to understand that administrative reform is not just a mechanical exercise. One needs to understand the sociology and psychology of organizations, drawing on some of the lessons of institutional and behavioral economics that this chapter was concerned with.

Why does the problem of obstructive bureaucracy persist in India? Having joined government as a senior member from a career totally outside it, I got an insight into this that the more jaded may not have. Once you are part of the coterie at the top—leading policymakers and politicians who confer behind closed doors in Delhi, corporate honchos who have broken into this top circuit and a few sundry others—you do not face any of the hassles that India's poor administration gives rise to. During my nearly three years in the North Block, when I needed to renew my driving license, I could do it as fast as in the most efficient nations. My assistant would phone the relevant authority and get it done effortlessly. At year's end paying taxes were no hassle either, since some of the people I worked with in the Ministry of Finance had contacts in the department dealing with taxes. Renewing a passport was a shoo-in. For India's top bureaucrats it is easy to begin to think that they live in Singapore, in terms of efficiency. For this small carved-out segment of society, India does seem like a remarkably efficient country. Since much of India's bureaucracy—from those who run the domestic administrative service, through the police administration, to the foreign service—is a life-long service, for the coterie at the top whose members have over many years steadily reached this gated lifestyle, the memory of what it feels like to be on the outside is faint. For them it is psychologically very difficult to appreciate what life is like outside.

Since I entered the gated community by practically jumping over the wall, the memory of what life in terms of all interaction with government was outside the wall was fresh. I did not have to read papers and scour through data to be aware of this but simply to recall of what my interaction with government was like before my leap.

During my time in government I would get an occasional glimpse of how living in the ivory tower distorted thinking. I remember a heated discussion in June 2010 when we were discussing deregulating petrol and diesel prices. The policymakers spoke angrily about how the rich corporate honchos freely drove around their large sports utility vehicles using subsidized petrol and diesel which the government provided. They argued, rightly, that allowing these prices to rise would make these users of gasoline more cost-conscious and they would use their cars a little less and effect some essential economy for the nation. What did not seem to strike any of them is that all of us in that room got our petrol and diesel not at a subsidized price but effectively for free, since having a car with a full gas tank and driver was part of our senior government life. Hence, if we truly wanted demand to be curtailed during times of gasoline shortage, along with letting prices rise, we needed to take away this very expensive perquisite which is a part of life in government bureaucracy.

It is critical for India to disrupt the comforts of the elite if the nation is to do well and achieve inclusive growth. To do this, we have to act both on changing the rules of governance and on mindsets. For changing the rules of governance, the nation needs a major administrative reform. Much of India's rules of administration are inherited from Britain. India's problem is that it has held on to those rules more steadfastly than Britain and other Commonwealth nations. India has a similar problem with higher education, as we shall see in chapter 10. So a commission needs to be set up, which will study countries such as Britain, Australia, and Singapore, which have a similar heritage but have managed to modernize, and recommend how the nation can make it easier for the small firms to run their businesses and ordinary individuals to live their lives.

A study of this kind will invariably take us into some details of democratic governance systems. Democratic decision making in government can take two forms that are polar opposites. One, which may be called an "overlapping organization," tries to let everyone in government participate in every decision. The other, which I shall call "partitioned organization," makes sure that every person has a say over a certain domain, which has negligible overlap with others' domains. Practical considerations make these two extremes impossible in reality. All democratic decision-making systems have to lie somewhere between the two extremes. My contention is that India has veered too close to the former. Every file needs clearance by too many people, which slows down the process greatly. Of course, the bureaucrat has a source of comfort in this system because when a decision goes wrong, it is difficult to apportion blame. However, India needs to shift toward a system of decision making that is closer to partitioned organization.

This has a direct lesson, in case a commission for administrative reform along the lines I have suggested is actually set up. Do not have a large body of people constituting the commission all of whom have to sign up on the final document. This will ensure the production of an anodyne report with very few serious suggestions, as happened with some previous administrative reform commissions. In other words, the administrative reforms commission itself should not be an example of an overlapping organization.

But, in parallel with this, we also need to work on mindsets. Bureaucrats have to be made to realize that their aim is to aid people's lives and facilitate their functioning, instead of trying to find the culprit and starting from the presumption that everyone is one.[10] Such a refocusing of the target of work can change daily functioning because then we will judge our work satisfaction by this new objective. Some of these changes in mindsets do occur gradually and from within. But that often takes too long. This should be a primary responsibility of the political leaders holding office. Since their lives at the top are often curtailed by the five-year election cycle, they have less of a vested interest in the system and so may have a greater incentive to set the ball rolling for change.

India's economy now has enough strength that it will continue to develop anyway. The hustle and bustle of India today hopefully is the sound of its engine revving up. But, if its administrative system can be reformed, this could give the nation a burst of life and growth not seen in its recent history. While there are many reforms and policy initiatives that are important and have been discussed elsewhere in this book, an efficient bureaucracy can play a pivotal role for all of them.

10   The Road Ahead

India's Prospects

The Indian economy today stands at the crossroads. From here on, it could trundle along the way it has done, reasonably well in recent times, or it could take off. What makes the current juncture exciting is that the prospect of a major takeoff is real in a way it has never been before. It is a confluence of many factors that has given rise to this.

First, the global economic landscape has shifted dramatically in ways that create advantages for all developing economies. Cheap and efficient labor can no longer be kept out of the global labor market through the use of unfair trade and immigration practices, aided by the lack of appropriate technology. The steady march of technology, particularly the ability to transmit work over long distances at negligible cost, has altered the landscape altogether; and there are indications that this march is going to continue for a while. This has created opportunities not just for India but also for any emerging economy that is able to keep its own house in order by providing basic infrastructure, law and order, an independent judicial system to mediate in disputes, and an enabling milieu for enterprise and investment.

Second, and this is more specific to India, India invested early in what for most emerging economies turns out to be the biggest stumbling block in the long run. I am referring here to the choice made by the founding fathers to create an open, secular, and democratic society. Whether this was the right objective to strive for so soon after the nation's birth will continue to be debated till the cows go out again in the morning. But, having done it, this is now an advantage. The 2014 national election is a good example. The debates were rancorous and loud, and were conducted via every possible media, but the election, stretched out over a month, happened smoothly and the results were accepted by the winners and the losers alike as representing the verdict of the electorate. This is a remarkable achievement for a developing country that only recently graduated from being classified as a low-income economy to a lower middle-income one. India shifted from "low income" to "lower middle-income" in the World Bank's classification table between 2008 and 2009.

Closely related to this is a foreign policy matter that is likely to be of advantage to India. I am referring here to the natural alignment of interests between the United States and India, founded on the commitment of both nations to secularism and democracy.[1] The relations between these two countries over the last sixty or seventy years have been complicated. In the early 1950s, there was an opportunity of alignment, when a newly independent India was unsure and trying to establish its identity in the international space. There was a lot of genuine interest in America to reach out, and there were some remarkable early U.S. ambassadors, notable among them Chester Bowles and John Kenneth Galbraith,[2] who were progressive thinkers and played a vital role. This is reflected in some early writings, such as Eleanor Roosevelt's book based on her travels through India in 1952. She talks about the ambassador and his wife's effort to build a bridge between the two nations: "The impact of the Bowleses on India was made largely by the warmth they brought to diplomacy. Their life and their ways were not those of the average diplomatic couple. They insisted on moving into a smaller house, though there were those who feared American prestige might suffer thereby. They sent their children to an Indian public school instead of to the school usually attended by diplomats' children. And, what is more, the children were not driven to school; they bicycled" (Roosevelt 1953, 115–116).[3]

Nevertheless, the relationship between the two countries did not pan out according to script. While there were many who were genuine in their effort to build strong bonds between the two large democracies, it must not be forgotten that the early 1950s were also the time of McCarthyism in the United States, when any but a narrow mainstream opinion was quickly labeled as "un-American" and dissenters persecuted. This was no doubt reflected in foreign policy as well. India's independence of ideas, so clearly articulated by the nation's founding fathers, notably Nehru, which would later be codified into the nonaligned movement, was difficult for the United States of those times to accept.

It is often remarked that India does not have a foreign policy. Whether or not this is true for contemporary India, it was certainly not the case in the early years of the nation. Nehru's policy of nonalignment stemmed not from realpolitik but a moral commitment; but it nevertheless had enormous aspiration. As Rao (2014, 14) has recently observed, "[Nehru] was ambitious about foreign policy, and India's role in the world, navigating between two opposing blocs, confronting issues of war and peace, and leaving an indelible global imprint in a way India has not been able to do, since." One sees elements of a similar constructive cooperation and what one may call "politics of decency" in President Obama's foreign policy. This is often met with criticism from those who equate foreign policy with power and subjugation, even though it is arguable that, in the long run, a value-based foreign policy leaves a more indelible mark on the world.

Interestingly, Eleanor Roosevelt had an instinctive grasp of this, and she summed it up well in writing about the early "distrust" between the two nations: "We can all understand, I think, that no one likes the rich uncle who flaunts his wealth in the face of your poverty; who will help you perhaps—but on his own terms; who will send you to college, if you like—but only to the college of his choice" (Roosevelt 1953, 114). These inherently contradictory propensities, to encourage democracy in nations and to make choices for them, became a stumbling block. This also explains why, contrary to the rhetoric, some nations led by military rulers and not too respectful of their own democracies found it easier to build bridges with the United States of that period. This, as already remarked in chapter 2, peaked in 1971, during Bangladesh's war of Independence, when Nixon's government sided openly with Pakistan's military regime of Yahya Khan, trying to crush the independence movement.

This has now undergone a sea change, thanks to the changing global topography of power. By the early years of this century, it was evident that the hope some in the United States may have had, following the fall of the Soviet Union, that it would be a uni-polar world, was unrealistic. If that wasn't going to happen, it was important to build bridges with nations committed to democracy and secularism.[4] With the rise of global terrorism, this was even more important. India was the natural candidate for this. And the fact of Indian professionals having moved to the United States in large numbers and becoming prominent in the intellectual and political life of the nation bolstered this. For India, still a lower middle-income nation struggling to grow economically, this is a valuable link. This coming together of mutual interests between the United States and India allows for a more balanced relation than was ever possible in the past and this creates new opportunities for India's economy.[5]

Third, the Indian economy, after three or four decades of near economic stagnation since Independence, instituted major reforms in the early 1990s that resulted in a rise in growth from 1994. But, as we saw in chapter 2, India's elevated growth is still in its early stages and in fact the engines spluttered a little over the last two or three years. If the nation is to build on the economy's superior performance from the mid-1990s, consolidate, and sustain its growth, there is a lot that needs to be done.

Finally, the nation recently witnessed a dramatic change of leadership. Between the start of my writing this book and finishing it, India has seen a new government with a different political mandate win an election and take power. This makes for new risks, and also new opportunities. If for no other reason, the citizenry is often willing to accept policy shifts that come with a new government, which it would not accept from the incumbent. Hence, any new government, whether or not it has a different mandate, brings with it the scope for change which the old government would not have. In addition, this is a government that has come to office with an explicit political commitment to growth and efficiency.

All these factors militate to open up new possibilities for India. My close association with policymaking in India and my reading of the evidence lead me to believe that India has the ability to take the road toward economic takeoff. More specifically, it is entirely within the realm of possibility for the country to join the ranks of industrialized nations (defined by an income of at least $10,000 per annum, per capita) by 2040, and bring chronic poverty to an end well before that. This will entail maintaining a GDP growth rate of approximately 8.5 percent per annum, combined with intelligently designed policies directed at helping and creating new opportunities for the poor.

This is an exciting project and not from a narrow nationalist point of view. Reaching out to any mass of citizens in any country who have endured diminished lives because of poverty would be a worthwhile venture. Through the configuration of global forces, hard work, a few visionary political leaders, and some luck, India stands poised to deliver on this; and it will be sad if the nation does not seize the moment.

Determination is necessary for this but determination alone will not do it. Economic policymaking at the helm of a nation or a multilateral organization or even a local government is one of the most challenging tasks. One needs a lot of professional input into the design of a nation's takeoff. A policy that looks good on the face of things can have a negative macroeconomic fallout in seemingly unconnected parts of the economy, for instance, by triggering off an economy-wide price increase. Modern economic theory gives us a handle on this and we need to utilize it for successful policymaking. To counter this by saying that in distant history nations did rise with little knowledge of economics and statistics is like claiming modern medicine is not necessary because historically many people lived through illnesses and epidemics and survived without modern medicine.

There is no single source for the art of economic policymaking. It is important to use the guidance of statistics and data—in short, knowledge of past regularities;[6] there is need to rely on good description, of the kind that one often encounters in anthropology;[7] but one also has to use economic theory and deductive reasoning. This closing chapter may be viewed as a pamphlet of instructions, which, while not a sure-fire toolkit, for there is no such thing in economics, lays out some of the rules of economic policymaking at the helm and as such should be of use to the Indian policymaker as well as to students of development economics. I present this in a somewhat unusual way, first, with a concrete example—an intervention that the Indian government can initiate almost immediately, and which can yield huge benefits to the nation; and second, by laying down some general principles of successful policy intervention at the highest level of government. The next two sections are devoted to, respectively, these two tasks.

The intervention that I am going to describe pertains to education and shows how India has the potential to be a global hub for higher education and research. There are many other examples one can give of useful policy initiatives—from the conduct of fiscal and monetary policy to reforming labor laws, and the modalities of distributing benefits to the poor. Some of these ideas have already been discussed in the book. But there is no such thing as a complete compendium of desirable policies. No one has compiled such an exhaustive list. Moreover, times and contexts change, the political mood of the nation varies, creating new opportunities for policies that may have been impossible earlier and closing avenues that may have been open earlier. Hence, in the end, all one can hope for is that those at the helm will have the wisdom and astuteness to use some basic principles to navigate the waters. Through history, enormous blunders have been made, unleashing famines and deaths and hyperinflations because of policy mistakes. There is no foolproof method for preventing these but one can arm oneself with some basic principles that can minimize these risks.

Striking Gold with Higher Education

There have been sectors in India which took off not because of major policy interventions and expenditures by government but simply because some constraints were removed, and by adjusting some nuts and bolts of the economy. A good example of this is India's services sector and, in particular, the sector dealing with information technology (IT), which took off in the early 1990s and was a major driver behind India's overall excellent growth performance since the mid-1990s. As one of the founders of Infosys, and India's IT success, Narayana Murthy (2000) pointed out, this sector did not take off because of fiscal infusions or large government help but simply because the reforms of the 1990s removed artificial hurdles and facilitated business and enterprise. In addition, this was a sector that was unregulated and so did not, for the most part, come under the choking grip of the Indian government's bureaucracy.

A similar line is taken by Ratan Tata (2011), one of India's celebrated business leaders, in an essay on the Tata Group's extraordinary business history dating back to the mid-nineteenth century. He laments how the Group and, more generally, Indian manufacturing struggled under an overbearing regulatory system in the early decades after independence; this began easing twenty-five years ago when the liberalization policy began. He remarks how, if the right polices are in place, India can "leverage the country's scientific and engineering talent pool to create value" and benefit from globalization.

In this section I discuss and present a plan for a sector of the Indian economy that is raring to go and can take off with no long-run fiscal burden on the state, no major macropolicy shift, simply by making some virtually costless reforms to the regulatory system, adjusting some nuts and bolts, and having government give this sector an initial nudge.[8] This is the higher education sector. India has natural advantages that can enable it to quickly become a global hub for higher education, that is, as a center where students from around the world come to get quality education. The profit from this sector can be used to give a boost to education and research for the residents of India. This building up of human capital can, in turn, be a major catalyst for growth.

The two most important natural advantages are India's widespread use of the English language and its longstanding tradition of higher education and research. English is the global lingua franca; a tradition of language takes longer to pick up than technology and engineering skills and this tradition India has for reasons of history. While India's performance in terms of basic education and literacy has been woeful, it has a long history of excellence in higher education. India has a strange education system, where only a few receive an education, but those who do then get a good education all the way to the top. The first surviving[9] universities in India were founded in the mid-nineteenth century by the British. The Indian Association of the Cultivation of Science (IACS) was set up in Calcutta in 1876, with the aim of boosting pure-science research and teaching. It was in the laboratory of the IACS that Sir C. V. Raman discovered the "Raman effect." Soon after independence, the government started the Indian Institutes of Technology and, a little later, the Indian Institutes of Management. Unfortunately, India may now be beginning to lose the lead it had among emerging economies in higher education till as recently as two or three decades ago (Chatterjea and Moulik 2011). But these traditions have enough roots for us to be able to revive and build on them.

Through history, we have examples of how societies that nurtured higher education, research, and creativity also flourished in other ways. This was true for Greece three or four hundred years before the Christian era, for Italy in the fifteenth and sixteenth centuries, for Britain in the nineteenth and early twentieth centuries, and United States in our times. It would clearly be folly for India to ignore this sector in the light of this and India's innate advantages therein.

I got especially interested in this topic in 2008 when I was invited by the Government of India to serve on the Committee to Advise on Renovation and Rejuvenation of Higher Education, which produced its report in July 2009, popularly known as the "Yashpal Committee Report." Given my interest in education, I joined this committee with enthusiasm but it turned out to be a most disappointing experience. The committee went through the bureaucratic motions of meeting periodically and regurgitating old ideas. To my dismay, I discovered that a draft was circulated, which was described as approved by the entire committee, whereas I had never seen that draft and, when I did see it, I found much to disagree with. Eventually, the report came out with my dissenting note appended. And some of the ideas in that note have made their way into the policy recommendation for higher education that I am about to make.

In analyzing higher education, let us first try to understand why India is beginning to lose out, despite the natural advantages and the early lead it had. The reason India is beginning to trail in higher education and research is not that it is doing anything differently but because it is not doing anything differently. The nation has stuck diligently to the same model which once worked well but is increasingly unviable. The tendency to have higher education serviced largely by the state and to have it controlled centrally, such as by the University Grants Commission (UGC) and also the All India Council of Technical Education (AICTE), has had a deleterious effect on this sector.

India has over six hundred universities.[10] To try to control and finance so many universities so that they all have the same standard is to ensure they all have a poor standard. It felt it had to control the quality of universities tightly, and this has had a stifling effect on universities. To have universities of excellence, we have to create space for universities of nonexcellence. This would not be a disaster, given that the teaching needs of a nation as large as India are huge. For a large number of students, the need is for the acquisition of some basic skills. They do not need to be exposed to cutting-edge research and ideas. That can be left to the charge of a few universities, institutes, and colleges. The first step in getting to this is to allow different universities the freedom to set different standards, in terms of fees students pay, salaries professors get, and curricula. A good example of this is higher education and the university system in the United States. Of all the achievements of the United States, higher education and research probably stand out most. And there is hardly any centralized regulation of standards in the United States. Not surprisingly, the United States has both some of the greatest universities and some very mediocre ones.

One can find another example of this within India itself. Unlike the university system where the government felt obligated to uphold standards, there was no such pressure to uphold the standards of films being made in India. The consequence is for all to see. Bollywood is one of the world's big success stories. Some great films are made in Bollywood; and, in keeping with the preceding argument, a large number of very mediocre films also are made there.

To transform India's higher education sector, the first step is to reorganize the UGC. The UGC and AICTE have, over time, become like a licensing authority, creating barriers to entry and controlling what is taught, what is paid, what is charged, going into a level of minutiae which is a waste of time. At times we forget that the market with all its faults does perform certain functions reasonably well. Poorly performing colleges and educational institutes, if information about their performance is made easily available, will become low-tuition-fee teaching shops or get competed out of existence by the pressures of the market. Hence, the UGC should be reorganized to move away from being a licensing authority to an organization that uses a minimal regulatory structure for universities and colleges but, more importantly, makes available information about how the universities and colleges are doing in terms of the quality of education and the placement of students and maybe even provide a rating of all universities. Ratings, well done, can be a powerful instrument, helping potential students decide where to apply and whether the large fee of a certain college is worth paying. As such, ratings enable markets to function effectively.

Second, it is not possible even for a rich nation, let alone a developing economy, to finance over six hundred universities equitably and expect them all to be good. This means that we have to reconcile ourselves to the fact that there will be different kinds of universities, with different kinds of finance. This takes us to the touchy topic of salaries and research support. The old system of having a flat pay scale for all teachers, professors, and researchers in all universities across the length and breadth of the nation was once a good idea (and maybe in some distant future the world will return to this).[11] But it is not viable now. Several nations are switching over to a system of using star salaries and research budgets for especially talented researchers and teachers. This began in the United States. Many nations, including the UK and China, have gone in for a similar strategy. Given this fact of the world (about which India can do little), if India wants to have an attractive university system, it has to go for this model of salary variability.[12] One standard counterargument to this, which I often heard during my work on India's higher education committee in 2008 and 2009, was to point to the many talented professors and teachers currently working in Indian universities as proof that it is not salaries that attract people to this career. This is the classic biased-sample mistake—trying to deduce why people choose to be professors by drawing a sample entirely from those who chose to be professors. Evidently, those who chose to be professors under the current system do not place a big weight on financial incentives. But this does not negate the possibility that there are talented people who choose not to be professors because of the flat salary system.

Third, India needs to allow the private sector to come into the higher education sector easily and to open the door for collaboration with foreign universities. There need to be transparent rules and an enabling atmosphere for the private sector to invest in education. A concomitant of this is to create room for charging higher fees from students. For the sake of their reputation, private universities will of their own accord give scholarships to good and poor students, in order to be able to raise their reputations and charge more from less good but rich students (Basu 1989). It is true that the private sector will typically come into areas which are commercially viable, such as business and finance education, engineering, medicine and some areas of economics. There is nothing wrong with this. In fact, this will allow government to allocate its precious money to disciplines that are important for society in the long run but may not be commercially viable, such as mathematics, physics, economic theory, philosophy, and literature, and also to support poor students with grants and scholarships. Freed of a large part of the burden it currently bears quite unnecessarily it will be able to do the other tasks more effectively.

One major positive outcome is, if these changes are accompanied by a few additional reforms, India can become a global hub for education. This will bring in students and profit from around the world, which can be used to expand India's own domestic education and raise its gross enrollment ratio. This can also have the byproduct of strengthening the nation's links with the world. Indeed, this can be a game changer.

Usually, when we think of a global hub in an emerging economy, we think of students from mainly other developing countries going there to study. But that is not the model I am suggesting; that model will not in fact work. The main aim should be to attract students from rich countries. This is more by necessity than by choice. To see this it is important to recognize that the large flow of students from developing and low-income countries to industrialized countries occurs only partly for the education and, in larger measure, as a conduit to the high-paying job markets in those nations. In other words, in the minds of a majority of students from developing countries the education is merely a permit to stay on and work in that country. There is no way that India can compete on this. India is not an attractive destination for large numbers of educated and reasonably wealthy outsiders to want to come here to settle down and work. Hence, there will be no great demand for education in India for foreigners, simply as a passport to settling down in the country after the education. Hence, no matter how well India does in providing education, students of developing countries—Africa, other South Asian nations, Latin America, and parts of East Asia—are unlikely to come here in large numbers, pay high fees, and get a degree. Some will come but that cannot be the mainstay of the program.

For students from rich countries the calculations are different. They will anyway have the right to return to their own nation and other industrialized countries for work. Hence, they will want a degree from a good university, whether or not that university is located in a nation with an attractive and high-paying job market. It is this category of students that India can attract.

What I am suggesting is the idea of India as an education hub for students from around the world, from rich and poor nations. However, the dominant flow will be from rich countries because of the reasons I have stated and pure arbitrage possibilities. A college student's tuition fee in the United States is currently around $50,000 or roughly Rs. 3,000,000 a year. Given the purchasing power parity difference between the two nations, it is possible for India to offer a similar education for an annual tuition fee of $10,000. When you add to this the cost-of-living advantage, over a four-year period, it is possible for a student to save considerably more than $160,000. This is a substantial sum of money. If this market is opened up, there will be large flows of students from rich countries—and not only those in which education is private and expensive as in the United States but also nations where the state pays and may encourage students to go to India to get their education and save the exchequer money.

This arbitrage gap is so large that no government funding is needed for this. Once clear, transparent rules are written down, the private sector will have every interest in entering this sector. What has to be ensured—and for this the state is important—is that there is no misinformation used in attracting students. Private teaching institutes have been known to misinform incoming students about their faculty, job placement record, and even fees, tucking some charges under the carpet to be discovered by students once they have enrolled. Laws will be needed to control such practices but not to fix fees and salaries and create red tape that ultimately chokes the system. To facilitate accessibility to higher education, new ideas have been proposed concerning income-contingent loans (see Chatterjee et al. 2011), but these too will need some laws to be amended.

This is not all. Many a good plan is laid low for the most trivial of reasons—this is what I meant earlier in speaking about the nuts and bolts of an economy. To have these schools flourish we need to create special visa rules. No student will want to come to India to study with visas for three months, six months, or even a year, for fear that halfway through the course his or her visa may not be renewed. So there will have to be changes in visa regulations for students, giving them permission to stay three or four years at one issuance. Even common courtesy in India's visa offices around the world will be important for students applying for a visa to feel comfortable about heading to India; and on this there is scope for improvement, to put it mildly.

These look like rather minor quibbles to bring up in a book on the broad sweep of the Indian economy. But that is precisely the point. Big successes and, equally, large disasters often occur because of the failure of small things.[13]

None of the policies discussed in this section involve budgetary support from government—nothing substantial, in any case. It involves some creative interventions, changes in rules and regulations, and an enthusiastic leadership. But with these, India can unleash a sector, namely, the knowledge sector, which can, in turn, be pivotal in helping the country take off and build a vibrant economy.

The Invisible Hand, Markets, and Interventions

Policymakers at the helm of a nation need to know a lot but, even more importantly, they need to know what they do not know. The biggest policy blunders in history, such as China's Great Leap Forward in 1958, which unleashed the most severe famine in recorded human history, or the ill-conceived reparations policy that led to the German hyperinflation of 1923, occurred because leaders overestimated their knowledge and ability. The reason why knowing one's limitations is critical is that for any national economy, even the smallest ones, what the leader knows and can directly do will be severely limited. Economic leadership entails knowing one's limitations and having judgment about where one can directly act, and where one cannot and must draw on other people's expertise and knowledge and provide an enabling atmosphere so that people can provide what people need. This entails treading a fine line between intervening directly and letting markets function. Getting this right is what good governance is all about.

One of the central and powerful ideas in economics, of which any policymaker at the helm of a nation needs to have a modicum of understanding, is that of the "invisible hand." This refers to the remarkable observation of Adam Smith that the order we see in an economy, whereby the butcher, the brewer, and the baker work beyond their own immediate needs to bring meat, drinks, and bread to other people's dinner tables, does not indicate the presence of the spirit of charity, divine power, or royal edict, but relies largely on the self-interest of ordinary people going about their daily chores and the coordinating power of the market. The laws of the invisible hand of the market are like the laws of the winds and the waves. The policymaker needs to understand and use the invisible hand to guide the economy along. This is what John Stuart Mill (1867, 17) was referring to when he so elegantly spoke,[14] referring to sailors going out to the high seas: "The winds and the waves are very unfeeling. Would you advise those who go to sea to deny the wind and the waves—or to make use of them, and find the means of guarding against their dangers?"

The idea of the invisible hand cuts both ways. It means that you should not try to do everything yourself; but it does not mean that all should be left to unfettered market forces. The example of government policy in the previous section illustrates this well. There are many parts of the higher education sector of a nation in which ordinary individuals and firms can be left to operate and meet the demands. This is true, as we have seen, of the commercially viable disciplines like finance, business, and engineering. The individuals and firms may well work in their own interest but they will, nevertheless, meet the needs of society. There is good reason for the government, which is usually overstretched anyway, to design an education system where these tasks are left to the private sector and the invisible hand.

But to leave it all to the market, as some market fundamentalists propose, would be folly. Smith put forth his idea of the invisible hand of the market with caution and qualification. For a whole host of ideologues the caveats fell by the wayside and this powerful idea came to acquire the status of dogma with which to celebrate selfishness and unfettered markets, and risk government shutdowns and fiscal catastrophe. There are many needs of society which may be vital but where a commercial operation, driven by the profit motive, is not viable. To leave these to private enterprise will mean either corruption and exploitation, or leaving large amounts of demand unmet.

Where the policymaker at the helm of a nation tries to deliver directly and where he or she simply creates an enabling atmosphere and leaves it to private individuals to deliver is partly derived from the knowledge of basic economics and past evidence. Much of this book was devoted to sketching these in the context of the Indian economy. But this is also in part based on common sense and deductive reasoning. Let me give an example how flaws in policy recommendations can be spotted by using pure reason. Take trade and openness. In the light of the recent volatility faced by emerging economies in response to adjustments to monetary policy in industrialized nations, important questions have arisen about openness and the role of interventions in trade to curb current account deficits. There is a fundamentalist school that opposes virtually all curbs to openness. One argument that is given to defend this extreme ideological position is the following: There is no economy on earth that is closed and has grown rapidly; therefore, government should not put any restriction on trade and foreign capital flows.

To see that the claim is flawed one does not need to study tomes or collect data. Simple, intuitive reasoning takes us there. The claim is actually doubly flawed. First, the "therefore" has no basis. There can be many reasons why there may be no nation that is closed and has grown rapidly. This would, for instance, be true if there were no economies that were closed. If that was the reason why there were no economies that were closed *and* grew rapidly, this would say nothing about what closedness does to growth. Second, the claim overlooks the fact that the earth as a whole is a totally closed economy, and it has grown rather well over the years. Indeed, based on this and the fact that there is no other known economy that is totally closed, the ideologue on the other side could point out how "all totally closed economies have grown rapidly," which would be a valid observation, but totally misleading.

Another mistake, at times made by well-intentioned grassroots activists is to suppose that good actions can come only from good intentions. This crops up most often when discussing the role of the private sector. In India, this comes up in many areas, such as the airline industry. Air India, India's state-run airline, provides poor-quality service and routinely notches up large losses, which the government has to subsidize using taxpayer money and displacing other more urgent expenditures. But the privatization of Air India is a taboo topic in government. When on rare occasions the topic comes up and it is pointed out that it is high time that Air India was privatized, a standard response is: Do you think the private sector entity—be it an Indian company or an international group—that buys up Air India will do so because it is interested in the welfare of ordinary travelers and social good?

The fact that this question is even asked shows our naivety. The answer is, obviously, no. However, the fact that the private sector is driven primarily by the urge to make more profit does not mean that it will not provide valuable service to passengers and play a socially useful role. That is precisely the idea behind Smith's invisible hand. The policymaker's task is to harness the profit-making urge of private individuals and corporations to generate socially valuable goods and services. A good analogy is the flowing river. It has no interest in providing electricity to the residents in the region. But we can nevertheless harness the energy of the river's flow to create electricity and enhance living conditions of ordinary people.[15]

We can see this in the higher education example given earlier. Students in rich countries desire good education, but like most people, they will seek to acquire this at as low a cost as possible. Firms in India are eager to sell education to rake in a reasonable financial return. Neither is interested in any large objective for the nation. What the previous section showed is that by changing some of India's regulatory structure, we can harness these two forces to create human capital and growth in the nation.

A big hindrance to good policy is public opinion. Certainly in democracies, but also in more totalitarian settings, leaders do not like to veer too far from popular opinion. Often, the right policies do not get adopted not because policymakers do not know what these are, but out of a fear that the *people* will object to them. It follows that an important task of those at the helm of a nation is to educate the general public so that the popular opinion is founded in reason and knowledge, and, by implication, policies that are chosen are better.

This problem of populism is compounded by the common proclivity among politicians and policymakers to live for the next morning's headlines. We of course know from standard political economy models that politicians in a democracy will have a penchant for short-term popularity because their aim is to win the next election; they don't usually care about earning kudos two decades after they are dead and gone. What I am pointing to here is short-termism which is over and above this. This probably has roots in the human tendency to hyperbolic discounting—placing an irrationally high weight on immediate gains and losses. In politics, this translates into an obsession with the next morning's headlines. A policy that may not win plaudits the next day but will deliver benefits a year later often gets sidelined because of this phenomenon of political hyperbolic discounting.

This is the reason why we so frequently go for immediate, visible gains, and are willing to give up larger gains that come much later. The education plan I proposed in the previous section runs this risk. Since in the initial stage it will step on some vested interests and entail transactions costs and the benefits will come after a lag, even though the benefits will be disproportionately larger than the costs, there will be a propensity on the part of politicians to stay with the status quo. It is only a visionary leader who can look beyond the immediate headlines and take these kinds of initiatives.

Development without Borders

In closing it is worth reminding the reader that in today's world, which, thanks to the march of technology, is rapidly shrinking, the development project of any nation has to be viewed as a development project of the world. As India matures, it must not stop at its own boundaries but bring to the table of ideas a commitment and a conscience for global development. Fortunately, this internationalism, tolerance of diversity, and secularism was written into the early script of India, from the poetry and essays of Rabindranath Tagore, through the writings of Gandhi, to the statements by the founding fathers at the dawn of the nation. There have been lapses in these no doubt, but at the same time, these are the principles that make up the idea of India.

These ideas resonated through the speech by Radhakrishnan, the first president of the nation, delivered in the Indian parliament on August 14,

1947: "We are lucky in having for our leader one who is a world citizen, who is essentially a humanist . . . if India gains freedom, that freedom will be used not merely for the well-being of India but for *vishwa kalyana*—for world peace, the welfare of mankind."[16]

This was an unusual speech because it is rare for a leader at the moment of independence, after a hard fought battle for freedom, to step beyond national concerns to remind the people of the nation's larger global, humanist commitment. It was unusual for another, technical reason. Nehru had asked Radhakrishnan to speak immediately after his own speech, with a request to continue speaking till just up to midnight so that the assembly could take the pledge at the dawn of the nation. Radhakrishnan did exactly that, concluding at the midnight hour when he passed the baton on to the assembly, in what later came to be described as "an oratorical time-bound relay race."

The subject of this monograph was India's economy, and that is what the preceding pages tried to cover as comprehensively as is possible within the confines of a slim volume. I argued that India is at a juncture where it can take on the mantle of the world's major growth driver, and transform itself into an economic powerhouse with enormous influence on the world economy. The book has discussed a vast range of policies, from large macroeconomic interventions to ground-level microinitiatives, ideas that can be adapted to the needs of other developing nations. But even as India and all nations strive for higher and sustainable growth and overall national development, there is one lesson that the world would do well to take away from India's founding fathers. Beyond the boundaries of each nation, there is a larger but nevertheless fairly small world that we all share; and ultimately, the nationalisms of the day must make way for a global agenda that all peoples, irrespective of their narrow identities, can shape and cherish.

Notes

Preface

1. It is worth clarifying that in speaking about theory I am not talking about mathematical economics. The bulk of mathematical economics is, it is true, an exercise in theory but theory goes beyond that and there is scope for using it across disciplines in the social sciences. As such, I am using the term closer to the sense in which it is used in Swedberg's recent book on social theory (Swedberg 2014), where he cites, among economists, Thomas Schelling and Albert Hirschman as practitioners of this method.

1   Arriving in Lutyens's Delhi

1. I had argued elsewhere (Basu 1986; 2000, chapter 6) that this intriguing fact, namely, the essential vacuousness of power, is true not just for soft, cooperative governments but, paradoxically, also for ruthless, totalitarian states.

2   India's Growth Story

1. Mumbai: Jaico Publishing House, 1975. All quotations are from p. 107.

2. To prevent miscommunication, let me add that in India, "revenue deficit" is defined as the gap between the consumption expenditure (revenue expenditure) of the government and its current revenues (revenue receipts).

   "Fiscal deficit" is the difference between the total expenditure of the government and the total non-debt-creating receipts of the government. It measures the gap between the government consumption expenditure including loan repayments and the income from tax and non-tax revenues. A good source of such definitions is the website Arthapedia, maintained by the Indian Economic Service: http://www.arthapedia.in/index.php?title=Home_Page.

3. In the remainder of this chapter I have drawn from multiple sources, referenced in appropriate places in footnotes. In addition, I have drawn extensively from my earlier chapter, "The Indian Economy up to 1991 and Since," in Basu 2004. The references presented without citation are to be found in that chapter.

4. These are quoted in Wolpert 1996, 150.

5. The letters quoted are from pages 1332 and 1330, respectively, of Howe and Frankfurter 1953. It should be pointed out that Laski was a major influence in early Indian thinking (see Kramnick and Sheerman 1993).

6. See Rudra 1996, especially chapter 11, which was completed by T. N. Srinivasan, following Rudra's untimely death.

7. The fiscal year in India runs from April 1 to March 31 of the following year. Hence the dual, hyphenated reference to years when quoting annual Indian statistics.

8. I should clarify that since India's population, at that time, was growing well above 1.4 percent, per capita income did decline that year, even though overall GDP growth was positive. That is in fact the only year of negative per-capita income growth since 1980.

9. A remarkably candid account of the devastation caused by the famine may be found in Jisheng 2008. Jisheng also draws attention to the overlooked fact that Zhou Enlai originally coined the phrase "the leap forward."

10. The above paragraph, including the data cited, draws on Basu 2009. See also Lin 1999; Lin, Cai, and Li 1996. For more recent comparative analysis of China and India, see Prestowitz 2005; Khanna 2007; Pant 2007; Bardhan 2008; and Rao 2014.

11. In an engaging recent article, Mehta 2014 talks about the challenge of trying to size up Nehru in retrospect and the risk of "condescension of hindsight." He points out how, as is the case for so many major thinkers in history, self-doubt was an inherent part of Nehru's intellectual makeup.

12. For India's complicated yet vital relation with the United States, see Malone 2011, chapter 7.

13. Even today India happens to be the biggest recipient of remittances from abroad, raking in around $70 billion per annum. However, other flows into India have picked up even more, thereby relegating remittances to a relatively smaller role.

14. For a comprehensive account of the state of India's economy and the challenges faced at that juncture, see Jalan 1991.

15. The Indian reforms of 1991–1993 and the subsequent growth prospects of the Indian economy have been analyzed and dissected arguably more than any other

episode of the economy, since independence. See, for a small sampler, Nayyar 1996; Bardhan 1998; Forbes 1999; Srinivasan 2000; Ahluwalia 2002; Mohan 2002; Basu 2004; Rakshit 2004; Rao 2004; Reddy 2004; Rodrik and Subramanian 2004; Virmani 2006; Panagariya 2008; and Bhagwati and Panagariya 2013.

16. A comprehensive analysis of India's industrial sector and the role of controls can be found in Mohan 1992. See also I. J. Ahluwalia 1991.

17. For a trenchant critique, see Bhagwati 1993.

18. This is not to deny that India still has some distance to go in creating an efficient ethos for new small enterprises to enter and function effectively. As I argue later, India's cumbersome, bureaucratic regulatory system remains one of the biggest stumbling blocks for the economy's growth.

19. Much has been written on this subject. The brief analysis presented here draws on Basu 2003. For a fuller analysis of the East Asian crisis, see Stiglitz 2002. See also McKibbin and Martin 1999.

20. See Harrod 1939; Domar 1946; Solow 1956; Swan 1956; Romer 1986; and Lucas 1988.

21. Among more recent works in a similar vein, see Khanna 2007; Nilekani 2009; French 2011; and Das 2012.

22. There were also reminders of the tough, Machiavellian world that leaders inhabit. During the dinner, I asked Kissinger if he and Mao Zedong felt any warmth toward each other. After all, they came from two powerful countries, with many similar concerns, and they had met several times. He did not answer the question directly but he clearly liked this topic, for he held forth at length. From his answer it appeared there was a grudging warmth between them if for no other reason than the loneliness at the top. He said Mao was a person of "great stature" and "he filled the room." Mao told Kissinger that to understand Mao he should know what Mao told the president of Romania when the latter came to see him and urged him to make peace with Russia. Mao first said, "Never." He would wage ten thousand years of war against Russia. Then he paused and said that since the president had come such a long distance to urge Mao, Mao would agree to make it nine thousand years of war. Mao turned to Kissinger and said that was how easygoing he was. He could give up a thousand years of war at the slightest urging. (I may add I have heard variants of this story and my guess is that Mao liked it so much that he repeated it several times, and was unfussy about the details.)

23. I use the expression in the sense of Robin Matthews's CLARE group. He founded this elite discussion group of economists in 1977. It is believed that CLARE referred to Cambridge, London, And the Rest of England.

24. In reality, given that there will be transactions costs, the bank may not be able to recoup $110 but in fact a little less; however, that is unlikely to change the argument in most cases.

25. There were of course many more complications to this major financial event than the one feature I just focused on. As is known, most of the biggest investment banks and other financial groups were rescued using taxpayer money on the ground that they were allegedly too big to be allowed to fail. This meant that the biggest players were protected; for such players the rule was, effectively: if they made a profit that was for them to keep, but if they made a loss that was for others to bear. The literature on the crisis is large; see Johnson 2009 and Stiglitz 2010 for lucid accounts.

26. A formal model trying to explain this occurs in Basu 2011c.

27. It is widely believed that in terms of purchasing power parity (ppp)-adjusted GDP, China will overtake the United States some time in 2014. This is not as momentous a fact as some make it out to be, since political power depends much more on GDP than on ppp-adjusted GDP. With this caveat in mind, it is possible to do an exercise of updating GDPs using the 2011 ppp-adjustments, which were released in July 2014, and extending recent growth-rates forward to find crossover points. According to my calculation as of now, by this method, China crossed over the United States on October 10, 2014.

28. See Swaminathan Aiyar's article "Black Money Saves Financial Sector," in *Times of India*, March 30, 2008.

29. UAE's importance is not as a destination for trade but as a hub where goods go and then travel onward to other nations.

30. Later it would dip further, to just below 5 percent, and then rise again. By the first quarter of 2015, GDP growth was aabove 7 percent.

31. See Rajan 2010; Stiglitz 2010; Schäfer 2012; Pisani-Ferry, Sapir, and Wolff 2013; and Basu and Stiglitz 2015.

32. For analyses of the roots of India's democracy and the challenges faced on this score by the nation, see Khilnani 1999; Sen 2004; Guha 2007; Bose 2013; and Varshney 2013.

33. See Sen 1976; Stiglitz, Sen, and Fitoussi 2009; and Basu 2000, 2010.

3   Inflation

1. This term is usually used to describe central bank operations that try to move short- and long-term interest rates in different directions, such as when in September 2011 the U.S. Federal Reserve bought long-term treasury bonds and sold short-term ones in an effort to lower long-term bond yields interest rates relative to short-term ones.

2. Some of the arguments presented here are drawn from a more extended discussion in Basu 2011d.

3. All inflation numbers, unless explicitly stated otherwise, refer to annual inflation, that is, the growth rate of the price index on a year-on-year basis.

4. For a detailed, phased analysis of India's inflationary experience during 2009 and 2010, see Mohanty 2011.

5. When analyzing inflation in India, throughout this chapter I shall be using the WPI-based inflation numbers. On the few occasions when other indicators are used, this will be made explicit.

6. For an excellent analysis of the changing nature of this inflation, see Rakshit 2011. The multiple sources of India's recent inflation are discussed by Mishra and Roy (2011), and Goyal (2014); see also Sudipto Mundle's article "To Curb or Not to Curb: Traditional Inflation Fighting Methods May Land Us in Stagflation," in *Times of India*, June 8.

7. I am grateful to M. C. Singhi, senior economic adviser in the Ministry of Commerce and Industry, for suggesting this procedure for comparing the two data series and then doing the necessary statistical computation.

8. This is broadly in keeping with the view expressed in V. K. R. V. Rao's (1952) celebrated paper. For a critical assessment of this, see Patnaik 2012.

9. This is not to deny the substantial literature on non-Walrasian general equilibria, where markets clear without relative price movements. While theoretically these models are of great interest, they rely on systems of rationing that have few counterparts in our everyday life and so will be ignored here.

10. What is considered tolerable inflation varies from nation to nation and the source of the opinion. Most industrialized nations target to keep inflation below 2 percent per annum. Emerging economies like India are more lax and begin to act when inflation exceeds 4 or 5 percent; though some argue it can be allowed to go even higher, to 6 or 7 percent.

11. It has been argued (Government of India 2011, chapter 2) that this principle of one economy/one central bank has been weakened in recent times. With globalization the world economy is increasingly beginning to look like a single economy, but, to the extent that the world has many central banks with the right to create money, we are tending to get back to the kind of world we worked hard to get out of. This is one phenomenon (multiple money-creating authorities in an increasingly unique global economy) that is dramatically altering the nature of inflation in recent times. As Reddy (2011, chapter 4) warned in 2009, the injection of liquidity around the world to jumpstart various economies caught in recession created the risk of inflation. Subsequent experience has borne this out.

12. This system has evolved over time. The main instrument of liquidity management, the Liquidity Adjustment Facility was introduced in 2000. The concept of repo auctions was introduced in May 2001. As Jalan (2001, 180) noted, the market

responded to these changes positively "with an appreciable rise in turnover and a decline in volatility." From now on, there will be no reason to treat the repo and reverse repo as separate variables, since at the time of the monetary policy review on May 3, 2011, the Reserve Bank of India declared that it was freezing the spread between the repo and reverse repo at 100 basis points. If the repo is set at x percent, by definition the reverse repo will be (x-1) percent.

13. For an analysis of the Indian repo market, see Bandopadhyay 2012.

14. Recently, the RBI has also tried to use the savings account interest rate as a monetary policy instrument, raising it in May 2011 from 3.5 percent to 4.0 percent.

15. Inflation can also be affected by changes in the exchange rate regime and policy concerning capital account convertibility (see Tarapore 2002). However, in recent years there has not been any major shift in these policies for these to be important factors in explaining shifts in the inflation rate. In general, some authors have argued that monetary policy transmission in India is weak and that a possible line of impact on prices is via the exchange rate (Bhattacharya, Patnaik, and Shah 2011).

16. For philosophical accuracy, it may be pointed out that even in engineering it is not written in stone, though the relationships are more stable there than in banking science.

17. The notion of "liquidity" is not as obvious as popular discourse makes it out to be. There is the question about why a mere change in the portfolio of what a person holds should alter liquidity. I am unable to answer this question here and in any case I doubt there is a known answer to it. The problem will be briefly elaborated upon in this chapter (without resolution).

18. There are also endogenous explanations for why the credit market may not clear in equilibrium and, in particular, market imperfection can lead to credit rationing (Stiglitz and Weiss 1981). It should however be pointed out that the argument I will present would not work in an obvious way if the cause of the interest rate rigidity was in the manner of Stiglitz and Weiss (ibid.).

19. The argument may also hinge critically on what the cause of the interest rigidity is, in the first place. It is possible to argue that my analysis does not work, at least not in any straightforward manner, when the initial rigidity is caused by the Stiglitz and Weiss (1981) type of argument. But, minimally, this warns us that the nature of the connection between interest rate and liquidity may be more complex than is popularly assumed. And it points to the need for research on the intricate connection between interest rates and liquidity.

20. This is related to what is known in the literature as the "immiserization theorem" (Bhagwati 1958).

21. For a general empirical investigation into inequality, poverty, and inflation in India, see Mishra and Roy (2011). Kohli (2012) analyzes the political economy of

India's high incidence of poverty despite its success with growth. For an analysis of the connection between growth and poverty and the environment see Ferro, Rosenblatt, and Stern 2004.

22. I have in this chapter, for the most part, stayed away from the classic debate about macroeconomic trade-offs between inflation and other growth-related variables (see Chitre 2010 for a discussion in the Indian context). A recent paper by Dholakia and Sapre (2011) finds little evidence of the traditional Phillips-curve type of negative relation between inflation and unemployment in India.

4   Fiscal and Other Macroeconomic Policies for an Emerging Economy

1. I am using the term "government" loosely to include autonomous bodies such as the central bank and regulatory authorities.

2. The dating of *Arthashastra* is not without controversy. The most commonly accepted view is that Kautilya was actually Chanakya, the philosopher and adviser to the emperor Chandragupta Maurya. Chanakya lived from 350 to 283 BC; and so conjecture is that the book was written within that period. However, some scholars have argued that Kautilya was not Chanakya but a scholar who lived and wrote some three centuries after Chanakya (see Kautilya 1992, introduction).

3. Social norms and culture, topics that I turn to later in the book, also play a role in tax compliance and hence in raising the tax-to-GDP ratio (see Besley and Persson 2014).

4. We know, in retrospect, that it is foolish to draw too sharp a distinction between a guarantee and a comfort letter. Under certain legal interpretations, a comfort letter becomes like a guarantee. It is not surprising that in raising investment a comfort letter from government is so effective. For my argument here, the distinction however is not important. All I want to show here is that there are situations where giving multiple guarantees is less onerous on government than giving a single guarantee.

5. There were later reports chaired by S. S. Tarapore, which also played a role in shaping the nature of current and capital account convertibility in India (see Mohanty 2011 for a discussion).

6. Policies for helping domestic exporters or importers can go beyond mere exchange rate management to subtle policy combinations involving the management of interest rates and capital flows (Basu and Morita 2006; Adam and Moutos 2012).

7. *Financial Times*, September 7, 2011, p. 1.

8. See Government of India 2012.

9. One class of analysts has argued that widespread expectations of inflation lead government to behave in ways—such as running large deficits—that in fact help fulfill those expectations (Sargent 1982; Mankiw 2010, chapter 13). One way to break this link is for government to visibly alter its rules of behavior, such as making an open and credible commitment to maintaining lower deficits in the foreseeable future.

10. The preceding somewhat frivolous reference to Brouwer is because Brouwer specified a set of sufficient conditions under which a function will have a fixed point. If a forecast function has no fixed point, we are caught in the trap suggested by Ahamed. It is impossible to make an accurate forecast. Otherwise, we can make an accurate forecast but simply have to take account of the self-referential problem of the forecast itself influencing the outcome.

5 Globalization and the Challenge of Development

1. While this is not germane to the policymaker or the student of economics, I would be negligent if I did not point out that *hilsa* is the tastiest fish in the world. Its high content of Omega-3 makes it a worthwhile diet even from a purely nutritional perspective. The only hurdle for those not tutored to handle it from early childhood is its high density of fine bones. The British, during their long colonial rule in India, having learned the magic of *hilsa*, and not wanting to lose its limited forces of colonial exploitation to accidents with the fishbone, created the recipe for what came to be called smoked *hilsa*, which miraculously melts the bones while retaining the taste.

2. See Schäfer 2012; Pisani-Ferry, Sapir, and Wolff 2013; Basu and Stiglitz 2015.

3. The exception was Germany, which, thanks to the great robustness of its economy and strong fiscal situation, did get some inward flow.

4. Some of my predecessors in the job of CEA—especially before the opening up of India in the 1990s—told me that every morning at work the first thing they did was to check the prices of essential goods in markets around India and how the various Indian stock markets were doing. For me, on most days, the first thing I did was to check how the Eurozone was doing because much was happening there and one could be sure that whatever happened would within days and maybe even hours begin to affect India's domestic markets and the exchange rate vis-à-vis other currencies.

5. The special policy challenges for emerging market economies that arise from spillovers in today's globalized world are described well in the article "How Emerging Markets Deal with Global Spillovers" by Alok Sheel, in *Business Standard*, January 25, 2014. The author stresses the need for macro policy innovation in developing countries and as such is in keeping with the line taken in this monograph.

6. My concern here is with economic policies in a globalized world; but this has a political counterpart that is as compelling. In Mahbubani's (2008, 51) words, "global theory" has not kept pace with "global practice." Economic globalization has run ahead of political institutions at the global level, giving rise to tensions that will ultimately have to be solved in the political arena.

7. Inequality can be viewed in many ways—by using different measures and also by viewing it across groups (see Subramanian 1997; Dutta 2002; Subramanian and Jayaraj 2012. In the case of India, for reasons of history, caste inequality is important. Fortunately, economists are now taking an interest in this and there is better enumeration and analysis of this problem (see Deshpande 2011). A revealing study of the grip of caste identities on the minds of those who live in caste-dominated societies is provided in Hoff and Pandey 2006. See also Iversen and Raghavendra 2006.

8. Interestingly, this is not just a statement about the nature of the world but also in a sense is based in pure reason. As has been stressed in many places, when we talk of inequality and shared prosperity we should mean this not just across people at a point of time but also across generations. This compels us to be sensitive to climate change and to protecting the environment. However, as we tried to show in Basu and Mitra (2003), the principles of equality over time runs into *logical* inconsistencies with some other perfectly reasonable axioms, such as one that says that if one income stream dominates the other at all points of time then that should get a higher welfare score. For a discussion of this conundrum explicitly in the context of intergenerational welfare distribution, see, for instance, Asheim and Tungodden 2004 and Roemer 2011.

9. This also flies in the face of conventional wisdom that with globalization and growth there should be convergence and raises important questions about how this may be countered, especially in poor nations where the growing inequality is particularly painful (Marjit and Acharyya 2006).

10. It is possible to think of parameters under which this will not be true.

11. Total equality is also achieved by setting the tax rate at 100 percent, but I will not expend effort explaining why this is not a good idea. I am assuming that there is another point where the post-tax income of the rich and the income of the poor become the same and I am calling that the "equality tax."

6   Food and Poverty

1. The number for 2012 is based on the "Tendulkar poverty line," which is not too far from the global extreme poverty line of $1.25, ppp-adjusted, which is used for all other years.

2. See Sen 1976, 1981; Anand 1983; Foster, Greer, and Thorbecke 1984; Ray 1988, chapter 8; Deaton and Drèze 2002; Deaton and Kozel 2005; Himanshu and Sen 2004;

Alkire and Foster 2011; Lanjouw and Murgai 2009; Ray and Mishra 2012; Reddy and Pogge 2010; Calvo and Dercon 2013; Chen and Ravallion 2013; Subramanian 1997, 2011; Ravallion 2014.

3. While I shall describe and analyze mainly the food subsidy system in India, one of the most significant sources of government support in India occurs through fuel and energy subsidies. See Gangopadhyay, Ramaswami, and Wadhwa 2005; some of the critical issues are also discussed in the 2020 Report of the Expert Group on "Pricing Methodology for Diesel, Domestic LPG and PDS Kerosene," chaired by Kirit Parikh.

4. For a compelling study of this, see Drèze and Sen 2013. As Mishra (2013) observes in his review of this book, the Indian leaders did not match up to leaders in socialist countries in terms of human development investments in education and health, "nor did they unleash, like their counterparts in South Korea and Japan, entrepreneurial energies in the country's protected private sector."

5. The chapter draws on Basu 2011b.

6. I was in government when this law, also known as the Right to Food Act, was being drafted. I believe that making basic and essential foods a right is as it should be. But one must be wary of conferring too many rights, because with each right comes an obligation and to provide rights in areas where it is not possible to fulfill them is to demean the status of a right and damage the fabric of a law-abiding society. The reason why a "right to employment" is not a good idea is that the policy that could achieve full employment in a large country is not yet known. The idea that we can move toward full employment by having the government create jobs is flawed. You can deliberately create jobs in one village, one thousand villages, ten thousand villages. What most policymakers do not realize and many economists do not either is that such actions have macroeconomic consequences. Through movements in prices and interest rates, such action can exacerbate unemployment and poverty elsewhere. So in each village where you directly intervene, you may see benefits, but when you study the Indian economy as a whole, you may not see the level of achievement you would expect by adding all this up, because of the macro-collateral impact of these policy interventions.

7. See *The Economist*, April 9, 2014, 58–59.

8. T. N. Ninan makes this point effectively in his article "Intent vs. Delivery," in *Business Standard*, April 3, 2010. The article rightly points to the need to direct some of the zest that we have shown to analyze the quantity to be given at subsidized rate to how this may actually be delivered. The decision concerning the quantity is moot if we do not resolve the mechanism question. Bhaskar Dutta points to the concurrence of high prices and overflowing warehouses in his article "Stamp of Possibility: Food Stamps May Wipe Out Some Corruption in the PDS," in *The Telegraph*, August 4, 2010. There are also different ways of giving out a subsidy—as goods and services, as cash, or by making it conditional on a certain kind of behavior. The first and the

second options are discussed in several places in this book. I do not go into conditional cash transfers in any detail here but it is a large topic (see, for instance, Das, Do, and Ozler 2004; Fiszbein and Schady 2009).

9. Subsequent work shows that there is some improvement in performance (Khera 2011). Nevertheless, it remains grossly suboptimal.

10. Actually it is not politically unpalatable once we recognize that human beings are very similar innately and the differences we see in the behavior of different groups are a response to their histories and also possible equilibrium responses to one another. This in turn means that societies can undergo changes in these qualities. The qualities of honesty and trustworthiness in a group have value to the group that may not be there for each individual. Societies that manage to inculcate these traits in their individuals tend to prosper economically. Given variations in each group's history and experience, trust levels can vary across nations, communities, and gender (Landa 1995; Fukuyama 1996; Chaudhuri and Gangadharan 2007). I discuss some of these issues in Basu (2010) and, in the context of India, in chapter 9 of this book. To that extent it is imperative to try to inculcate the quality of honesty in society. But that does not change the fact that in designing policy we have to take into account people as they are, not as they ought to be. This is the single biggest underlying flaw in the design of India's policies.

11. This was what prompted the sitting justices of the Supreme Court of India on July 27, 2010, to admonish the government for wasting procured food grains. This has also been widely reported in the popular media. For some compelling accounts, see, for instance, "India Lets Grain Rot Instead of Feeding the Poor," by S. Halarnkar and M. Randhawa, and "After Rot, Panel Moves to Stem Grain Drain," by Z. Haq in *Hindustan Times*, of July 27 and July 30, 2010, respectively.

12. For a recent comprehensive treatise on the subject, see Vaidyanathan 2009.

13. See note 11.

14. For a brief description of the PDS and its evolution and also other related programs, see Desai et al. 2010.

15. In turning to this, it must be stressed that this must not detract us from the need to invest more in agriculture and boost productivity (Dev and Rao 2010). The distribution of food grain to the needy, which is the subject matter of this chapter, and policies for raising agricultural productivity are not substitutes; both need to be pursued simultaneously.

16. It is also arguable that under certain parameters transferring food to some households confers positive externalities on others (Angelucci and De Giorgi 2009).

17. It should be pointed out, in fairness to the ration shop owners, that the government sets the official prices for them to receive and sell food grain with such a slender profit margin that, if the store owners were totally honest, they would not be

able to make a living wage from running a ration shop full time (Khera 2010). Clearly, we are caught in a vicious cycle. Prices are set based on the assumption that store owners will earn money illegally and store owners comply.

18. For a short, lucid description of such a system, see Nandakumar's article "Food Coupons: The Way Forward," in *Economic Times*, April 27, 2010. While the proposal discussed there is not identical to the one in the "Economic Survey 2009–2010" (Government of India 2010) the broad thrust is the same.

19. The idea of using coupons or smart cards to give the subsidy directly to the household is not a novel idea. It has been tried in several nations, including Sri Lanka and the United States. Several commentators on the Indian economy have proposed variants of it (see Jha and Ramaswami 2010; Standing et al. 2015).

20. The recent book by Standing et al. (2015) documents, based on empirical studies, a remarkable list of benefits from better nutrition to empowerment that a system of direct transfers can confer on society.

21. According to the Reserve Bank of India's estimate, eight-notes-per-million pieces of paper currency circulating in India are fake.

22. All this is not to deny that payment in kind also has some advantages. Theoretical arguments have been constructed to show that in situations with asymmetric information, in-kind transfers may have advantages, in particular, that of self-selection (see, for instance, Blackorby and Donaldson 1988; Singh and Thomas 2000). On balance, however, it seems to me that the advantages of payment in coupons or smart card outweigh the disadvantages.

23. For a recent analysis of the economics of cash transfers, with illustrations from the Brazilian experience, see Vyasulu 2010.

7   The Nuts and Bolts of the Economy

1. The most prominent example of an O-ring-based theory is the work of Kremer (1993); for a discussion, see Basu 1997.

2. This plumbing metaphor has been used more than once by *The Economist*. See, for instance, "Of Plumbing and Promises," *The Economist*, February 25, 2012.

3. I persisted with this in the next two annual "Economic Surveys," in which the respective chapter 2s were titled "Micro-Foundations of Macroeconomic Development" and "Micro-foundations of Macroeconomic Policy (see Government of India 2010, 2011, 2012).

4. I have discussed this at some length in Basu 2007, 2010.

5. The arrival and flourishing of M-Pesa or mobile money in Kenya, which has helped foster financial inclusion among poor people, enabling them to borrow,

lend, and start up small enterprises, is an example of this. In many countries this is not possible because of regulatory restrictions. This is not an argument for a carte blanche and for removing all regulation, but it urges us to be careful when we set up impediments to mutually convenient contracts and trade.

6. Basu 2010; Satz 2004.

7. See also Neeman 1999; Genicot 2002.

8. Elsewhere (Basu 2003, 2007), I develop the concepts of "inviolable preferences" and "maintainable preferences" and a consistent normative criterion based on these, which would enable government to ban voluntary harassment but not the right of the homeowners to sell their homes.

9. I am referring here to the growth models of Harrod 1939; Domar 1946; Solow 1956; and Swan 1956.

10. The fact of there being people who do not understand the complexities of contracts is a great advantage to others looking for individuals to exploit. There were reports, following the subprime crisis in the United States, of financiers making rosters of people who defaulted, not in order to avoid them in the future but in fact to do business with them because they are likely to be people who do not understand contracts.

11. See Ashraf, Karlan, and Yin 2006; Karna Basu 2011; and World Bank 2014b. Even without going into behavioral economics, there are enough intricacies in finance, for instance to do with liability structures, that can be utilized for efficiency and exploitation (see, for instance, Ghatak 1999).

12. See Bhaduri 1973.

13. It is this build up to enormous size, starting small, which makes a Ponzi appear like an inverted pyramid, and that is the reason why it is often referred to as a pyramid scheme.

14. Here is the general rule for those with interest in understanding the details of how Ponzis are set up. In period m, sell 2^{m-1} cars, and to each buyer offer shares worth $\frac{1}{2}^{2m-1}$ of all future profit of the company, starting from that period.

15. More generally, the link between the world of money and finance on the one hand, and goods and human well-being on the other, remains ill understood. What seems obvious often ceases to be so when one thinks hard. I used to routinely respond to airlines urging travelers to put the loose change which they would never use again as they crossed international boundaries in a pouch to be used for charity by the airline. But think. If you do put money, which would have idled in a drawer, back into circulation via an airline's well-meaning effort at corporate social responsibility, you are effectively increasing the total amount of money circulating in the world. Hence, you will have created a small upward pressure on prices, which is an

unkind thing to inflict on unwitting consumers around the world. Till some mathematical economist resolves this conundrum, I am left in a dilemma each time I fly; and nowadays I give or do not give my loose change depending on the stage of my reasoning.

8 Law and Economics

1. For a widely cited survey of the connection between corruption and development, see Bardhan 1997.

2. This was clear from a ruling of the Delhi High Court in the *Bharadwaj Media Private Limited v. State*, 2008 146 DLT 108 (Del): 2008 (1) CCR 11: 2008 (2) Crimes 244.

3. Interestingly, it had been used in special cases even before the concept had been formally "discovered" (see, for instance, Dixit 1980).

4. The two most notable (and confused) ones in this genre were in *The Hindu* and *The Telegraph*.

5. *The Economist* ("A Novel Way to Combat Corruption: Who to Punish?" May 5, 2011) and *La Monde* ("Faut-il legaliser la corruption?" by Paul Seabright, May 24, 2011) would later publish supportive articles on this; and CNN International would devote a segment of its popular *GPS* program to this (May 16, 2011); see also Xingxing Li, "Bribery and the Limits of Game Theory: The Lessons from China," *Financial Times*, May 1, 2012. More recently, there have been some research-based extensions and evaluations of this argument: see Kenny, Klein, and Sztajerowska 2011; Gandhi, Pethe, and Tandel 2012; Songchoo and Suriya 2012; Spengler 2014; Borooah 2012; Sundell 2014; Abbink et al. 2014; Dufwenberg and Spagnolo 2014; Oak 2014; Basu, Basu, and Cordella 2014.

6. This is not just a casual claim but has scholarly grounding, as argued by Amartya Sen (2005).

7. As is increasingly recognized now, and will be discussed later, social norms and institutions also play a major role. I argued this with a simple illustration in Basu 1983. See also Myerson 2004 and Guha and Guha 2012.

8. In some cases of rent control, landlords are allowed to raise the rent from one year to another but at some prespecified rate.

9. Besley and Burgess (2004) provide interesting evidence that supports this hypothesis. For fuller statements of my argument see Basu, Fields, and Debgupta 2009. See also Singh 2012 and Martin Rama, "Which Labor Reforms Will Make a Difference," *Economic Times*, July 4, 2014.

10. If you felt one way out for a firm that has expanded beyond long-run survival is to declare insolvency and to close out, that is not easy either in India. As the World

Bank's latest *Doing Business* data show, it takes on average 4.3 years to resolve insolvency and close a business in India. And it is not the case that this has to happen because closing a business is an innately cumbersome process, because in Singapore the same takes nine months, in Norway ten months, in the United Kingdom one year, and in China 1.7 years (see World Bank 2014a).

11. Formal proofs of this may be found in Basu 2003, 2007.

12. I argued this "ink on paper" view in Basu 1993 and developed this further in Basu 2000.

13. See Mailath, Morris, and Postlewaite 2003 and Basu 2000, 2010 for analysis of the "focal point approach" to law and economics. See also Cooter 1998; McAdams 2000, and Dixit 2007.

14. It is possible to take this idea further to locate clusters of choices by each player rather than one action on the part of one player. This would have us looking for not focal points but focal sets (see Myerson 2006).

15. It will be argued later that economists have often contributed to our flawed understanding by taking too narrow a view of what is self-enforcing by assuming that human beings are totally self-centered. In reality, people care about others, or at least have the innate propensity to do so (though we can damage the innate hardwiring) and are also guided by social and cultural norms (Basu 2000a, 2010). I shall discuss some of this in chapter 9.

16. I believe that the prescription laws in developed countries are unnecessarily cumbersome and compel people to go to doctors when they really do not need to, and I appreciate the relative freedom from this in India.

17. It is interesting that the Indian government's official survey of the economy has also begun to pay attention to this—see Government of India 2011, 2012.

18. In fairness it must be recalled that the USSR broke up the previous year. The Communist Party that had ruled from 1917 finally gave up. Over the next five years, Russia's national income would shrink by half. So 1992 was a period of turmoil and chaos.

9   The Social and Organizational Foundations of Economic Development

1. See Kahneman and Tversky 1979; Sunstein 1996; Rabin 1998; Gigerenzer and Todd 1999; Fehr and Gächter 2000; Platteau 2000; Rao and Walton 2004; Mullainathan 2005; Thaler and Sunstein 2008; Basu 2000, 2010; Kahneman 2011; Benabou and Tirole 2011; Rubinstein 2014. For a comprehensive statement of the subject in the context of development, see the recent World Development Report of the World Bank (2014b). For a sweeping survey of the evolution of this kind of thought from William Petty, through Adam Smith, to contemporary times with observations on

institutions like the World Bank, see Stathakis and Vaggi 2006. Questions pertaining to social norms have been raised in the context of household dynamics (A. M. Basu 1992; Agarwal 1997), migrant networks and community cohesion (Dhillon, Iversen, and Torsvik 2013; Munshi 2014), and political conflict (Kuran 1988; Varshney 2003). How do we reconcile conflict, violence, and nationalism, for instance, with individual rationality? Varshney (2003) makes a compelling case not for abandoning rationality but for broadening the concept.

2. These may in turn have roots in evolution, whereby groups exhibiting ruthless self-interest naturally make way for people with altruism and other-regarding norms (Bowles and Gintis 2005; Alger and Weibull 2013).

3. With a set of innovative, game-theoretic experiments he shows how players show different proclivity to be instinctive or contemplative. It is possible, however, to take this a step further and argue that people have different domains where they are instinctive and where they are contemplative. In some cultures, when you see a queue, you instinctively go and join it at the end. In other cultures, you ponder whether to break the queue, and if so where to do so, or to simply join the queue at the end. Our history, experience, and context create these propensities. Whether or not a group of people will prosper could depend critically on where they use instinctive choice and where they use contemplative choice. See, for instance, Barrett 1997; Fershtman and Weiss 1998; Harrington 1999; Gintis 2009.

4. All this of course has large fiscal implications (see Muralidharan et al. 2014).

5. What these noneconomic drivers are is poorly understood. The main reason for this is that much of mainstream economics had taught us that there are no such drivers. The first step in understanding what the noneconomic drivers are is to recognize their importance. Fortunately, that has happened now and we are beginning to take rudimentary steps in identifying them (World Bank 2014b).

6. Basu and Van 1998; Basu 2000; Hoff and Stiglitz 2001; Emerson and Souza 2003; Edmonds 2007.

7. Goffman 1963; Besley and Coate 1992; Lindbeck, Nyberg, and Weibull 1999; López-Calva 2003.

8. See Basu 1995, 2000. One common norm that makes societies prone to multiple equilibria is the propensity of human beings to cooperate and forego opportunities for free-riding if they know that others are cooperating and foregoing their opportunity to free-ride. Some striking recent research shows that this is fairly universal trait (Martinsson, Pham-Kanh, and Villegas-Palacio 2013). This has large implications for society. In one society where people believe everyone is corrupt, everyone will be corrupt. Once this society manages to break away from this to develop a behavior pattern where most people are not corrupt, most people will be not corrupt. This shows that to change some of the bad equilibra, we may not need persistent intervention but rather a short period of deliberate intervention to shift society to the better pattern of behavior, which then becomes self-enforcing.

9. Despite my criticism of the bureaucracy and politics at the helm, it will be wrong not to acknowledge the *individual* talent of India's top policymakers. I would, time and again, be surprised by the skill and talent of India's leading bureaucrats and policymakers. The wealth of knowledge and analysis they brought to the table was outstanding. One remarkable example of this was when I tried to get Finance Minister Pranab Mukherjee to write an entry on "Budget Making" for the *New Oxford Companion to Economics in India*, which I was editing with Annemie Maertens. The days rolled by, the economy lurching from one challenge to another, and we worried the piece would never get written. Finally, we decided that the only way to get it done was to have him speak extempore, record it, and then begin work with the draft. It ended up a most remarkable forty-five minutes of commentary, from memory, starting with the budget of Liaquat Ali Khan (who would later be prime minister of Pakistan), just before India's independence, to current times, and was packed with data, references to the relevant articles of India's Constitution, landmark dates, and anecdotes. The finance minister also informed us about why India has the strange custom of a separate Railway Budget, a practice that dates back to 1924. With a few marginal changes, "Budget Making" was ready for print (see Mukherjee 2012). My diary of that period is full of such examples of individual talent and collective inertia. The only way to understand this is to think of India's top administration as a group of ace drivers, locked in a traffic jam. The challenge of improving India's administration is, therefore, one of breaking up the jam.

10. While I am at it, here is another tip for interpreting bureaucrats. On joining the Indian government I learned quickly something I later discovered is not unique to India: faced with a question, bureaucrats never say that they do not have an answer. In case they do not, they answer the question for which they do. Thus, for example, if you ask what caused the country's industrial growth to tank last year, you may have to settle for the answer: What is more important is agriculture and the agriculture sector did well the previous year because of the new policy of subsidized seed distribution.

10   The Road Ahead

1. This is not all coincidence but is partly rooted in the fact that the remarkable man who drafted India's constitution, Bhimrao Ramji Ambedkar, was influenced deeply by Thomas Jefferson. For Ambedkar, drafting the nation's constitution was not just an exercise in displaying his outstanding intellect, but also a deeply emotional task for he was born in the Mahar caste, which is classified as one of India's "untouchable" castes. He knew well the pain and humiliation of societal exclusion, and was committed to building a nation that would be inclusive and founded in universalism (Jadhav 2013). The same philosophical predilection was to be found in Rabindranath Tagore's poetry and his controversial essay decrying narrow-minded nationalism (Tagore 1918).

2. Bowles was U.S. ambassador to India from 1951 to 1953 and again for a few months in 1963. Galbraith was ambassador from 1961 to 1963.

3. I may add here that while I cannot vouch for the cycling, the school choice may not have been too bad given that one of those children turned out to be a distinguished economist.

4. There is scope for debate on the semantics of the word "secularism" in India and the United States, and more generally, the West. In the United States, unlike in India, this is not a matter of public declaration as much as implicit acceptance. Sanjay Subrahmanyam (2013, chapter 3, 22) argues that this is in general true of the West: "Neither Tony Blair nor Mrs. Thatcher has ever used the word in a speech that I can remember. The only Europeans who use some sort of term like this are the French, with their idea of *laicite*. . . . [T]he term [secularism] has a political weight in India that it has never had in the West. . . . Thus, 'secularism' has become almost as Indian a word as 'preponed.'" It is, nevertheless, a principle of quiet adherence in the United States.

5. A statement of this coming together of not just values but also interests was deftly analyzed by India's foreign secretary at that time (2005) and preeminent foreign policy expert, Shyam Saran, in an address to the Carnegie Endowment for International Peace in Washington, D.C.: "Transforming India-US Relations: Building a Strategic Partnership" (see carnegieendowment.org/files/indianfsdec21.pdf). The recent announcement of India having invited (the first time ever) a U.S. president to attend the Republic Day parade in January 2015 and President Obama's acceptance of the invitation is also leading to a lot of analysis in the media. See, for instance, the analysis of Seema Sirohi, "Letter from Washington," *Economic Times*, November 16, 2014.

6. On this, giant strides have been made in the last one to two decades through the spread of randomized trial method. This method has been in wide use in epidemiology for a long time but its entry into development economics is recent. Randomized trials have yielded rich insights into which microinterventions work and which do not. A celebrated finding using the method in India was that of Chattopadhyay and Duflo (2004), who established that having women leaders in local governments improved the provision of public goods, such as a potable water supply. This is just one example. For numerous other results unearthed by this method, see, for instance, Banerjee and Duflo 2009, 2011; Deaton 2010. However, even here the claims made often exceed what can legitimately be claimed. As I have tried to show in Basu 2014, better use of theory and deductive reasoning could help even here in eliciting the right knowledge from the findings of randomized trials (see also Mookherjee 2005; Rodrik 2009; Manski 2013).

7. Description, it is worth adding, is not a mundane task as economists often make it out to be. Good description, as Sen (1980) reminds us, entails choice, for not all

that one sees can or should be described. It involves skill and judgment for one has to decide "which details to focus on and which to leave out" (Swedberg 2014, 41).

8. In our cynical moments we wonder if a simple nudge can really be all that holds back a major change. To counter this doubt I can only recount the somewhat jaded story of a man whose car broke down on a highway. After a lot of futile effort by him to repair it, he reluctantly took it to a roadside garage. The mechanic examined the engine and said he could do it for 500 rupees. The man agreed, upon which the mechanic took out a hammer and gave a sharp knock. The car started and he asked for his money. The man looked upset and said, "500 hundred rupees for just one knock?" The mechanic responded, "It is actually 10 rupees for the knock and 490 for knowing where to place it." This is one of the tales I heard from Mrinal Datta Chaudhuri, sitting in the Coffee House of the Delhi School of Economics that I described in chapter 2.

9. This qualifier is necessary because India was home to the world's oldest university—Nalanda, which was flourishing by the fifth century AD, with students and teachers from multiple nations, prominently India and China. It was destroyed in the twelfth century by a Turkish attack and subsequently lay in ruins.

10. For one of the most comprehensive studies of India's higher education sector, see Agarwal 2009. See also Kapur and Mehta 2004.

11. I cannot deny that in some ways I hope that will happen.

12. I discussed some details of how this can be done in my dissenting note to the Yashpal Committee Report: http://prayatna.typepad.com/education/2009/07/full -text-of-kaushik-basus-dissent-note-to-the-yashpal-committee-report.html.

13. There are examples galore from modern behavioral economics of how small hurdles foil many a large plan and program (Thaler and Sunstein 2009; Kahneman 2011; World Bank 2014b). I have direct experience from my field work in Jharkhand, where poor peasants opted to go to the local moneylender for their borrowing needs instead of to the banks because they found the banks' procedures and paperwork daunting, thereby agreeing to pay an interest rate of 10 percent per month instead of the 18 percent per annum that the banks offered.

14. This was in an inaugural address delivered to the University of St. Andrews in 1867 (Mill 1867).

15. There is no contradiction between this line and the argument made in chapter 9 that what drives people varies and can also be changed and we have to keep up the effort to make them more accountable to the larger interests of society. But this is a much more long-term agenda.

16. For this and the quotation in the next paragraph, see Mukherjee 2007, 182, 178.

References

Abbink, Klaus, Utteeyo Dasgupta, Lata Gangadharan, and Tarun Jain. 2014. "Letting the Briber Go Free: An Experiment on Mitigating Harassment Bribes." *Journal of Public Economics* 111:17–28.

Acharyya, Rajat, and Sugata Marjit. 2000. "Globalisation and Inequality: An Analytical Perspective." *Economic and Political Weekly* 35 (39): 3503–3510.

Adam, Antonis, and Thomas Moutos. 2012. "Capital Importers Pay More for Their Imports." CESifo Working Paper No. 3723.

Agarwal, Bina. 1997. "'Bargaining' and Gender Relations: Within and Beyond the Household." *Feminist Economics* 3 (1): 1–51.

Agarwal, Pawan. 2009. *Indian Higher Education: Envisioning the Future.* New Delhi: Sage.

Ahamed, Liaquat. 2009. *Lords of Finance: The Bankers Who Broke the World.* New York: Penguin Books.

Ahluwalia, Isher J. 1991. *Productivity and Growth in Indian Manufacturing.* New Delhi: Oxford University Press.

Ahluwalia, Montek S. 2002. "Economic Reforms in India since 1991: Has Gradualism Worked?" *Journal of Economic Perspectives* 16 (3): 67–88.

Aiyar, Swaminathan. 1999. "India's Economic Prospects: The Promise of Services." Center for Advanced Study of India Occasional Paper No. 9, University of Pennsylvania.

Akerlof, George A. 1970. "'The Market for 'Lemons': Quality Uncertainty and the Market Mechanism." *Quarterly Journal of Economics* 84 (3): 488–500.

Alger, Ingela, and Jörgen W. Weibull. 2013. "Homo Moralis—Preference Evolution under Incomplete Information and Assortative Matching." *Econometrica* 81 (6): 2269–2302.

Alkire, Sabina, and James Foster. 2011. "Counting and Multidimensional Poverty Measurement." *Journal of Public Economics* 95 (7–8): 476–487.

Anand, Sudhir. 1983. *Inequality and Poverty in Malaysia: Measurement and Decomposition.* London: Oxford University Press.

Angelucci, Manuela, and Giacomo De Giorgi. 2009. "Indirect Effects of an Aid Program: How Do Cash Transfers Affect Ineligibles' Consumption?" *American Economic Review* 99 (1): 486–508.

Asheim, Geir, and Bertil Tungoddenl. 2004. "Resolving Distributional Conflicts between Generations." *Economic Theory* 24:221–230.

Ashraf, Nava, Dean Karlan, and Wesley Yin. 2006. "Tying Odysseus to the Mast: Evidence from a Commitment Savings Product in the Philippines." *Quarterly Journal of Economics* 121 (2): 635–672.

Auerbach, Robert. 1982. *Money, Banking and Financial Markets.* New York: Macmillan.

Bandopadhyay, Tamal. 2012. "Repo Market." In *New Oxford Companion to Economics in India*, ed. Kaushik Basu and Annemie Maertens, 597–600. New Delhi: Oxford University Press.

Banerjee, Abhijit, and Esther Duflo. 2009. "The Experimental Approach to Development Economics." *Annual Review of Economics* 1 (1): 151–178.

Banerjee, Abhijit, and Esther Duflo. 2011. *Poor Economics: A Radical Rethinking of the Way to Fight Global Poverty.* New York: Public Affairs Press.

Bardhan, Pranab. 1997. "Corruption and Development: A Review of Issues." *Journal of Economic Literature* 35 (3): 1320–1346.

Bardhan, Pranab. 1998. *The Political Economy of Development in India.* Oxford: Oxford University Press. Expanded edition with an epilogue on the political economy of reform in India.

Bardhan, Pranab. 2008. "Economic Reforms, Poverty and Inequality in China and India." In *Arguments for a Better World: Essays in Honor of Amartya Sen*, ed. K. Basu and R. Kanbur, 49–58. Oxford: Oxford University Press.

Barrett, Scott. 1997. "The Strategy of Trade Sanctions in International Environmental Agreements." *Resource and Energy Economics* 19 (4): 345–361.

Basu, Alaka Malwade. 1992. *Culture, the Status of Women, and Demographic Behaviour: Illustrated with the Case of India.* Oxford: Clarendon Press.

Basu, Karna. 2011. "Hyperbolic Discounting and the Sustainability of Rotational Savings Arrangements." *American Economic Journal: Microeconomics* 3 (4): 143–171.

Basu, Karna, Kaushik Basu, and Tito Cordella. 2014. "Asymmetric Punishment as an Instrument of Corruption Control." World Bank Policy Research Working Paper No. 6933.

Basu, Kaushik. 1983. "On Why We Do Not Try to Walk Off without Paying after a Taxi-Ride." *Economic and Political Weekly* 18 (201): 2011–2012.

Basu, Kaushik. 1986. "One Kind of Power." *Oxford Economic Papers* 38 (2): 259–282.

Basu, Kaushik. 1989. "Technological Stagnation, Tenurial Laws, and Adverse Selection." *American Economic Review* 79 (1): 251–255.

Basu, Kaushik. 1993. *Lectures in Industrial Organization Theory*. Oxford: Blackwell Publishers.

Basu, Kaushik. 1997. *Analytical Development Economics: The Less Developed Economy Revisited*. Cambridge, MA: MIT Press.

Basu, Kaushik. 2000. *Prelude to Political Economy: A Study of the Social and Political Foundations of Economics*. New York: Oxford University Press.

Basu, Kaushik. 2003. "Globalization and the Politics of International Finance: The Stiglitz Verdict." *Journal of Economic Literature* 41 (3): 885–899.

Basu, Kaushik. 2004. *India's Emerging Economy: Performance and Prospects in the 1990s and Beyond*. Cambridge, MA: MIT Press.

Basu, Kaushik. 2006. "Gender and Say: A Model of Household Behaviour with Endogenously Determined Balance of Power." *Economic Journal* 116 (511): 558–580.

Basu, Kaushik. 2007. "Coercion, Contract and the Limits of the Market." *Social Choice and Welfare* 29 (4): 559–579.

Basu, Kaushik. 2009. "China and India: Idiosyncratic Paths to High Growth." *Economic and Political Weekly* 44 (38): 19–25.

Basu, Kaushik. 2010. *Beyond the Invisible Hand: Groundwork for a New Economics*. Princeton: Princeton University Press.

Basu, Kaushik. 2011a. *An Economist's Miscellany*. New Delhi: Oxford University Press.

Basu, Kaushik. 2011b. "India's Foodgrain Policy: An Economic Theory Perspective." *Economic and Political Weekly* 46 (5): 37–45.

Basu, Kaushik. 2011c. "A Simple Model of the Financial Crisis of 2007–2009, with Implications for the Design of a Stimulus Package." *Indian Growth and Development Review* 4 (1): 5–21.

Basu, Kaushik. 2011d. "Understanding Inflation and Controlling It." *Economic and Political Weekly* 46 (41): 50–64.

Basu, Kaushik. 2012. "How to Devalue Exchange Rates, without Building up Reserves: Strategic Theory for Central Banking." *Economics Letters* 117 (3): 758–761.

Basu, Kaushik. 2014. "Randomisation, Causality and the Role of Reasoned Intuition." *Oxford Development Studies* 42 (4): 455–472.

Basu, Kaushik, and Patrick M. Emerson. 2000. "The Economics of Tenancy Rent Control." *Economic Journal* 110 (466): 939–962.

Basu, Kaushik, Gary S. Fields, and Shub Debgupta. 2009. "Labor Retrenchment Laws and Their Effect on Wages and Employment: A Theoretical Investigation." In *New and Enduring Themes in Development Economics*, ed. Bhaskar Dutta, Tridip Ray, and E. Sommanathan, 181–206. Hackensack, NJ: World Scientific Publishing.

Basu, Kaushik, and Annemie Maertens. 2008. "The Pattern and Causes of Economic Growth in India." *Oxford Review of Economic Policy* 23 (2): 143–167.

Basu, Kaushik, and Tapan Mitra. 2003. "Aggregating Infinite Utility Streams with Intergenerational Equity: The Impossibility of Being Paretian." *Econometrica* 71 (5): 1557–1563.

Basu, Kaushik, and Hodaka Morita. 2006. "International Credit and Welfare: A Paradoxical Theorem and Its Policy Implications." *European Economic Review* 50 (6): 1507–1528.

Basu, Kaushik, and Joseph E. Stiglitz. 2015. "International Lending, Sovereign Debt and Joint Liability: An Economic Theory Model for Amending the Treaty of Lisbon." Forthcoming in *Economic Journal*.

Basu, Kaushik, and Pham Hoang Van. 1998. "The Economics of Child Labor." *American Economic Review* 88 (3): 412–427.

Basu, Kaushik, and Jörgen Weibull. 2003. "Punctuality: A Cultural Trait as Equilibrium." In *Economics for an Imperfect World: Essays in Honor of Joseph Stiglitz*, ed. Richard Arnott, Bruce Greenwald, Ravi Kanbur, and Barry Nalebuff, 163–182. Cambridge, MA: MIT Press.

Benabou, Roland, and Jean Tirole. 2011. "Laws and Norms." NBER Working Paper 17579.

Besley, Timothy, and Robin Burgess. 2004. "Can Labor Regulation Hinder Economic Performance? Evidence from India." *Quarterly Journal of Economics* 119 (1): 91–134.

Besley, Timothy, and Stephen Coate. 1992. "Understanding Welfare Stigma: Taxpayer Resentment and Statistical Discrimination." *Journal of Public Economics* 48 (2): 165–183.

Besley, Timothy, and Torsten Persson. 2014. "Why Do Developing Countries Tax So Little?" *Journal of Economic Perspectives* 28 (4): 99–120.

Bhaduri, Amit. 1973. "A Study in Agricultural Backwardness under Semi-Feudalism." *Economic Journal* 83:120–137.

Bhaduri, Amit. 1977. "On the Formation of Usurious Interest Rates in Backward Agriculture." *Cambridge Journal of Economics* 1:341–352.

Bhagwati, Jagdish. 1958. "Immiserizing Growth: A Geometrical Note." *Review of Economic Studies* 25 (3): 201–205.

Bhagwati, Jagdish. 1993. *India in Transition: Freeing the Economy.* Oxford: Clarendon Press.

Bhagwati, Jagdish, and Arvind Panagariya. 2013. *Why Growth Matters: How Economic Growth in India Reduced Poverty and the Lessons for Other Developing Countries.* New York: Public Affairs.

Bhattacharya, Rudrani, Ila Patnaik, and Ajay Shah. 2011. "Monetary Policy Transmission in an Emerging Market Setting." IMF Working Paper WP/11/5.

Blackorby, Charles, and David Donaldson. 1988. "Cash versus Kind, Self-Selection, and Efficient Transfers." *American Economic Review* 78 (4): 691–700.

Borooah, Vani. 2012. "Corruption in India: A Quantitative Analysis." *Economic and Political Weekly* 47 (28): 23–25.

Bose, Sumantra. 2013. *Transforming India: Challenges to the World's Largest Democracy.* Cambridge, MA: Harvard University Press.

Bosworth, Barry, Susan Collins, and Arvind Virmani. 2007. "Sources of Growth in the Indian Economy." NBER Working Paper No.12901.

Bourguignon, François, and Christian Morrisson. 2002. "Inequality among World Citizens: 1980–1992." *American Economic Review* 92 (4): 727–744.

Bowles, Samuel, Steven Durlauf, and Karla Hoff. 2006. *Poverty Traps.* Princeton: Princeton University Press.

Bowles, Samuel, and Herbert Gintis. 2005. "Can Self-Interest Explain Cooperation?" *Evolutionary and Institutional Economics Review* 2 (1): 21–41.

Burns, Nicholas. 2014. "Passage to India: What Washington Can Do to Revive Relations with New Delhi." *Foreign Affairs* 93 (5): 132–143.

Cagan, Phillip. 1956. "The Monetary Dynamics of Hyperinflation." In *Studies in the Quantity Theory of Money*, ed. Milton Friedman, 25–117. Chicago: University of Chicago Press.

Calvo, Cesar, and Stefan Dercon. 2013. "Vulnerability to Individual and Aggregate Poverty." *Social Choice and Welfare* 41:721–740.

Chanda, Rupa. 2012. "Services-Led Growth." In *The New Oxford Companion to Economics in India*, ed. Kaushik Basu and Annemie Maertens, 472–479. New Delhi: Oxford University Press.

Chatterjea, Arka, and Satya Moulik. 2012. "Academic Research." In *New Oxford Companion to Economics in India*, ed. Kaushik Basu and Annemie Maertens, 1–7. New Delhi: Oxford University Press.

Chattopadhyay, Raghabendra, and Esther Duflo. 2004. "Women as Policy Makers: Evidence from a Randomized Policy Experiment in India." *Econometrica* 72 (5): 1409–1443.

Chatterjee, Shoumitro, Mausumi Das, Seher Gupta, and Tridip Ray. 2011. "Education Financing Policy: Income-Contingent Loans and Educational Poverty Traps." Mimeo. New Delhi: Indian Statistical Institute.

Chaudhuri, Ananish, and Lata Gangadharan. 2007. "An Experimental Analysis of Trust and Trustworthiness." *Southern Economic Journal* 73 (4): 959–985.

Chaudhury, Nazmul, Jeffrey Hammer, Michael Kremer, Karthik Muralidharan, and F. Halsey Rogers. 2006. "Missing in Action: Teacher and Health Worker Absence in Developing Countries." *Journal of Economic Perspectives* 20 (1): 91–116.

Chen, Shaohua, and Martin Ravallion. 2013. "More Relatively-Poor People in a Less Absolutely-Poor World." *Review of Income and Wealth* 59 (1): 1–28.

Chitre, Vikas. 2010. "Monetary and Fiscal Policy for Inclusive Growth." Mimeo. Pune: Indian School of Political Economy.

Clifford, Mark. 1994. *Troubled Tiger*. London: M. E. Sharpe.

Cohen, Stephen P. 2001. *Emerging Power: India*. Washington, DC: Brookings Institution Press.

Cooter, Robert. 1998. "Expressive Law and Economics." *Journal of Legal Studies* 27 (S2): 585–607.

Das, Gurcharan. 2012. *India Grows at Night: A Liberal Case for a Strong State*. New Delhi: Penguin.

Das, Jishnu, Quy-Toan Do, and Berk Ozler. 2004. "Conditional Cash Transfers and the Equity-Efficiency Debate." World Bank Policy Research Working Paper No. 3280.

De, Supriyo. 2012. "Fiscal Policy in India: Trends and Trajectory." Working Paper, Ministry of Finance, New Delhi.

Deaton, Angus. 2010. "Instruments, Randomization, and Learning about Development." *Journal of Economic Literature* 48 (2): 424–455.

Deaton, Angus, and Jean Drèze. 2002. "Poverty and Inequality in India: A Re-Examination." *Economic and Political Weekly* 37 (36): 3729–3748.

Deaton, Angus, and Valerie Kozel. 2005. "Data and Dogma: The Great Indian Poverty Debate." *World Bank Research Observer* 20 (2): 177–199.

Desai, Meghnad. 1991. "Human Development: Concepts and Measurement." *European Economic Review* 35 (2): 350–357.

Desai, Sonalde, Amaresh Dubey, Brij L. Joshi, Mitali Sen, Reeve Venneman, and Abusaleh Sharif. 2010. *Human Development in India: Challenges for a Society in Transition.* New Delhi: Oxford University Press.

Desai, Sonalde, and Devaki Jain. 1994. "Maternal Employment and Changes in Family Dynamics: The Social Context of Women's Work in Rural South India." *Population and Development Review* 20 (1):115–136.

Deshpande, Ashwini. 2011. *The Grammar of Caste.* New Delhi: Oxford University Press.

Dev, Mahendra. 2008. *Inclusive Growth in India: Agriculture, Poverty, and Human Development.* New Delhi: Oxford University Press.

Dev, Mahendra, and N. Chandrasekhara Rao. 2010. "Agricultural Price Policy, Farm Profitability and Food Security." *Economic and Political Weekly* 40 (26): 174–182.

Dhar, Prithvi Nath. 2000. *Indira Gandhi, the "Emergency," and Indian Democracy.* New Delhi: Oxford University Press.

Dhillon, Amrita, Vegard Iversen, and Gaute Torsvik. 2013. "Employee Referral, Social Proximity, and Worker Discipline." CESinfo Working Paper No. 4309.

Dholakia, Ravindra H., and Amey A. Sapre. 2011. "Speed of Adjustment and Inflation: Unemployment Tradeoff in Developing Countries: Case of India." Indian Institute of Management (IIMA) Working Paper No. 2011-07-01.

Dixit, Avinash. 1980. "The Role of Entry Deterrence." *Economic Journal* 90 (1): 95–106.

Dixit, Avinash. 2007. *Lawlessness and Economics: Alternative Modes of Governance.* Princeton: Princeton University Press.

Dixit, Avinash. 2015. "How Business Community Institutions Can Help Fight Corruption." Forthcoming in *World Bank Economic Review.*

Domar, Evsey. 1946. "Capital Expansion, Rate of Growth, and Employment." *Econometrica* 14 (2): 137–147.

Drèze, Jean, and Amartya Sen. 2013. *An Uncertain Glory: India and Its Contradictions.* Princeton: Princeton University Press.

Dufwenberg, Martin, and Giancarlo Spagnolo. 2014. "Legalizing Bribe Giving." Forthcoming in *Economic Inquiry.*

Dutta, Bhaskar. 2002. "Inequality, Poverty and Welfare." In *Handbook of Social Choice and Welfare, Volume 1*, ed. K. Arrow, A. Sen, and K. Suzumura, 597–633. Amsterdam: Elsevier.

Edmonds, Eric V. 2007. "Child Labor." *Handbook of Development Economics* 4:3607–3709.

Eichengreen, Barry, and Poonam Gupta. 2014. "Tapering Talk: The Impact of Expectations of Reduced Federal Reserve Security Purchases on Emerging Markets." World Bank Policy Research Working Paper, No. 6754.

Emerson, Patrick M, and André Portela Souza. 2003. "Is There a Child Labor Trap? Intergenerational Persistence of Child Labor in Brazil." *Economic Development and Cultural Change* 51 (2): 375–398.

EPW Research Foundation. 2011. "Is the Growth in Bank Credit a Serious Concern?" *Economic and Political Weekly* 46 (23): 71–77.

Fehr, Ernst, and Simon Gächter. 2000. "Fairness and Retaliation: The Economics of Reciprocity." *Journal of Economic Perspectives* 14 (3): 159–181.

Ferguson, William. 2013. *Collective Action and Exchange: A Game-theoretic Approach to Contemporary Political Economy*. Stanford, CA: Stanford University Press.

Ferro, Manuela, David Rosenblatt, and Nicholas Stern. "Policies for Pro-Poor Growth in India." In *India's Emerging Economy: Performance and Prospects in the 1990s and Beyond*, ed. K. Basu, 153–182. Cambridge, MA: MIT Press.

Fershtman, Chaim, and Yoram Weiss. 1998. "Social Rewards, Externalities and Stable Preferences." *Journal of Public Economics* 70 (1): 53–73.

Fiszbein, Ariel, and Norman Schady. 2009. "Conditional Cash Transfers." World Bank Policy Research Report No. 47603.

Forbes, Naushad. 1999. "Technology and Indian Industry: What Is Liberalization Changing?" *Technovation* 19 (6): 403–412.

Foster, James, Joel Greer, and Erik Thorbecke. 1984. "A Class of Decomposable Poverty Measures." *Econometrica* 52 (3): 761–766.

Frank, Katherine. 2002. *Indira: The Life of Indira Nehru Gandhi*. New York: HarperCollins.

French, Patrick. 2011. *India: A Portrait*. New York: Alfred Knopf.

Fukuyama, Francis. 1996. *Trust: The Social Virtues and the Creation of Prosperity*. New York: Free Press.

Gandhi, Sahil, Abhay Pethe, and Vaidehi Tandel. 2012. "Unravelling the Anatomy of Legal Corruption." *Economic and Political Weekly* 47 (21): 55–62.

Gangopadhyay, Shubhashis, Bharat Ramaswami, and Wilima Wadhwa. 2005. "Reducing Subsidies on Household Fuels in India: How Will It Affect the Poor?" *Energy Policy* 33 (18): 2326–2336.

Garcia, Márcio, Diego Guillén, and Patrick Kehoe. 2010. "The Monetary and Fiscal History of Latin America." Mimeo. Princeton University.

Genicot, Garance. 2002. "Bonded Labor and Serfdom: A Paradox of Voluntary Choice." *Journal of Development Economics* 67: 101–127.

Ghatak, Maitreesh. 1999. "Group Lending, Local Information and Peer Selection." *Journal of Development Economics* 60 (1): 27–50.

Gigerenzer, Gerd, and Peter M. Todd. 1999. *Simple Heuristics That Make Us Smart.* New York: Oxford University Press.

Gintis, Herbert. 2009. *The Bounds of Reason: Game Theory and the Unification of the Behavioral Sciences.* Princeton: Princeton University Press.

Goffman, Erving. 2009. *Stigma: Notes on the Management of Spoiled Identity.* New York: Simon and Schuster.

Gokarn, Subir. 2012. "An Assessment of Recent Macroeconomic Developments." *RBI Bulletin* 66 (1): 41–46.

Government of India. 2010. *Economic Survey 2009–2010.* New Delhi: Ministry of Finance and Oxford University Press.

Government of India. 2011. *Economic Survey 2010–2011.* New Delhi: Ministry of Finance and Oxford University Press.

Government of India. 2012. *Economic Survey 2011–2012.* New Delhi: Ministry of Finance and Oxford University Press.

Government of India. 2014. *Economic Survey 2013–2014.* New Delhi: Ministry of Finance and Oxford University Press.

Goyal, Ashima. 2014. "Understanding the High Inflation Trend in India." Asian Development Bank South Asia Working Paper No. 24.

Granovetter, Mark. 1985. "Economic Action and Social Structure: The Problem of Embeddedness." *American Journal of Sociology* 91 (3): 481–510.

Greif, Avner. 1993. "Contract Enforceability and Economic Institutions in Early Trade: The Maghribi Traders' Coalition." *American Economic Review* 83 (3): 525–548.

Guha, Ashok S, and Brishti Guha. 2012. "The Persistence of Goodness." *Journal of Institutional and Theoretical Economics JITE* 168 (3): 432–443.

Guha, Ramachandra. 2007. *India after Gandhi: The History of the World's Largest Democracy.* New Delhi: Harper Collins.

Hahn, Frank. 1982. *Money and Inflation*. Oxford: Blackwell Publishers.

Harrington, Joseph E. Jr. 1999. "Rigidity of Social Systems." *Journal of Political Economy* 107 (1): 40–64.

Harrod, Roy F. 1939. "An Essay in Dynamic Theory." *Economic Journal* 49 (193): 14–33.

Hashimoto, Takehiko. 2008. "Japanese Clocks and the History of Punctuality in Modern Japan." *East Asian Science, Technology and Society* 2 (1): 123–133.

Himanshu and Abhijit Sen. 2004. "Poverty and Inequality in India." *Economic and Political Weekly* 39 (38): 18–24.

Hoff, Karla, and Priyanka Pandey. 2006. "Discrimination, Social Identity, and Durable Inequalities." *American Economic Review* 96 (2): 206–211.

Hoff, Karla, and Joseph Stiglitz. 2001. "Modern Economic Theory and Development." In *Frontiers of Development Economics: The Future in Perspective*, ed. Gerald M. Meier and Joseph E. Stiglitz, 389–459. New York: Oxford University Press.

Howe, Mark DeWolfe, and Felix Frankfurter. 1953. *Holmes-Laski Letters, Volume 2*. Cambridge, MA: Harvard University Press.

Hume, David. 1758. "Of the First Principles of Government." In *Essays: Moral, Political and Literary*. Indianapolis: Reprinted Liberty Fund.

Iversen, Vegard, and P. S. Raghavendra. 2006. "What the Signboard Hides: Food, Caste and Employability in Small South Indian Eating Places." *Contributions to Indian Sociology* 40 (3): 311–341.

Jadhav, Narendra. 2013. *Ambedkar: Awakening India's Social Conscience*. New Delhi: Konark Publishers.

Jalan, Bimal. 1991. *India's Economic Crisis: The Way Ahead*. New Delhi: Oxford University Press.

Jalan, Bimal. 2001. "Indian Banking and Finance: Managing New Challenges." In *India's Economy in the 21st Century*, ed. R. Kapila and U. Kapila, 37–54. New Delhi: Academic Foundation.

Jha, Shikha, and Bharat Ramaswami. 2010. "How Can Food Subsidies Work Better? Answers from India and the Philippines." Asian Development Bank Working Paper Series No. 221.

Jhabvala, Renana, Sapna Desai, and Jignasa Dave. 2010. *Empowering Women in an Insecure World: Joining Sewa Makes a Difference*. Ahmedabad: SEWA Academy.

Jisheng, Yang. 2008. *Tombstone: The Untold Story of Mao's Great Famine*. London: Penguin Books UK.

Johnson, Simon. 2009. "The Quiet Coup." *The Atlantic*, May.

Kahneman, Daniel. 2011. *Thinking, Fast and Slow*. New York: Farrar, Straus and Giroux.

Kahneman, Daniel, and Amos Tversky. 1979. "Prospect Theory: An Analysis of Decision under Risk." *Econometrica* 47 (2): 263–291.

Kanbur, Ravi. 2004. "On Obnoxious Markets." In *Globalization, Culture and the Limits of the Market: Essays in Economics and Philosophy*, ed. S. Cullenberg and P. Pattanaik, 39–64. New Delhi: Oxford University Press.

Kanbur, Ravi, and Lawrence Haddad. 1994. "Are Better Off Households More Unequal or Less Unequal?" *Oxford Economic Papers* 46 (3): 445–458.

Kapur, Devesh, and Pratap Bhanu Mehta. 2004. "Indian Higher Education Reform: From Half-Baked Socialism to Half-Baked Capitalism." Center for International Development Working Paper 103.

Kautilya. 1992. *The Arthashastra*. Trans. L. N. Rangarajan. New Delhi: Penguin Books.

Kenny, Charles, Michael Klein, and Monika Sztajerowska. 2011. "A Trio of Perspectives on Corruption: Bias, Speed Money and 'Grand Theft Infrastructure.'" World Bank Policy Research Working Paper, No. 5889.

Keynes, John Maynard. 1936. *The General Theory of Employment, Interest, and Money*. London: Macmillan.

Khanna, Tarun. 2007. *Billions of Entrepreneurs: How China and India Are Reshaping Their Futures—and Yours*. Boston: Harvard Business Review Press.

Khera, Reetika. 2010. "India's Public Distribution System: Utilization and Impact." *Journal of Development Studies* 47 (7): 1038–1060.

Khera, Reetika. 2011. "Trends in Diversion of Grain from the Public Distribution System." *Economic and Political Weekly* 46 (21): 106–114.

Khilnani, Sunil. 1999. *The Idea of India*. New York: Farrar Strauss Giroux.

Kohli, Atul. 2012. *Poverty Amid Plenty in the New India*. Cambridge: Cambridge University Press.

Kramnick, Isaac, and Barry Sheerman. 1993. *Harold Laski: A Life on the Left*. New York: Allen Lane.

Kremer, Michael. 1993. "The O-Ring Theory of Economic Development." *Quarterly Journal of Economics* 108 (3): 551–575.

Kremer, Michael, Karthik Muralidharan, Nazmul Chaudhury, Jeff Hammer, and F. Halsey Rogers. 2005. "Teacher Absence in India." *Journal of the European Economic Association* 3:658–667.

Kudaisya, Megha. 2003. *The Life and Times of G. D. Birla*. New Delhi: Oxford University Press.

Kuran, Timur. 1988. "Ethnic Norms and Their Transformation through Reputational Cascades." *Journal of Legal Studies* 27 (S2): 623–659.

Landa, Janet Tai. 1995. *Trust, Ethnicity and Identity: Beyond the New Institutional Economics of Ethnic Trading Networks, Contract Law and Gift Exchange*. Ann Arbor: University of Michigan Press.

Lanjouw, Peter, and Rinku Murgai. 2009. "Poverty Decline, Agricultural Wages, and Nonfarm Employment in Rural India: 1983–2004." *Agricultural Economics* 40 (2): 243–263.

Levine, Robert V., Laurie J. West, and Harry T. Reis. 1980. "Perceptions of Time and Punctuality in the United States and Brazil." *Journal of Personality and Social Psychology* 38 (4): 541–550.

Li, Xingxing. 2012. "Bribery and the Limits of Game Theory—the Lessons from China." *Financial Times* (London).

Lilienfeld-Toal, Ulf von, Dilip Mookherjee, and Sujata Visaria. 2012. "The Distributive Impact of Reforms in Credit Enforcement: Evidence from Indian Debt Recovery Tribunals." *Econometrica* 80 (2): 497–558.

Lin, Justin Yifu. 1999. "Comparative Advantage Development Strategy and the Economic Development of Taiwan." In *Taiwan's Development Experience: Lessons on Roles of Government and Market*, ed. E. Thorbecke and H. Wan, 157–162. Boston: Kluwer Academic Press.

Lin, Justin Yifu, Fang Cai, and Zhou Li. 1996. *The China Miracle: Development Strategy and Economic Reform*. Hong Kong: Chinese University Press.

Lindbeck, Assar, Sten Nyberg, and Jorgen W. Weibull. 1999. "Social Norms and Economic Incentives in the Welfare State." *Quarterly Journal of Economics* 114 (1): 1–35.

López-Calva, Luis-Felipe. 2003. "Social Norms, Coordination, and Policy Issues in the Fight against Child Labor." In *International Labour Standards*, ed. K. Basu, H. Horn, L. Romain, and J. Shapiro, 256–266. Oxford: Blackwell.

Lucas, Robert E., Jr. 1988. "On the Mechanics of Economic Development." *Journal of Monetary Economics* 22:3–42.

Mahbubani, Kishore. 2008. *The New Asian Hemisphere: The Irresistible Shift of Global Power to the East*. New York: Public Affairs.

Mailath, George, Stephen Morris, and Andrew Postlewaite. 2001." Laws and Authority." Mimeo. University of Pennsylvania.

Malone, David M. 2011. *Does the Elephant Dance? Contemporary Indian Foreign Policy*. Oxford: Oxford University Press.

Mankiw, Gregory N. 2010. *Principles of Macroeconomics.* New York: Worth Publishers.

Manski, Charles. 2013. *Public Policy in an Uncertain World.* Cambridge, MA: Harvard University Press.

Marjit, Sugata, and Rajat Acharyya. 2006. "Trade Liberalization, Skill-Linked Intermediate Production and the Two-Sided Wage Gap." *Journal of Economic Policy Reform* 9 (3): 203–217.

Martinsson, Peter, Nam Pham-Kanh, and Clara Villegas-Palacio. 2013. "Conditional Cooperation and Disclosure in Developing Countries." *Journal of Economic Psychology* 34:148–155.

McAdams, Richard. 2000. "A Focal Point Theory of Expressive Law." *Virginia Law Review* 86:1649–1729.

McKibbin, Warwick J, and Will Martin. 1999. *The East Asian Crisis: Investigating Causes and Policy Responses.* Washington, DC: World Bank Publications.

Mehta, Pratap. 2014. "Bigger than the Sum of His Imperfections." *Open Magazine* 14, November.

Milanović, Branko. 2010. *The Haves and the Have-Nots: A Brief and Idiosyncratic History of Global Inequality.* New York: Basic Books.

Mill, John Stuart. 1859. *On Liberty.* London: Dent and Sons. Reprinted 1971.

Mill, John Stuart. 1867. *Inaugural Address Delivered to the University of St. Andrews, Feb. 1st, 1867.* London: Longmans, Green, Reader, and Dyer.

Mishra, Pankaj. 2013. "Which India Matters?" *New York Review of Books*, November 21.

Mishra, Prachi, and Devesh Roy. 2011. "Explaining Inflation in India: The Role of Food Prices." Mimeo. Washington, DC: IMF and IFFPRI.

Mohan, Rakesh. 1992. "Industrial Policy and Controls." In *The Indian Economy: Problems and Prospects*, ed. Bimal Jalan, 85–115. New Delhi: Penguin.

Mohan, Rakesh. 2002. "A Decade after 1991: New Challenges Facing the Indian Economy." *Reserve Bank of India Bulletin* 56:771–788.

Mohanty, Deepak. 2011. "Monetary Policy Response to Recent Inflation in India." Speech delivered on September 3, Indian Institute of Technology (IIT), Guwahati.

Mookherjee, Dilip. 2005. "Is There Too Little Theory in Development Economics Today?" *Economic and Political Weekly* 40 (40): 4328–4333.

Mukherjee, Pranab. 2012. "Budget Making." In *The New Oxford Companion to Economics in India*, ed. Kaushik Basu and Annemie Maertens, 44–48. New Delhi: Oxford University Press.

Mukherjee, Rudrangshu. 2007. *The Great Speeches of Modern India*. New Delhi: Random House India.

Mullainathan, Sendhil. 2005. "Development Economics through the Lens of Psychology." In *Annual World Bank Conference in Development Economics 2005: Lessons of Experience*, 45–70. New York: Oxford University Press.

Munshi, Kaivan. 2014. "Community Networks and the Process of Development." *Journal of Economic Perspectives* 28 (4): 49–76.

Muralidharan, Karthik, Jishnu Das, Alaka Holla, and Aakash Mohpal. 2014. "The Fiscal Cost of Weak Governance: Evidence from Teacher Absence in India." NBER Working Paper No. 20299.

Murphy, Kevin M., Andrei Shleifer, and Robert W. Vishny. 1989. "Industrialization and the Big Push." *Journal of Political Economy* 97 (5): 1003–1026.

Murthy, N. R. Narayana. 2000. "Making India a Significant IT Player in This Millennium." In *India: Another Millennium*, ed. Romila Thapar, 212–240. New Delhi: Viking and Penguin Books.

Murthy, N. R. Narayana. 2004. "The Impact of Economic Reforms on Industry in India: A Case Study of the Software Industry." In *India's Emerging Economy: Performance and Prospects in the 1990s and Beyond*, ed. K. Basu, 217–222. Cambridge, MA: MIT Press.

Myerson, Roger. 2004. "Justice, Institutions, and Multiple Equilibria." *Chicago Journal of International Law* 5 (1): 91–107.

Myerson, Roger. 2006. "Fundamental Theory of Institutions: A Lecture in Honor of Leo Hurwicz." Mimeo. Department of Economics, Chicago University.

Nayyar, Deepak. 1996. *Economic Liberalization in India: Analytics, Experience and Lessons*. Kolkata: Orient Longman.

Neeman, Zvika. 1999. "The Freedom to Contract and the Free-Rider Problem." *Journal of Law Economics, and Organization* 15:685–703.

Nehru, Jawaharlal. 2004. *The Discovery of India*. Gurgaon, Haryana: Penguin Books India.

Nilekani, Nandan. 2009. *Imagining India: Ideas for the New Century*. London: Penguin.

Oak, Mandar. 2013. "Legalization of Bribe Giving When Bribe Type Is Endogenous." University of Adelaide Research Paper 2013-06. Forthcoming in *Journal of Public Economic Theory*.

Oh, Jinhwan. 2011. "Spatial Adaptation of the Murphy-Shleifer-Vishny Model, with Special Reference to World Development Report 2009 and Korean Examples." Working Paper. International University of Japan.

Panagariya, Arvind. 2008. *India: The Emerging Giant*. New York: Oxford University Press.

Pankaj, Ashok, and Rukmini Tankha. 2010. "Empowerment Effects of the NREGS on Women Workers: A Study in Four States." *Economic and Political Weekly* 45 (30): 45–55.

Pant, Harsh. 2007. "India in the Asia-Pacific: Rising Ambitions with an Eye on China." *Asia-Pacific Review* 14:54–71.

Parfit, Derek. 1984. *Reasons and Persons*. New York: Oxford University Press.

Patel, I. G. 2004. *Glimpses of Indian Economic Policy: An Insider's View*. New Delhi and Oxford: Oxford University Press.

Paternostro, Stefano. 1997. "The Poverty Trap: The Dual Externality Model and Its Policy Implications." *World Development* 25 (12): 2071–2081.

Patnaik, Ila. 2012. "Tariffs." In *The New Oxford Companion to Economics in India*, ed. Kaushik Basu and Annemie Maertens, 676–677. New Delhi: Oxford University Press.

Patnaik, Prabhat. 2012. "Inflation." In *The New Oxford Companion to Economics in India*, ed. Kaushik Basu and Annemie Maertens, 381–382. New Delhi: Oxford University Press.

Piketty, Thomas. 2014. *Capital in the Twenty-First Century*. Cambridge, MA: Harvard University Press.

Pisani-Ferry, Jean, André Sapir, and Guntram Wolff. 2013. "EU-IMF Assistance to EuroArea Countries: An Early Assessment." Bruegel Blueprint Series No. 19.

Platteau, Jean-Philippe. 2000. *Institutions, Social Norms, and Economic Development*, vol. 1. New York: Psychology Press.

Polanyi, Karl. 1944. *The Great Transformation*. Boston: Beacon Press.

Prasad, Eswar S. 2014. *The Dollar Trap: How the US Dollar Tightened Its Grip on Global Finance*. Princeton: Princeton University Press.

Prestowitz, Clyde V. 2005. *Three Billion New Capitalists: The Great Shift of Wealth and Power to the East*. New York: Basic Books.

PROBE. 1999. *Public Report on Basic Education in India*. New Delhi: Oxford University Press.

Rabin, Matthew. 1998. "Psychology and Economics." *Journal of Economic Literature* 36 (1): 11–46.

Radford, Robert A. 1945. "The Economic Organisation of a POW Camp." *Economica* 12:189–201.

Rajan, Raghuram G. 2010. *Fault Lines: How Hidden Fractures Still Threaten the World Economy*. Princeton: Princeton University Press.

Rajwade, A. V. 2012. "The Fall of the Rupee: Background, Remedy, and Policy." *Economic and Political Weekly* 47 (2): 10–14.

Rakshit, Mihir. 2004. "Some Macroeconomics of India's Reform Experience." In *India's Emerging Economy: Performance and Prospects in the 1990s and Beyond*, ed. Kaushik Basu, 83–114. Cambridge, MA: MIT Press.

Rakshit, Mihir. 2011. "Inflation and Relative Prices in India 2006–10: Some Analytics and Policy Issues." *Economic and Political Weekly* 46 (16): 41–54.

Rana, Kumar, Abdur Rafique, and Amrita Sengupta. 2002. *The Pratichi Education Report: The Delivery of Primary Education*. New Delhi: The Pratichi India Trust.

Rangarajan, Chakravarthi. 2009. *India: Monetary Policy, Financial Stability, and Other Essays*. New Delhi: Academic Foundation.

Rao, Govinda. 2004. "State-Level Fiscal Reforms in India." In *India's Emerging Economy: Performance and Prospects in the 1990s and Beyond*, ed. Kaushik Basu, 115–150. Cambridge, MA: MIT Press.

Rao, Nirupama. 2014. "The Politics of History: India and China, 1949–1962." Mimeo. Brown University.

Rao, Vijayendra, and Michael Walton, eds. 2004. *Culture and Public Action*. Stanford, CA: Stanford University Press.

Rao, V. K. R. V. 1952. "Investment, Income and the Multiplier in an Underdeveloped Economy." *Indian Economic Journal* 56 (2): 55–67.

Ravallion, Martin. 2014. *The Economics of Poverty*. Oxford and New York: Oxford University Press.

Rawls, John. 1971. *A Theory of Justice*. Cambridge, MA: Harvard University Press.

Ray, Debraj. 1998. *Development Economics*. Princeton: Princeton University Press.

Ray, Ranjan, and Ankita Mishra. 2012. "Multi-Dimensional Deprivation in the Awakening Giants: A Comparison of China and India on Micro Data." *Journal of Asian Economics* 23 (4): 454–465.

Reddy, Sanjay, and Thomas W. Pogge. 2010. "How Not to Count the Poor." In *Debates on the Measurement of Poverty*, ed. Sudhir Anand, Paul Segal, and Joseph Stiglitz, 42–85. New York: Oxford University Press.

Reddy, Y. V. 2004. "Monetary and Financial Sector Reforms in India: A Practitioner's Perspective." In *India's Emerging Economy: Performance and Prospects in the 1990s and Beyond*, ed. Kaushik Basu, 61–82. Cambridge, MA: MIT Press.

Reddy, Y. Venugopal. 2011. *Global Crisis, Recession and Uneven Recovery*. New Delhi: Orient Blackswan.

Reserve Bank of India. 2008. *Report on Foreign Exchange Reserves*. Mumbai: RBI.

Rodrik, Dani. 2009. "The New Development Economics: We Shall Experiment, but How Shall We Learn?" In *What Works in Development? Thinking Big and Thinking Small*, ed. Jessica Cohen and William Easterly, 24–47. Washington, DC: Brookings Institution Press.

Rodrik, Dani, and Arvind Subramanian. 2004. "Why India Can Grow at 7 Percent a Year or More: Projections and Reflections." *Economic and Political Weekly* 39 (16): 1519–1526.

Roemer, John. 2011. "The Ethics of Intertemporal Distribution in a Warming Planet." *Environment and Resource Economics* 48:363–390.

Romer, Paul M. 1986. "Increasing Returns and Long-Run Growth." *Journal of Political Economy* 94 (5): 1002–1037.

Roosevelt, Eleanor. 1953. *India and the Awakening East*. New York: Harper and Brothers.

Rubinstein, Ariel. 1979. "Equilibrium in Supergames with the Overtaking Criterion." *Journal of Economic Theory* 21 (1): 1–9.

Rubinstein, Ariel. 2014. "A Typology of Players: Between Instinctive and Contemplative." Mimeo. Tel Aviv University.

Rudra, Ashok. 1996. *Prasanta Chandra Mahalanobis: A Biography*. New Delhi: Oxford University Press.

Sachs, Jeffrey. 2005. *The End of Poverty: Economic Possibilities for Our Time*. New York: Penguin.

Sargent, Thomas J. 1982. "The Ends of Four Big Inflations." In *Inflation: Causes and Effects*, ed. R. E. Hall, 41–98. Chicago: University of Chicago Press.

Satz, Debra. 2004. "Noxious Markets: Why Should Some Things Not Be For Sale." In *Globalization, Culture and the Limits of the Market*, ed. P. Pattanaik and S. Cullenberg, 41–98. New York: Oxford University Press.

Schäfer, Hans-Bernd. 2012. "The Sovereign Debt Crisis in Europe, Save Banks Not States." *European Journal of Comparative Economics* 9:179–195.

Schelling, Thomas C. 1980. *The Strategy of Conflict*. Cambridge, MA: Harvard University Press.

Sen, Abhijit. 2002. *Report of the Committee on Long Term Grain Policy*. New Delhi: Commission for Agricultural Costs and Prices.

Sen, Abhijit, and Himanshu. 2005. "Poverty and Inequality in India: Getting Closer to the Truth." In *Data and Dogma: The Great Indian Poverty Debate*, ed. Angus Deaton and Valerie Kozel, 177–199. New Delhi: Macmillan.

Sen, Amartya. 1976. "Poverty: An Ordinal Approach to Measurement." *Econometrica* 44 (2): 219–231.

Sen, Amartya. 1980. "Description as Choice." *Oxford Economic Papers* 32 (3): 353–369.

Sen, Amartya. 1981. *Poverty and Famines: An Essay on Entitlement and Deprivation.* New York: Oxford University Press.

Sen, Amartya. 2004. "Democracy and Secularism in India." In *India's Emerging Economy: Performance and Prospects in the 1990s and Beyond,* ed. Kaushik Basu, 35–48. Cambridge, MA: MIT Press.

Sen, Amartya. 2005. *The Argumentative Indian: Writings on Indian History, Culture and Identity.* New York: Farrar, Straus and Giroux.

Shah, Ajay, and Ila Patnaik. 2007. "India's Experience with Capital Flows: The Elusive Quest for a Sustainable Current Account Deficit." In *Capital Controls and Capital Flows in Emerging Economies: Policies, Practices and Consequences,* ed. Sebastian Edwards, 609–644. Chicago: University of Chicago Press.

Singh, Jaivir. 2012. "Labour Laws." In *The New Oxford Companion to Economics in India,* ed. Kaushik Basu and Annemie Maertens, 430–434. New Delhi: Oxford University Press.

Singh, Nirvikar. 2004. "Information Technology and India's Economic Development." In *India's Emerging Economy: Performance and Prospects in the 1990s and Beyond,* ed. Kaushik Basu, 223–262. Cambridge, MA: MIT Press.

Singh, N. K., and Nicholas Stern. 2013. *The New Bihar: Rekindling Governance and Development.* New Delhi: Harper Collins.

Singh, Nirvikar, and Ravi Thomas. 2000. "Welfare Policy: Cash versus Kind, Self-Selection and Notches." *Southern Economic Journal* 66 (4): 976–990.

Sivasubramonian, S. 1997. "Revised Estimates of the National Income of India, 1900–1901 to 1946–1947." *Indian Economic and Social History Review* 34 (2): 113–168.

Solow, Robert M. 1956. "A Contribution to the Theory of Economic Growth." *Quarterly Journal of Economics* 70 (1): 65–94.

Songchoo, Tananya, and Komsan Suriya. 2012. "Competition to Commit Crime: An Economic Experiment on Illegal Logging Using Behavioral Game Theory." *Empirical Econometrics and Quantitative Economics Letters* 1 (1): 75–90.

Spence, Michael. 1973. "Job Market Signaling." *Quarterly Journal of Economics* 87 (3): 355–374.

Spengler, Dominic. 2014. "Endogenising Detection of Collaborative Crime: The Case of Corruption." *Review of Law and Economics* 10 (2): 201–217.

Srinivasan, T. N. 2000. *Eight Lectures on India's Economic Reforms.* New Delhi: Oxford University Press.

Standing, Guy, Sarath Davala, Renana Jhabvala, and Soumya Kapoor Mehta. 2015. "Basic Income: A Transformative Policy for India." London and New Delhi: Bloomsbury Academic.

Stathakis, George, and Gianni Vaggi. "Economic Development and Social Change: The Classical View and the Moderns." In *Economic Development and Social Change: Historical Roots and Modern Perspectives*, ed. George Stathakis and Gianni Vaggi, 1–26. London: Routledge.

Stern, Nicholas. 2007. *The Economics of Climate Change: The Stern Review.* Cambridge: Cambridge University Press.

Stiglitz, Joseph E. 2002. *Globalization and Its Discontents.* New York: W. W. Norton & Company.

Stiglitz, Joseph E. 2010. *Freefall: America, Free Markets, and the Sinking of the World Economy.* New York: W. W. Norton & Company.

Stiglitz, Joseph E, Amartya Sen, and Jean-Paul Fitoussi. 2010. *Report by the Commission on the Measurement of Economic Performance and Social Progress.* Paris: Commission on the Measurement of Economic Performance and Social Progress.

Stiglitz, Joseph E., and Andrew Weiss. 1981. "Credit Rationing in Markets with Imperfect Information." *American Economic Review* 71 (3): 393–410.

Subbarao, Duvvuri. 2011. "India and the Global Financial Crisis: What Have We Learnt?" K. R. Narayanan Oration, Australian National University, Canberra.

Subrahmanyam, Sanjay. 2013. *Is Indian Civilization a Myth?* New Delhi: Permanent Black.

Subramanian, S. 1997. *Introduction: The Measurement of Inequality and Poverty.* New Delhi: Oxford University Press.

Subramanian, S. 2011. "'Inclusive Development' and the Quintile Income Statistic." *Economic and Political Weekly* 46 (4): 69–72.

Subramanian, S., and D. Jayaraj. 2012. "The Evolution of Consumption and Wealth Inequality in India: A Quantitative Assessment." Mimeo. Chennai: Madras Institute of Development Studies.

Sundell, Anders. 2014. "Understanding Informal Payments in the Public Sector: Theory and Evidence from Nineteenth-Century Sweden." *Scandinavian Political Studies* 37 (2): 95–122.

Sunstein, Cass. 1996. "Social Norms and Social Roles." *Columbia Law Review* 96 (4): 903–968.

Swan, Trevor W. 1956. "Economic Growth and Capital Accumulation." *Economic Record* 32 (2): 334–361.

Swedberg, Richard. 2014. *The Art of Social Theory*. Princeton: Princeton University Press.

Tagore, Rabindranath. 1918. *Nationalism*. London: Macmillan.

Tarapore, S. S. 2002. "Capital Account Convertibility Revisited." In *India's Economy in the 21st Century: A Collection of Select Articles*, ed. R. Kapila and U. Kapila, 419. New Delhi: Academic Foundation.

Tata, Ratan. 2012. "Tata, the House Of." In *New Oxford Companion to Economics in India*, ed. K. Basu and A. Maertens, 677–679. New Delhi: Oxford University Press.

Thaler, Richard H, and Cass R. Sunstein. 2008. *Nudge: Improving Decisions About Health, Wealth, and Happiness*. New Haven, CT: Yale University Press.

Vaidyanathan, A. 2009. *Agricultural Growth in India: The Role of Technology, Incentives and Institutions*. New Delhi: Oxford University Press.

Varshney, Ashutosh. 2003. "Nationalism, Ethnic Conflict, and Rationality." *Perspectives on Politics* 1 (1): 85–99.

Varshney, Ashutosh. 2013. *Battles Half Won: India's Improbable Democracy*. New Delhi: Penguin.

Vaughan, Diane. 1996. *The Challenger Launch Decision*. Chicago: University of Chicago Press.

Veblen, Thorstein. 2007. *The Theory of the Leisure Class*. Oxford: Oxford University Press.

Virmani, Arvind. 2006. *Propelling India from Socialist Stagnation to Global Power: Policy Reforms*. New Delhi: Academic Foundation.

Von Tunzelmann, Alex. 2007. *Indian Summer: The Secret History of the End of an Empire*. London: Macmillan.

Vyasulu, Vinod. 2010. "Brazil's 'Fome Zero' Strategy: Can India Implement Cash Transfers?'" *Economic and Political Weekly* 45 (26/27): 89–95.

Wolf, Martin. 2004. *Why Globalization Works*. New Haven, CT: Yale University Press.

Wolpert, Stanley A. 1996. *Nehru: A Tryst with Destiny*. New York: Oxford University Press.

World Bank. 2014a. *Doing Business 2015*. Washington, DC: World Bank Group.

World Bank. 2014b. *World Development Report 2015: Mind, Society, and Behavior*. Washington, DC: World Bank Group.

Index

Name Index

Subject Index

Openness, 11, 141, 184. *See also* Trade
Operation Twist, 45
Organized labor, 145
Outsourcing, 33
Overtaking criterion, 131

Pakistan, 20, 144, 173, 205n9
Pareto principle, 114, 123
People's Bank of China, 42, 79
Permit raj, 11. *See also* Licensing
Policymaking, 3, 6, 12, 28, 44, 65, 86, 93, 95, 120, 147, 149, 174, 175
Policy puzzle, 46
Political hyperbolic discounting, 186. *See also* Hyperbolic discounting
Ponzis, 129–132, 201n13
Populism, 186
Poverty, 34, 61, 63, 90–92, 94–96, 99–103, 107, 109, 111, 130, 159, 173–174, 194n21, 197n1, 198n6
Power
authoritarian (*see* Totalitarianism)
government's, 2
Prediction. *See* Forecasting (economic)
Preferences, 114, 201n8
Price stabilization, 52, 111
Princeton University, 10
Principle of free contract, 122–124, 129, 145, 147, 148
Privatization, 185
Psychology, 50, 151, 157, 167. *See also* Cipher stroke
Psychologist, 24, 161
Public distribution system (PDS), 109, 111, 114–117, 198nn3, 8, 199n14
Punctuality, 22, 161–163

Quantitative Easing (QE), 64, 89

Raisina Hill, 1, 2, 166
Rashtrapati Bhavan, 1
Ratings, 179
Reasoning, 61–62, 95

deductive, 148, 175, 184
Recession, 36, 38, 40–42, 64, 72, 193n11
Recourse loan, non-recourse loan, 36
Reforms. *See* Economic reforms
Regulation, 11, 16, 96, 123, 127, 129, 130, 133, 176, 178, 182, 200n5
Rent control, 143–145, 202n8
Repo rate, 56–58, 60, 67, 82, 56, 193n12
Reputation, 180
Reserve Bank of India (RBI), 39, 51–2, 55–7, 76–9, 127, 193n12, 194n14, 200n21
Reverse repo rate, 56–58, 193n12
Right to Food Act, 100, 103, 198n6
Right to employment, 198n6
Russia, 14–15, 50, 155–156, 191n22, 203n18

Salad bowl stagflation, 63–64, 89, 193n6
Savings, 30–34, 43, 54–55, 59, 126, 128, 194n14
Schedule intervention, 79–81
Securities and Exchange Board of India, 132
Securities and Exchange Commission, 132
Self-enforcing outcome. *See* Game theory, Nash equilibrium
Self-interest, 92, 159, 169, 183, 204n2
Sen Rule, 7
Service sector, 29, 176. *See also* Finance (sector); Information technology (sector)
Shared prosperity, 92–96, 197n8
Sheremetyevo Airport, 155
Sherman Act, 135
Singapore, 16, 31, 34, 90, 122, 167, 168, 202n10
Smart card, 116, 200n19, 200n22
Social norms, 22, 43, 153–154, 156, 157–165, 195n3, 202n7, 203n15, 203n1, 204n2, 204n8
Social persuasion, 166